100 THINGS
BLACKHAWKS FANS
SHOULD KNOW & DO
BEFORE THEY DIE

Tab Bamford

TRIUMPH
BOOKS

Library of Congress Cataloging-in-Publication Data

Bamford, Tab, 1980–
    100 things Blackhawks fans should know & do before they die / Tab Bamford.
    p. cm.
  ISBN 978-1-60078-652-5
1. Chicago Blackhawks (Hockey team)—History. 2. Chicago Blackhawks (Hockey team)—Miscellanea. I. Title. II. Title: One hundred things Blackhawks fans should know and do before they die.
  GV848.C48B35 2011
  796.962'640977311—dc23

                                                        2011020190

This book is available in quantity at special discounts for your group or organization. For further information, contact:

Triumph Books LLC
542 South Dearborn Street
Suite 750
Chicago, Illinois 60605
(312) 939-3330
Fax (312) 663-3557
www.triumphbooks.com

Printed in U.S.A.
ISBN: 978-1-60078-652-5
Design by Patricia Frey
All photos courtesy of AP Images

For every fan who's committed to the Indian,
whether it's been since 1926 or 2010

Contents

Foreword

Having grown up a fan of the Original Six franchise Bruins in Boston, I really didn't understand the tradition in Chicago when I arrived. However, from my first moments in Chicago, I could tell I was in a special place. Everything was unique, from the way the Blackhawks organization was run and how it presented itself to how I was treated by the GM, the owner, and the coaches in the locker room.

Chicago is a championship city and one of the greatest sports cities in the country. Its love and passion for sports is unprecedented, and it has produced legendary teams in myriad sports throughout history. Some might say Boston and New York are better sports cities, but I was blessed to witness mayhem on...and off...the ice in Chicago. For my money, Chicago and Philadelphia are the two greatest sports cities around...period.

I have a lot of really special memories from my days in Chicago; playing for the Blackhawks was a truly amazing experience. The team's jersey and logo are loved and adored worldwide but have a special meaning to the team itself. I'll never forget my first game, when I was only 18 years old...coming into the locker room, where the team hangs up all the players' jerseys in the stalls. Seeing my name sewn on the back of one of those white jerseys with the Blackhawks emblem was an indescribable feeling. I think that's when I really got it. I remember two things distinctly from that game: how nervous I was and how proud I was to be wearing the best jersey in all of professional sports.

Chicago is one of the friendliest and most beautiful cities in the world and one of the best cities to live in as well as visit. The fans in Chicago made it fun for me to go to the rink every day, and they made it exciting to get ready to play games. The team knew the fans were going to be on their game, so we better be on ours.

And when we were on, the fans would respond in a mad fervor. I recall the 1991 All-Star Game, which we played at Chicago Stadium during the Gulf War. The cheers I got from the fans that night and the way the fans embraced the game and treated the military were incredible. I had a great game that night, with a goal and three assists. That night is one of those special moments from my time in Chicago that I'll never forget.

Chicago Stadium was an institution in Chicago and one of the things that made the Blackhawks so special. The place oozed tradition, and the fans made it exciting. From the singing of the National Anthem and the atmosphere it created to all the memorable moments that occurred in those hallowed walls, the history of that building will never be matched. I have the distinction of scoring the final goal by a Blackhawks player at Chicago Stadium, against the Toronto Maple Leafs.

These small stories are just the tip of the iceberg. The Chicago Blackhawks are one of the most storied and important teams in hockey history. This book gives a unique insight into the team's history and provides a list of the 100 things all Blackhawks fans should know and do in order to truly call themselves fans. It will enhance any Blackhawks fan's library!

—Jeremy Roenick

Acknowledgments

For a lifelong fan and season-ticket holder, writing this book was a labor of love. I consider it an honor and privilege to be a Blackhawks fan, and I love their rich history. That being said, I couldn't have written this book without a little help.

Thanks to Adam Jahns of the *Chicago Sun-Times* and Tim Sassone of the *Daily Herald* for a number of great conversations about the team, especially Jahns during the 2010 Stanley Cup Finals. Also, big thanks to Jimmy Greenfield at ChicagoNow.com, David Kaplan of Comcast SportsNet Chicago and WGN Radio, and Dennis Bernstein and Dave Pagnotta of the *Fourth Period* magazine and thefourthperiod.com for their fantastic support.

A shout-out to the folks in Section 302 at the United Center as well. The 300 level at the U.C. is a special place, and there's a great group of fans in 302 for every Hawks home game.

Thanks to my wonderful wife, Kristin, for putting up with me disappearing to my man cave until 1:00 AM while the Hawks are on the West Coast and taking care of our kids while I'm at the United Center. Our two sons, Matt and Bobby, are lucky to have such a wonderful mother.

My parents and in-laws were a huge help as well, especially my mother-in-law, who hung out with the boys while I disappeared to write. Without my family's support, this couldn't have happened.

Finally, thanks to my grandfather for encouraging me to write. I wish he were here to read this.

1 The Drought Is Over

As Patrick Kane sprinted down the ice shaking his fists in the air, before even the television cameras had found the game-winning goal sliding into the side of the net, the most spectacular resurrection in the history of professional team sports had reached its ultimate climax. On June 9, 2010, the Chicago Blackhawks were Stanley Cup Champions.

Step back for a moment and read that last sentence again.

After 49 years, the finality of this statement brought Bobby Hull, Jeremy Roenick, and thousands of Chicagoans who had given their hearts to the franchise for generations to tears when Jonathan Toews hoisted the Cup above his head.

And what better team to represent the history of the Chicago Blackhawks than this roster? Consider where the players on the championship team came from: Patrick Sharp and Ben Eager kissed the Cup on the ice surface they weren't good enough to play on full-time; the Flyers dealt both of them to the Hawks for relatively little in return. Andrew Ladd, once the fourth overall pick in the draft, who won a ring playing for opposing Philadelphia Flyers coach Peter Laviolette in Carolina, saw those same Hurricanes give up on him when they dealt him to Chicago. Kris Versteeg, a fifth-round draft choice, didn't factor into Boston's long-term plans enough for the Bruins to keep him. Tomas Kopecky was Detroit's leading hitter prior to signing with Chicago, but the Red Wings didn't want to bring him back. Dustin Byfuglien didn't impress many scouts; 244 players were drafted before him. Troy Brouwer was drafted after 213 other players. Niklas Hjalmarsson watched 107 other names get called before the Blackhawks tabbed him on draft day. Heck,

Antti Niemi was too old to be considered for the league's top rookie honors; he was never drafted and signed with the Hawks as a free agent at 24 a couple seasons prior to winning the Cup.

With the rare exceptions of Brent Seabrook, Jonathan Toews, and Patrick Kane being high draft picks (Duncan Keith was a second-round selection) or big-money free agents like Brian Campbell or Marian Hossa, most of the players on this Blackhawks roster were afterthoughts and castaways. Which is perfect for this organization.

In the first two seasons after the lockout, the Blackhawks ranked 27th in attendance in the NHL in 2005–06 (13,319 average) and 29th in 2006–07 (12,727 average). Three years before winning it all, the Blackhawks had the second-worst average attendance in the league. Nobody wanted to watch a terrible team, and the Blackhawks were terrible.

Patrick Kane has hurled off his gloves and skates victoriously down the ice after scoring the Cup-clinching goal for the Blackhawks on June 9, 2010. It took several moments for anyone else to even realize he had scored, and Kane celebrated his goal alone until the goal was confirmed.

The bottom fell out in 2003–04, when the team finished the regular season with just 59 points. In fact, before Toews and Kane arrived, the team had just one season in the decade with more than 80 points in a season.

General manager Dale Tallon started convincing free agents to come to the Hawks by grossly overpaying them. At this point in the organization's history, it wasn't elite players coming to Chicago, though; we're talking about Tallon offering way too much money and far too many years to guys like Martin Havlat, Nikolai Khabibulin, and Brent Sopel despite them being older, injury prone, and possessing limited skill sets.

In the rookie seasons of Toews and Kane, 2007–08, the Blackhawks jumped to 19th in the league in attendance (16,814 average). The team also jumped into a tie for ninth place in the Western Conference with 88 points. It was apparent that the turn-around was starting.

In the summer of 2008 the Blackhawks were able to sell their vision to higher-profile free agents like Brian Campbell and Cristobal Huet but still had to overpay with both dollars and years to get them into the fold.

Team owners Rocky Wirtz and John McDonough were also able to sell their vision to the league, and the commissioner's office bought in; the Blackhawks were awarded the Winter Classic on New Year's Day in 2009 at Wrigley Field against the Detroit Red Wings.

On the ice, the team started to back up the seemingly irrational hopes of Wirtz and McDonough, and the response was overwhelmingly positive. The Blackhawks leapt to the top of the league in average attendance in each of the next two seasons.

But Chicago had seen this before. Since 1961 Hawks fans had seen Tony Esposito, Ed Belfour, Steve Larmer, Jeremy Roenick, Chris Chelios, Doug Wilson, Keith Magnuson, Denis Savard, and hundreds of other great players wear the Indian-head jersey and achieve wonderful personal feats, but the Stanley Cup hadn't landed on Chicago's West Side.

But the 2009–10 team was different. Those Blackhawks didn't have a superstar scoring 50 goals like Savard, Roenick, Hull, or Mikita. And they didn't have a god between the pipes like Glenn Hall or Esposito. But in this era of expansion, with the talent in the league and the length of the playoffs, the 2009–10 Blackhawks might prove to be the best team in the organization's history.

Tallon did a magnificent job of putting together a roster with perfectly complementary pieces. The way the organization developed players like Keith, Seabrook, and Hjalmarsson into top defensemen is a credit to management. And the faith the team put in their young stars, Kane and Toews, sticking with them through injuries and a rough first season with many highs and lows, showed patience most major-market sports teams cannot imagine.

In the same decade in which they won the Cup, the Blackhawks had been named the worst professional sports team in North America by *Fortune* magazine, a distinction that usually accompanies decades of miserable play. And yet while the L.A. Clippers of the world continue to wonder if/when they'll be able to develop a fighting chance at legitimacy, the Blackhawks reached the mountaintop in three short years.

2 Stan Mikita

In long history of the Chicago Blackhawks, no player stands ahead of Stan "Stosh" Mikita.

On October 19, 1980, No. 21 was the first to be retired by the organization, recognizing the contributions Mikita made while playing for 22 years in Chicago. He was one of the greatest two-way forwards of all time and remains the gold standard at center for the Hawks.

Born Stanislaus Guoth in Sokolce, Czechoslovakia (now Slovakia), Mikita emigrated to Canada in 1948 as an eight-year-old with his aunt and uncle, where he took their family name of Mikita. He wasn't blessed with an imposing body like other superstars of his generation, such as Bobby Hull and Gordie Howe; in the tradition of Bill Mosienko and the Bentley brothers, Stosh stood just 5'9" inches tall and weighed just 169 pounds.

After three years in the juniors, he got the call from Chicago in 1958 for a three-game tryout. When he stepped on the NHL ice, he became the first Czechoslovakian-born player in the NHL. That was the first step toward Stosh rewriting the Blackhawks and NHL record books.

In his second full season in the NHL, Stosh led the entire postseason with six goals as the Hawks marched all the way to the 1961 Stanley Cup. Though he would return to the Finals in the subsequent 19 seasons, he would never win another Cup in Chicago.

For his 22 years, though, Mikita provided Chicago with the opportunity to watch one of the best to ever play the game. He was named to the NHL's first All-Star team after the 1961–62 season, just the beginning of his recognition as arguably the best player of the decade.

He won the Art Ross Trophy as the league's top point producer for the first time in 1964 and would win it three more times during the decade, in 1965, 1967, and 1968. Since it was first awarded in 1948, only six players have won the Art Ross Trophy four times in a decade: Gordie Howe, Phil Esposito, Wayne Gretzky, Mario Lemieux, Jaromir Jagr, and Mikita.

The first time Mikita played in the NHL All-Star Game was also in 1964, and he would return eight more times. He played in the game every year between 1967 and 1975, except 1970.

While 1964 may have been the first time Mikita received league-wide recognition, the 1966–67 and 1967–68 seasons cemented Stosh as one of the all-time greats. In 1966–67 he tied the league record for points in a season (established by teammate Bobby Hull) with 97 points, winning his third Art Ross Trophy. He added the Hart Memorial Trophy that season as the league's MVP and also won the Lady Byng Memorial Trophy for being the most gentlemanly player in the game.

No player in NHL history, before or after Mikita, has won those three awards in the same season. And Mikita did it again the following season.

Blackhawks MVPs

The Hart Memorial Trophy is the oldest and most prestigious individual award in hockey, serving as the most valuable player award in the NHL. The winner is determined annually by the Professional Hockey Writers Association, and it has been awarded 85 times to 52 different players since it was first given in 1924.

Only three eligible Hart recipients—Tommy Anderson, Al Rollins, and Eric Lindros—have not been elected into the Hockey Hall of Fame, and many deserving players in the 1980s failed to win the award during Wayne Gretzky's stretch of eight consecutive wins.

The following Chicago Blackhawks players have earned the Hart Memorial Trophy as the most valuable player in the NHL:

- Max Bentley: 1945–46
- Al Rollins: 1953–54
- Bobby Hull: 1964–65, 1965–66
- Stan Mikita: 1966–67, 1967–68

The Conn Smythe Trophy—named for the Hall of Fame owner, general manager, and coach of the Maple Leafs—has been awarded to the most valuable player of the entire postseason in each year since 1964. Only one Blackhawks player—Jonathan Toews (2010)—has won the Conn Smythe Trophy.

Only three Blackhawks players have been named the All-Star Game MVP: Bobby Hull (1970, 1971), Eric Daze (2002), and Patrick Sharp (2011).

What makes that accomplishment even more intriguing is that Mikita, a fierce competitor, was one of the league's most penalized players early in his career. In four of his first six NHL seasons, Mikita served more than 100 penalty minutes, including a career-high 154 in the 1964–65 season. Yet, after piling up almost six hours of penalties in seven seasons, he was called for only 12 minutes of infractions in 1966–67, an astounding turnaround.

In his autobiography, *I Play to Win*, Stosh credits a conversation between his daughter and wife for his career taking a turn. Mikita writes that his daughter and wife were watching a game late in the 1965–66 season. When Stosh was called for a penalty, his daughter asked why her father spent so much time sitting alone. When Mikita's wife relayed the story to Stosh, he realized he needed to change his approach and remarkably did so the following year.

Stosh may have had his best season in 1972–73. He scored 83 points despite missing a quarter of the season with an injury. The Hawks reached the Stanley Cup Finals that year but lost again to Montreal.

When he hung up his skates for the final time in 1980, Mikita had played more games—1,394—than any other European-born forward in history, a distinction he still holds. In 1998 Mikita ranked 17th on *Hockey News'* list of the 100 greatest hockey players of all time, the highest ranking for any player born outside Canada.

Only two players, Alex Delvecchio and Steve Yzerman, have played longer for a single organization than Mikita did for Chicago. His longevity and commitment to the Blackhawks is one of the primary reasons that he is remembered as the greatest player in the team's history. But he certainly builds a strong case with his statistics.

Mikita ranks first in Blackhawks history with 1,467 points (14th in NHL history). His 541 goals rank second behind only his teammate Bobby Hull, and the mark is still among the top 30 in NHL history. Mikita's 926 career assists are 207 more than the second-highest total in Hawks history, by Denis Savard, and still ranks 17th in NHL history.

He also retired as, and still is, the organization's all-time leader in postseason points (150) and assists (91) and ranks third in goals (59) and playoff games (155).

In 1976 Mikita was awarded the prestigious Lester Patrick Trophy for contributions to the game of hockey in the United States. He was only the seventh player to receive the award.

He earned the ultimate honor, a place in the Hockey Hall of Fame, in 1983 and was inducted into the Slovak Hockey Hall of Fame in 2002. On Opening Night of the 2000–01 season, Mikita was one of three centers named to the Blackhawks 75th Anniversary Team.

No Blackhawks player committed more years or games to the organization than Mikita. He was one of the best players of the Original Six era and remains one of the best centers to ever play the game.

Early in the 2011–12 season, a statue of Mikita and Bobby Hull will be unveiled outside the United Center.

The Golden Jet

A popular discussion that takes place in bars often is whether or not players from the past could play with the athletes in the game today. Could Mickey Mantle hit Randy Johnson's fastball? Would Wilt Chamberlain dominate Shaquille O'Neal? How would an NFL defense today stop Jim Brown?

Bobby Hull could have played with any generation.

A stocky 190 pounds and a shade under six feet tall, Hull was an imposing offensive force on the ice starting in 1957–58. He burst on to the NHL scene as a brash 18-year-old and was the runner-up for the Calder Memorial Trophy with 47 points.

He was nicknamed "the Golden Jet" because of his blond hair and blazing speed up and down the ice; he was once clocked at 29.7 miles per hour skating down the ice.

An unsigned article from the March 12, 1966, edition of the *New York Times* states, "Bobby Hull is electrifying as he skates down the ice faster than any man in hockey. He shoots at 120 miles an hour—the hardest slap shot in the sport. There is little doubt among his opponents and fans that…Robert Marvin Hull is the most exciting player in the National Hockey League."

The next season, Hull improved his point total to 50, and the Blackhawks qualified for the playoffs. With Hull and Mikita up front, the Hawks were quickly developing into one of the most lethal scoring teams in the NHL. Armed with an unbelievable slap shot and ridiculous accuracy, Hull could put the puck anywhere in the net he wanted. When a radar gun clocked his shot at 118.3 miles per hour, it became understandable why goalies wanted to get out of the way.

He led the league in goals (39) and points (81) in his third season, and the Blackhawks returned to the postseason for a second consecutive year. In 1960–61, though, Hull and the Hawks would finally bring the ultimate prize back to Chicago. Of that team, Hull told John McGourty in a 2009 interview, "[We were] strong up the middle. We had perhaps the greatest goalie in the history of the game, Glenn Hall. We had Stan Mikita and Bill Hay at center and we had great defense with Al Arbour, who came over from Detroit; Jack Evans, who came to us from the Rangers; Dollard St. Laurent, who had done yeoman duty in Montreal; and homegrown defensemen Elmer Vasko and Pierre Pilote."

Hull scored four goals and added 10 assists in 12 postseason games that spring as the Hawks won the organization's third Stanley Cup.

And that was only the beginning of Hull's amazing career. Hull captured the Art Ross Trophy as the league's leader in points in 1960, 1962, and 1966 and was an NHL First Team All-Star 10 times (in 1960, 1962, 1964 to 1970, and 1972).

In 1965 Hull won his first Hart Memorial Trophy as the league's most valuable player. Despite being a physical player, he also won the Lady Byng Memorial Trophy in 1965. The next season cemented Hull's status as an all-time great.

In 1966 Hull became only the fourth player in 43 years to win the Hart Memorial Trophy in consecutive seasons (Howie Morenz, Eddie Shore, and Gordie Howe were the first three). That season, Hull became the first player in NHL history to score more than 50 goals when he beat Cesare Maniago on March 12 at the Chicago Stadium.

He finished the 1966 season with 54 goals, which was the highest total in any season during the Original Six era to that point. Three years later he would break his own record, scoring 58 in the 1968–69 season.

The 1966 season was just one of seven seasons during the 1960s in which Hull led the NHL in goal scoring, achieving the 50-goal plateau an astonishing four times in the decade. Fifty goals were scored by single players only six other times in the entirety of the NHL that decade!

However, not everything in Hull's life was as cool or successful as he was on the ice. A feud had been brewing between Hull and Blackhawks management for some time, and it came to a head in 1972. "They never offered me a contract," Hull told AOL's Chris Botta in 2010. "Do you really think I wanted to leave Chicago, the greatest city with the greatest sports fans in the world? I had five kids and a very extravagant wife. I'd be nuts to want to leave. I'd given the Blackhawks my blood and sweat for 15 years! I told them I thought I had five years—five good years—left in my body. They didn't even offer me one year."

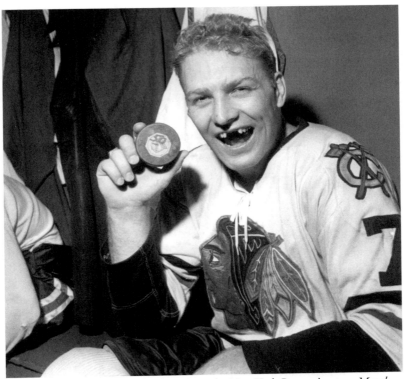

Bobby Hull holds the puck he drove into the New York Rangers' net on March 25, 1962, to score his 50th goal of the season and to tie the National Hockey League record in the final game of this regular season.

Despite all the blood, sweat, tears, and incredible play that Hull had given the Blackhawks, he accepted an unprecedented offer of $1 million from the Winnipeg Jets of the new World Hockey Association.

Because he jumped to the WHA, he was locked out of the 1972 Summit Series in Moscow. His brother and former teammate in Chicago, Dennis, did play for Team Canada despite considering a personal boycott on his older brother's behalf.

Hull's time in Chicago was remarkable. He was credited with popularizing the slap shot and, with Mikita, starting the trend of having a curved stick blade. He played 1,036 games in Chicago before his bitter divorce from the organization, and he is still the franchise's all-time leader with 604 goals. He scored an amazing 1,153 points. When he finally retired in 1980, he was the second-leading goal scorer and ninth-leading point scorer in NHL history. And those striking numbers don't include 303 goals and 335 assists in only 411 games in the WHA.

Hull was inducted into the Hockey Hall of Fame in 1983. He is best remembered wearing the same number—9—as his boyhood hero, Gordie Howe, but he also wore No. 7 and, when the Hawks won the Cup, No. 16 in Chicago. His jersey and No. 9 were retired by the Blackhawks on December 18, 1983.

When the *Hockey News* released its list in 1998 of the 100 greatest hockey players of all time, Hull was ranked eighth.

However, Hull was separated from the team and the city that he loved so much. It wasn't until Rocky Wirtz took over the franchise in the wake of his father's passing that Hull was brought back in.

In 2010 Brian Cazeneuve wrote, "[Rocky Wirtz] decided to dive into his past. Because he knew, with what we had, if he couldn't be proud of his past, they wouldn't have much of a future. And bringing back Esposito and Hull and Mikita was the icing on the cake."

When Hull was brought back as an ambassador with the Blackhawks organization, the history of the franchise was properly put back in one piece. The story was brought full circle when Hull joined eight of his teammates from the 1961 Cup team to hand the new banner to the 2010 champions on Opening Night of the 2010–11 season.

The Golden Jet is still one of the greatest players in the history of the Chicago Blackhawks and the greatest left wing to ever play the game.

4 Glenn Hall

When you consider how calm Glenn Hall was under pressure on the ice, it's interesting to know that his stomach was upset before every game.

The Blackhawks Hall of Fame netminder, known as "Mr. Goalie," threw up before every game he ever played. In fact, the Hawks used to keep a bucket handy just in case Hall needed it *during* the game as well. What's more amazing is that he got sick before 502 consecutive regular-season games.

Then again, it's understandable how someone might not be comfortable with between 20 and 50 shots coming at him without being protected by a mask.

Cal Ripken has baseball's all-time Iron Man record, having played in 2,632 straight games between 1982 and 1998. With all due respect to Ripken playing in every game for 16 years, Hall didn't wear a mask in one of his 502 starts and rarely missed even a minute of ice time. Even now, with improved safety equipment available for goalies at all levels, Hall's record will never be touched.

Looking back at the early parts of Hall's career, the Blackhawks were awfully fortunate to even have Hall. He first broke into the NHL with the Detroit Red Wings, where he was called up as a backup for the 1952 playoffs but didn't play in a single game. Still, the Wings put his name on the Stanley Cup with the rest of that championship team despite Hall having never played in an NHL game.

He didn't solidify his spot in Detroit until the 1955–56 season, when he replaced Terry Sawchuk. He would win the Calder Memorial Trophy as the league's top rookie after posting

12 shutouts that year. Hall played in every game in his first two seasons and was good for Detroit, playing in the All-Star Game in both seasons.

But there was a shake-up in the NHL after the 1956–57 season. Tommy Ivan, who had been in Detroit, signed with Chicago to be the Hawks' general manager, and he knew Hall well. When Hall and Ted Lindsay were put on the market, Ivan jumped at the opportunity and made one of the better trades in NHL history.

In one of his first games as a member of the Blackhawks, Hall already made history—in a bad way. His name became a trivia answer when he allowed Maurice "Rocket" Richard's 500th career NHL goal on October 19, 1957. However, allowing goals wasn't Hall's forte.

Once Hall arrived in Chicago, the Blackhawks' dynamics on the ice instantly changed. The Blackhawks of the late 1950s were a talented young group, and Hall joined Pierre Pilote, Stan Mikita, and Bobby Hull to turn around a franchise that had been a doormat for a generation.

He played for the Blackhawks for 10 years and clearly stood out as one of the preeminent netminders of his generation. Hall won two Vezina Trophies (1963, 1967) and played in eight All-Star Games as a member of the Blackhawks.

In 1961 Hall was a key part of the Blackhawks' Stanley Cup championship. The team struggled through the regular season, and Hall's 29–24–17 record reflected the parity in the six-team NHL at the time. He did, however, post a solid 2.51 goals-against average that year and was an All-Star.

When the playoffs started, though, Hall was incredible. He won the requisite eight games to earn the Stanley Cup and posted two shutouts and a 2.02 goals-against average for the postseason. He remembered that spring fondly in 2000 in the foreword for Brian McFarlane's *Original Six* series, when he wrote, "I was never so proud and happy as when the Hawks—third-place finishers behind

Blackhawks Vezina Winners

The Vezina Trophy is named for Georges Vezina, who was the goaltender in Montreal for 15 years until his career was cut short. He collapsed on the ice during a game in 1925, leading to his untimely death from tuberculosis in 1926.

The award has been presented annually since 1927, but it has not always gone to an individual. The first year it was awarded it was given to the most valuable goalie. In 1946, though, the criteria changed and, until 1981, the Vezina was awarded to the goaltender(s) of the team with the fewest allowed goals for the season.

Since 1981, however, it has again been given to the individual judged to be the best netminder in the league and is voted on by the general managers of each NHL team. The William M. Jennings Trophy is now awarded to the goalie/team allowing the fewest goals in the season.

The following Blackhawks have won the Vezina Trophy, either as the league's best goalie or when the Hawks led the league in goals allowed:

- Charlie Gardiner: 1931–32, 1933–34
- Lorne Chabot: 1934–35
- Glenn Hall: 1962–63
- Glenn Hall and Denis DeJordy: 1966–67
- Tony Esposito: 1969–70, 1973–74 (shared with Bernie Parent of the Philadelphia Flyers)
- Tony Esposito and Gary Smith: 1971–72
- Ed Belfour: 1990–91, 1992–93

The William M. Jennings Trophy has been awarded to a Blackhawks netminder on three occasions, all three times going to Ed Belfour (1990–91, 1992–93, 1994–95).

Montreal and Toronto in 1960–61—confounded the experts by capturing the Cup that spring…. What a sweet feeling! There is no sense of accomplishment quite like it."

Hall is remembered not only for his longevity but also as the godfather of the butterfly style of goaltending. He is credited by most goalie historians with either inventing the style or at least being the first goalie to use it regularly in the NHL.

Despite all of the success he brought to the Blackhawks, Hall is one of the many Hawks greats who did not finish his career in Chicago. At 36, he was left unprotected when the league expanded in 1967. The St. Louis Blues selected Hall in the expansion draft and, in his first season with the Blues, Hall led the expansion team to the Stanley Cup Finals, where they lost to a loaded Canadiens team.

One of the best-known images of Hall isn't even remembered because his face is not part of the photograph: it's the legendary picture of Boston's Bobby Orr scoring his dramatic Stanley Cup–winning overtime goal on May 10, 1970. Orr is sailing through the air, and then–St. Louis goalie Hall is reaching above his head to the crossbar as he falls backward.

The final numbers for Hall's Chicago tenure are fantastic. His 275 wins and 51 shutouts are both statistics that rank second in team history behind only Tony Esposito. He was elected into the Hockey Hall of Fame in 1975, and his No. 1 was retired by the team on November 20, 1988.

5 Savoir Faire

From birth, Denis Savard was bound to achieve legendary status playing hockey.

On February 4, 1961, Denis Cyr, Denis Tremblay, and Denis Savard were all born in the same neighborhood in Quebec. As the three young men grew up together, each was drawn to the ice and, as teenagers, they wound up on the same line in juniors in Montreal. The Les Trois Denis line came to prominence in Canada in large part because of its great success, but the legend grew when it was learned that the three boys with the same first name also shared a birthday.

In 1980 a 19-year-old Savard brought an astounding résumé to the NHL Draft: 455 points in only 214 games. His point production was a product of fantastic speed and a unique ability to carry the puck from end to end. In that year's draft class, Savard was the best center by a long shot.

The Blackhawks held the highest draft position in the organization's history that year—third overall—and needed someone to add scoring in the wake of Stan Mikita's retirement. When Montreal, the host team that year, passed on the local hero with the first overall pick and Winnipeg selected a defenseman, Savard would fall no further. Also, in the sixth round, with the 120th overall pick, they selected right wing Steve Larmer. Fate was being very, very kind to Chicago that summer.

Known as "Savoir Faire," Savard's impact was immediate. He started the 1980–81 season with Chicago and was credited with three assists in his first NHL game. When his rookie campaign ended, Savard had established a new Blackhawks rookie record with 75 points.

In his second season, Savard found a left wing to skate with in Al Secord. The physical forward was a perfect fit with the flying Savard, and the two combined to have a great season. Secord scored 44 goals, while Savard jumped to sixth in the NHL with 119 points. After being eliminated in the first round of the playoffs in his rookie season, the Blackhawks advanced all the way to the Campbell Conference Finals.

The 1982–83 season marked the genesis of arguably the greatest line in the history of the Chicago Blackhawks. The kid the Hawks had selected in the sixth round in 1980, Larmer, finally got a permanent call-up to Chicago when Orval Tessier was named the head coach in Chicago. Tessier had coached Larmer in the minors and, despite management's objections, put Larmer on the top line with Secord and Savard.

Larmer scored 90 points and captured the Calder Memorial Trophy that year, while Savard's 121 points ranked third in the NHL. The Hawks won the Norris Division by a comfortable eight points and advanced all the way to the Campbell Conference finals, where they met the Edmonton juggernaut.

Unfortunately, the Campbell Conference in the 1980s was nearly impossible to win. Because of the Hall of Fame–laden Oilers teams—which won the Stanley Cup in 1984, 1985, 1987, 1988, and 1990—the first decade of Savard's career faced a concrete ceiling. During the decade, Savard topped 100 points in five seasons and scored at least 30 goals in seven consecutive seasons. If not for Wayne Gretzky's Oilers, the 1980s may have belonged to Savard and the Blackhawks.

In 1988–89, however, the Blackhawks made a coaching change. Mike Keenan was brought in to get the Hawks over the hump and past the Oilers, and his track record of struggling to get along with star players would take aim at the team's best player: Savard.

The two never saw eye to eye and, in the summer of 1990, Savard was traded to his hometown Canadiens in exchange for young defenseman Chris Chelios. Like so many great Blackhawks before him, Savard was dealt out of Chicago at the end of his career.

Savard played well in Montreal, but injuries robbed him of the explosive speed he displayed in his early career. He scored 179 points in 210 games for the Habs over three seasons but reached the climax of his career as a member of the 1993 Stanley Cup champions. Unfortunately, Savard was injured and did not dress for the Cup-clinching game.

After a brief period with the Tampa Bay Lightning, Savard was reacquired by the Blackhawks during the 1994–95 season. As had been the story throughout Savard's career, he led the Hawks with

18 points in the 1995 postseason, but the Hawks were eliminated in the Conference Finals. Savard ultimately retired in the same sweater he wore in his first NHL game in 1997 and was inducted into the Hockey Hall of Fame three years later.

In his Chicago career, Savard scored 377 goals and added 719 assists. His 1,096 points still rank third in franchise history behind only Mikita and Bobby Hull. During their time together, Savard and Larmer accounted for over 700 goals and finished their careers just as close to each other among the Blackhawks' all-time leaders as they were on the ice.

Savard is also responsible for the four largest single-season point totals in the organization's history, with his career-best 131 from the 1987–88 season still the gold standard among all Blackhawks. He was the first Hawks player to eclipse the 100-point plateau in his sophomore season. He represented the Hawks in six All-Star Games. In 131 postseason games in Chicago, Savard posted 145 points. Both of those rank second only to Mikita in team history.

On March 19, 1998, his No. 18 was retired by the organization. He was also named one of the centers on the team's 75th Anniversary Team.

Unlike many of the team's great players that had left the organization in the previous three decades, Savard stayed with Chicago. He moved to the bench, where he served as an assistant coach from 1997 to 2006. When Trent Yawney was fired midway through the 2006–07 season, Savard was named the interim head coach.

During the 2007–08 season, Savard proved to be the perfect mentor for two budding stars who had joined the team: Patrick Kane and Jonathan Toews. Both of the young forwards appeared to share a unique personal and professional relationship with Savard, and the two did as well in their first seasons as Savard had in his.

However, after only four games in the 2008–09 season, the organization decided to make a change on the bench. Savard was relieved as head coach and replaced with Joel Quenneville. In the official statement released by the team, then-GM Dale Tallon said the following about his former teammate and close friend Savard: "Denis is forever a part of our organization."

Indeed he is. One month after he was fired as head coach, Savard joined Hull, Mikita, and Esposito as a Blackhawks ambassador. Savard gave 24 years of professional service to the Blackhawks organization—as either a player or coach—and represents the commitment to the Indian-head sweater to generations of fans.

The Original Six

The Original Six. The phrase brings so many thoughts and emotions into the front of hockey fans' minds. A reverence for the six franchises that founded the National Hockey League runs so deep that…well, the misconception that there were only six professional hockey teams that started the NHL continues to be a popularly accepted myth.

The National Hockey League was born in 1917, and only two of the franchises considered among the Original Six were part of that inaugural season. However, each of the Original Six franchises were founded within a decade of each other and, more importantly, lasted.

The original NHL consisted of 10 teams but, like the rest of North America, the impact of the Great Depression was too much to handle for more than one-third of the league. During the 1920s, the league lost the Pittsburgh Pirates, Montreal Maroons, and Ottawa Senators to financial instability.

During World War II, teams in every sport were experiencing unique, trying circumstances. While baseball players like Ted

Williams and Joe DiMaggio were fighting overseas, the NHL faced its own problems as an international sports league. During the war, the Blackhawks were forced to play without two of their best players—Doug and Max Bentley—because of travel restrictions.

The number of teams playing in the league was also impacted by the war. The Brooklyn Americans left the league because of a lack of available players in 1942, leaving only six teams remaining.

The truth about the Original Six is that the six teams that financially survived both the Great Depression and World War II were the sum total of the National Hockey League from 1942 until a large-scale expansion in 1967. Those six teams are:

The Chicago Blackhawks

The Boston Bruins

The Detroit Red Wings

The New York Rangers

The Montreal Canadiens

The Toronto Maple Leafs

During the Original Six era (25 years), only four of the six teams won a Stanley Cup championship; Boston and New York were shut out, and the Blackhawks won only the one title in 1961.

One of the great criticisms of the league during this period was that the six teams would play the regular season, but four would advance into the playoffs. Obviously familiarity breeds contempt in a league five times the size of those Original Six, so the rivalries built in those years ran deep between the players and fans.

In 1967 the league dramatically doubled its size by adding six more teams: the California Seals, Los Angeles Kings, Minnesota North Stars, Philadelphia Flyers, Pittsburgh Penguins, and St. Louis Blues. The expansion did not sit well with many Canadian fans because, as you might notice from the locations, none of the new teams were in Canada.

This was only the beginning, though. In 1972 the World Hockey Association was formed and started offering enormous contracts to many NHL stars, including a number of notable Chicago players. By 1974 the NHL had expanded to 18 teams.

Over the years, though, the Original Six teams have been separated by quality and expansion. Divisions, conferences, and realignment have made Original Six matchups more rare, especially with the Blackhawks and Red Wings in the Western Conference and the other four in the Eastern Conference.

There has been a great deal of conjecture over the years about the continued importance—and relevance—of the Original Six. In a 2007 series for ESPN.com, Scott Burnside wrote, "For many fans, the Original Six concept is similar to steam engines and black-and-white television—charming but distant."

While some national analysts may feel that the dust gathering on the concept of the Original Six grows with time, there will forever be a special place in the hearts of fans for the rivalries that have grown over the decades between these teams. As long as names like Hull, Howe, and Richard hold a place of respect in the history books, these six cities will honor their pasts.

Whether it's the Bruins and Habs, Leafs and Rangers, or Red Wings and Blackhawks, any time two Original Six teams face off, it's a special event.

7 Pierre Pilote

When most fans think back to the great offenses the Blackhawks put on the ice in the 1960s, the names that come to mind immediately are Hull and Mikita. What many forget is that the Hawks

Pierre Pilote poses in 1962.

also featured one of the greatest offensive defenseman in the game at the time in Pierre Pilote.

Pilote broke into the NHL in 1955–56, playing 20 games for the Blackhawks and contributing eight points. In the 1950s that kind of point production from a defenseman was unheard of, and the Hawks were sure they had found a gem on their blue line. The following season, he made the roster coming out of training camp and didn't have to worry about job security again for 12 more years.

In the late 1950s Pilote teamed up with Elmer "Moose" Vasko to form arguably the best defensive pair in the game. As the Blackhawks began improving as an organization under the leadership of general manager Tommy Ivan in the late 1950s, Pilote was a constant on the blue line. He played in 376 consecutive games, including five straight seasons without missing a game.

What made Pilote's iron-man status more impressive is that he was known as one of the toughest players in the game; he was never afraid of a scrap and wouldn't turn down an opponent's offer to fight. Legend recalls that he once knocked out both Henri and Maurice Richard in the same altercation.

He was also a wonderful shot-blocker, who was always willing to put his body between the shooter and the net. Pilote was always known as one of the most intelligent players in the game who had a great concept of spacing on the ice, which helped him to become one of the premier offensive blueliners of his era.

"There're always 10 or 15 square feet of space somewhere that you can skate into and be available to get the puck, get the pass, and make another move," Pilote told NHL.com in 2008. "That's what hockey is all about, and that's what you try to teach young players. The most important guy is not the one with the puck but the guy in position to receive it."

Pilote's career took an enormous step in the 1961 playoffs. During that historic postseason, Pilote had impactful goals—each one was game-tying or game-winning—and added 12 assists in 12 games.

The following season, Pilote was named the Blackhawks' captain, a role he would hold from 1961 to 1968. During that stretch of time, he was named an NHL First-Team All-Star five times (1963–67) and became only the second player in NHL history to win three straight Norris Trophies (1963–65).

Since the Norris Trophy was initially awarded in 1954, only four players have won the award given to the league's best defenseman three consecutive years: Doug Harvey, Pilote, Bobby Orr, and Nicklas Lidstrom. Pilote was also the first Blackhawks player to win the award.

Before the 1968–69 season, Pilote was traded to the Toronto Maple Leafs for forward Jim Pappin.

When Pilote retired after one season with the Leafs, his 498 points were the fourth-highest total for a defenseman in history. Only Red Kelly (823), Bill Gadsby (568), and Doug Harvey (540) had made a bigger statistical impact from the blue line than Pilote had in his 890-game NHL career.

"Growing up, I was a big Chicago Blackhawks fan, so I watched Pierre Pilote and Elmer Vasko, Doug Jarrett, and all those guys that played on that team," remembered Larry Robinson, the great Montreal rearguard. "Before Orr, there was Pierre and Doug Harvey. Those were the guys who pioneered defensemen taking the puck and rushing up the ice with it and tried to control the play."

Today, Pilote still ranks fourth among all Blackhawks defenseman with 477 points (behind Doug Wilson, Bob Murray, and Chris Chelios). His 400 assists trails only Wilson, and his 821 games in the Indian-head sweater is the third-most of all Hawks defenseman (behind Murray and Wilson). He also piled up 1,205 penalty minutes, which was the team record when he retired.

When the money was on the table, though, not many were better than Pilote. He posted 60 points (eight goals, 52 assists) in

Blackhawks Captains

There have been 34 men named captain of the Chicago Blackhawks, starting with Dick Irvin in 1926. Throughout the years, a number of Hall of Famers have worn the *C* on their chests in Chicago, including Charlie Gardiner, Pierre Pilote, Stan Mikita, Denis Savard, and Chris Chelios.

On July 17, 2008, Jonathan Toews was named the youngest captain in Blackhawks history (and the third-youngest in the history of the league behind Vincent Lecavalier and Sidney Crosby) at the tender age of 20 years, 79 days.

Here is the complete list of captains in Blackhawks history:

Dick Irvin: 1926–29

Duke Dutkowski: 1929–30

Ty Arbor: 1930–31

Cyclone Wentworth: 1931–32

Helge Bostrom: 1932–33

Charlie Gardiner: 1933–34

John Gottselig: 1935–40

Earl Seibert: 1940–42

Doug Bentley: 1942–44, 1949–50

Clint Smith: 1944–45

John Mariucci: 1945–46, 1947–48

Red Hamill: 1946–47

Gaye Stewart: 1948–49

Jack Stewart: 1950–52

Bill Gadsby: 1952–54

Gus Mortson: 1954–57

Ed Litzenberger: 1958–61

Pierre Pilote: 1961–68

Pat Stapleton: 1969–70

Pit Martin: 1975–77

Stan Mikita: 1975–77

Keith Magnuson: 1976–80

Terry Ruskowski: 1979–82

Darryl Sutter: 1982–87

Bob Murray: 1985–86

Denis Savard: 1988–89

Dirk Graham: 1988–95

Chris Chelios: 1995–99

Doug Gilmour: 1999–2000

Tony Amonte: 2000–02

Alex Zhamnov: 2002–04

Adrian Aucoin: 2005–07

Martin Lapointe: 2005–07

Jonathan Toews: 2008–Present

82 postseason games with the Blackhawks. Only Wilson has more career postseason points from the Blackhawks' blue line.

Pilote was inducted into the Hockey Hall of Fame in 1975 and ranked 59th on the *Hockey News* list of the 100 greatest hockey players of all time in 1998. On November 12, 2008, his No. 3 was retired by the Blackhawks, an honor he shares with Keith Magnuson.

 Tony O

The conventional approach wasn't Tony O's style.

Tony Esposito's family was well known in hockey circles because of his older brother, Phil. But unlike Phil, Tony wasn't an aspiring forward with an uncanny ability to put the puck in the net. To the contrary, Tony enjoyed keeping the puck out.

And rather than following the career path of most elite hockey players in the 1960s, Tony didn't play in juniors. Instead, he decided to attend Michigan Tech University, where he won an NCAA Championship and earned first-team All-American honors three times.

Because he chose college over juniors, though, some questioned if the younger Esposito would every make it as a professional. But his route to the pros wasn't the only part of his game that didn't conform to convention.

Esposito employed the same butterfly style between the pipes that Glenn Hall did for years in Chicago. It wasn't pretty, but it worked. Bobby Orr, who played with Esposito in Chicago at the end of his career, describes it this way in Brian McFarlane's *The Blackhawks*: "He looks like hell in goal. The guy does everything wrong. He gives us shooters all kinds of openings and he doesn't play the angles very well. Heck, he doesn't even keep his legs together, giving you big holes to shoot at. But when you shoot at them, they're gone. He closes them up. He's amazingly quick. And the thing is, he gets the job done."

Esposito's career didn't begin easily, either. He signed with the Montreal Canadiens, who had perhaps the greatest goalie depth in the game at that point. Gump Worsley was their starter, and

Chicago Blackhawks coach Billy Reay holds up goalie Tony Esposito's hand after the Blackhawks defeated the Montreal Canadiens to win the Eastern Division championship on April 6, 1970.

they had a young prospect named Ken Dryden developing. But, because Esposito was older and more mature, he got the call late in the 1968–69 season to replace injured Rogie Vachon as Worsley's replacement.

He showed some brief glimpses of his abilities with two shutouts in 13 games that season—including one against big brother Phil and the Bruins—and would have his name engraved on the Stanley Cup when the Habs won the championship that spring.

But, because Worsley was the present and Dryden the future in Montreal, Esposito was not protected by the Habs when the annual intraleague draft took place that summer. Chicago GM Tommy Ivan was looking for a capable backup and snatched up Esposito. Ivan hadn't planned on Esposito taking over as the Hawks' primary netminder for the next decade, but Esposito forced his way into the lineup.

What Esposito did in his rookie season was unheard of: not only did he bring the Calder Memorial Trophy home, but he was also the runner-up for the Hart Memorial Trophy after establishing a new record with 15 shutouts in his first season. His 2.17 goals-against average was good enough to land him the Vezina Trophy as well. He was only the third goalie to win the Vezina catching right-handed. The Blackhawks won the West division the next year and advanced all the way to the Stanley Cup Finals, where they ultimately lost to Esposito's former employer, Montreal.

In his third season, Esposito posted the lowest goals-against average of his career (1.77) and again won the Vezina Trophy, this time sharing it with backup Gary Smith. He represented the Blackhawks in five consecutive All-Star Games (1970–74) and won the Vezina three times in the first half of the decade (1970, 1972, and 1974). In 1972 Esposito also represented Canada in the Summit Series in Moscow. He was the first goalie to defeat Russia in that tournament. Esposito returned to the All-Star Game in 1980 for a sixth and final time.

Again defying conventional wisdom, when Esposito played in the 1981 Canada Cup, he did so representing the United States. He had acquired dual citizenship during his days in Chicago, and when Canada failed to extend an invitation to him, he decided to play for the USA.

Unlike many other great players in the team's history, Esposito finished his career in Chicago. In total, he played 15 years between the pipes for Chicago before retiring in 1984. He still ranks seventh in NHL history—just in front of his Chicago predecessor, Hall—with 423 victories but was third when he retired. His 76 career shutouts are tied for ninth in NHL history with Ed Belfour.

In 1988 Tony O was honored by both the Blackhawks and the league. His No. 35 was retired at the Chicago Stadium, and he was inducted into the Hockey Hall of Fame. In 1998 he ranked 79th on the *Hockey News* list of the top 100 greatest hockey players of all time.

Ten years later, on March 19, 2008, the Blackhawks welcomed Tony O back into the family when they held Tony Esposito Night and formally introduced him as a Blackhawks ambassador. Fittingly, then-Blackhawks goalie Nikolai Khabibulin pitched a shutout that night, and the Hawks won 5–0.

Gramps

In 1980 the Chicago Blackhawks drafted a right wing that would define consistency. Selected 120th overall, Steve Larmer was a smooth-skating scoring forward in the tradition of Mikita. It wasn't an immediate impact, though; Larmer was demoted in each of his first two seasons and played only seven games before earning a permanent spot on the roster.

In 1980–81, his first professional season, Larmer was sent back to juniors with the Niagara Falls Flyers. That season he exploded with 55 goals and 133 points in only 61 games.

The following season he again failed to lock down a spot with the NHL club and was sent to the AHL. That may have been the critical point in Larmer's career, though, as he was introduced to coach Orval Tessier.

Tessier quickly fell in love with Larmer's game and played him heavily that season. He scored 38 goals and 44 assists and helped the New Brunswick Hawks advance deep into the playoffs with six goals and 12 points in 15 postseason contests.

The following year, Tessier was promoted to be the head coach in Chicago, and he brought Larmer with him. Once Larmer settled in on the Blackhawks' top line, it became apparent that the Blackhawks were back on the map in the NHL.

In the 1982–83 season, Larmer scored 43 goals and added 47 assists, and his 90 points were good enough to win the Calder Trophy as Rookie of the Year. He was skating next to Hall of Famer Denis Savard and enforcer Al Secord on what may have been the fastest line in the NHL, and he factored heavily into Savard posting 121 points that season.

Known as "Gramps," Larmer defined the wing position, indeed the Blackhawks, for over a decade. He was a two-time All-Star (1990, 1991) and continues to be an icon of longevity in Hawks history. Larmer played in 884 consecutive games in his 10-plus seasons in Chicago, scoring 923 points and leaving the franchise with a career plus-minus of +182. His 884 straight games played is an NHL record for most consecutive games played with the same team, and the third-longest consecutive-games streak in league history.

Larmer scored 30-plus goals in nine seasons and broke Jim Pappin's club record for points by a right-winger with 101 in 1990–91.

He also played a huge role in the 1991 Team Canada victory in the Canada Cup as well, when his breakaway goal against Mike Richter was the decisive tally in Team Canada's victory over Team USA in the final of the Canada Cup. He led the entire Canada Cup in goals (6) and ranked second in points (11) behind only Wayne Gretzky. He was honored as the Hockey News/Inside Hockey Man of the Year that year.

What might be the only part of Larmer's résumé more impressive than his streak of consecutive games played is the fact that the Blackhawks qualified for the postseason every season he wore the Indian-head sweater. Indeed, Larmer appeared in the playoffs in all 13 seasons he played regularly in the NHL.

Beyond the numbers Larmer was a class act. "He was one of the best forwards to ever play the game and, more importantly, one of the finest people I have ever met," said former teammate Doug Wilson.

Today Larmer ranks fourth in Blackhawks history in points (923), third in goals (406), fifth in assists (517), seventh in games played (891), and his plus-minus (+182) is the best in franchise history. He is also the organization's all-time leader with 49 game-winning goals.

Larmer was voted onto the Blackhawks 75th Anniversary Team by the fans in 2000.

In his great career, Larmer played 1,006 regular-season games, scoring 1,012 points (441 goals, 571 assists). He also scored 131 points (56 goals, 75 assists) in 140 career postseason games. He won the Stanley Cup with the New York Rangers in 1994.

Steve Larmer should be in the Hockey Hall of Fame.

10 '61

On paper there was no chance. The Blackhawks finished in third place, 17 points behind the Canadiens during the regular season. They didn't have anyone in the league's top 10 in points, had only two players—defenseman Pierre Pilote and goalie Glenn Hall—named to the NHL's second All-Star team, and didn't win a single postseason award.

In fact, the most impressive thing the team did the entire regular season was, in a game in which they were shut out by the New York Rangers, Reg Fleming racked up 37 penalty minutes. In one game!

When the playoffs began, the Hawks faced the overwhelmingly favored defending-champion Montreal Canadiens. The Habs came into the series featuring the league's most valuable player and leading scorer, Bernie Geoffrion; the top defenseman, Doug Harvey; and two great centers in Jean Beliveau and Henri Richard.

The young Blackhawks, however, had a developing young nucleus, and Glenn Hall was established as an elite netminder. With young stars Bobby Hull on one line and Stan Mikita centering "the Scooter Line," Chicago hoped for at least a fighting chance in the first-round series.

Chicago proved to have more than youth on their side and shocked the league by eliminating the Habs in six games. In the other semifinal series, the fourth-place Red Wings also pulled off the upset and defeated the Leafs in five.

When the two hated rivals got together in the Finals, it was the first time since 1938 that the Blackhawks would have the opportunity to win the ultimate prize. They had spend most of the

1950s essentially serving as a farm team for the Red Wings; the two teams shared common ownership, and the Norris Family preferred Detroit.

That year, the games in the Finals alternated home ice with each game. With the changing scenery, the teams also alternated wins through the first five games, heading back to Detroit for Game 6 with the Blackhawks leading the series three games to two. Hull scored the game-winning goal in Game 1, and Mikita had the winner in Game 3.

Each of the first four games were close, but the Hawks put the hammer down in a strikingly decisive 6–3 win at the Chicago Stadium in Game 5. Game 6 ended early as well, with the Hawks skating to a definitive 5–1 victory. Ab McDonald was credited with the Cup-clinching goal at 18:49 in the second period.

However, after the game, coach Rudy Pilous gave credit for the winner to Fleming, who tied the game with a short-handed tally. "Reggie Fleming's goal did it," Pilous told the *Montreal Gazette*. "That's when we won it. The goal only tied the game, but it took the starch out of them and gave us the zip we needed. What more could you ask than to score a goal when you are short-handed?"

The Blackhawks have qualified for the Stanley Cup Finals on a number of occasions, but 1961 was their only Cup championship between 1938 and 2010.

There are a couple great ways for fans to see some old film of the 1961 champions. In 2007 Sundown Entertainment released a DVD titled *The Forgotten Champs: The Story of the 1961 Stanley Cup Champion Chicago Blackhawks*. This is an insightful documentary looking back at the championship team.

More recently, in 2010 NHL Studios and Warner Home Video released a six-disc collection of the greatest games and moments in Blackhawks history. Included on the sixth disc is actual game footage of the entire final 14 minutes of Game 6 of the 1961 Finals. There is also some great interview footage from after the game.

Since Rocky Wirtz took over, the history of the Blackhawks is more available to fans. Seeing Hull, Mikita, Pilote, and other great Hawks of the past around the United Center isn't uncommon.

11 Hull's 51st

In 1966 *Time* magazine reported, "The only thing that stood between Chicago Black Hawk Bobby Hull and goal No. 51 was the entire National Hockey League. By rights, even that should not have been enough." And it wasn't.

It was March 12, 1966. The Chicago Blackhawks were hosting the New York Rangers, who had Cesare Maniago in net. At 5:34 in the third period, Lou Angotti pushed a pass to Hull, who unloaded one of his familiar missiles from about 40 feet out. Eric Nesterenko, who was providing a good screen on Maniago, got out of the way just in time for Hull to break the NHL's record for goals in a season. This was Hull's 51st goal of the season.

At the time, the 50-goal mark was one of the most hallowed records in North American sports. Only Rocket Richard and Boom Boom Geoffrion had accomplished the feat, but neither had eclipsed the magic number of 50. Oddly enough, Maniago was in the net as a member of the Toronto Maple Leafs when Geoffrion scored his 50th goal. "I'm already in the books for giving up Geoffrion's goal," Maniago said later. "Why should I worry about Hull's?"

The aftermath of the puck entering the net was overwhelming for even the effervescent Hull. A ten-minute standing ovation from the crowd at the Chicago Stadium was loud enough that Hull later admitted to having goose bumps.

Blackhawks Art Ross Winners

Originally awarded after the 1947–48 season, the Art Ross Trophy is awarded to the player who leads the NHL in points (goals and assists) at the end of the regular season.

The following members of the Chicago Blackhawks have won the Art Ross Trophy:

- Roy Conacher: 1948–49
- Bobby Hull: 1959–60, 1961–62, 1965–66
- Stan Mikita: 1963–64, 1964–65, 1966–67, 1967–68

Martin Kane summed it up in the March 21, 1966, edition of *Sports Illustrated* when he wrote, "When the red light that signifies a goal flashed on, the more than 20,000 fans in the stadium lost control. They littered the ice with debris that ranged from hats—both men's and women's—to confetti. As he skated toward the Black Hawk bench, Hull picked up one of the more ludicrous hats and put it on, getting a laugh because, after all, he was Bobby Hull, and no man in the history of the National Hockey League, give or take 50-game or 70-game seasons, had ever made such a goal before."

The next day, a Chicago disc jockey invited listeners to sent gifts to Hull—as long as there was a *51* involved in the gift somehow. On the list of items received at the Hull household in the coming days were 51 chocolate pucks, 51 litter bags for his cattle, 51 puck-shaped steaks, 51 weeks' worth of free tobacco, 51 frozen TV dinners, 51 mops, and 51 car washes. Chicago Bears linebacker Dick Butkus—No. 51—sent one of his jerseys over to Hull. Even Hull's wife was in on the receiving end of the achievement. She received 51 roses, 51 pairs of stockings, and a gold bracelet with 51 charms. But the gift that topped them all was a hockey stick with 51 diamonds embedded in it.

With the goal, Hull quietly set a second NHL record; this was his 21st power-play goal of the season. But the reason the crowd stood and cheered their hero as loudly—and as long—as they did was because he was now the NHL's scoring king. The event was front-page news across the country and was worthy of a lead story in both *Time* magazine and *Sports Illustrated*. Hull was on top of the hockey world.

He finished the 1965–66 season with 54 goals and also set a new NHL record with 97 points that season. He won the Art Ross Trophy and his second straight Hart Trophy as the league's MVP. No left wing would match his point total again until Washington's Alexander Ovechkin in 2007–08, 42 years later.

12 The National Anthem

During the 2010 Stanley Cup Finals, NHL officials wanted to know exactly how loud the United Center could get. Readings were taken during the first two games of the series against the Philadelphia Flyers, and the numbers were astounding. The highest reading was 122 decibels, as loud as a shotgun blast. And the loudest crowd roar didn't even take place during game action. It happened during the National Anthem.

After the crowd reached 121 decibels during the National Anthem before Game 1, a number of media members brought earplugs with them for Game 2. That was when the United Center crowd reached a level that the building hadn't seen since Michael Jordan retired.

As NHL.com reported, the tradition began in 1985: "Chicago's anthem tradition began during the 1985 conference finals against Edmonton. After dropping the first two games of the series on the road, Hawks fans entered Chicago Stadium on May 9 fully energized and ready to help their team get back into the series. The crowd was so excited they cheered all the way through the National Anthem—and the tradition stuck.

"'When I introduced the anthem, fans just started clapping and cheering,' said Harvey Wittenberg, the Blackhawks' public-address announcer from 1961–2001. 'That was the start of the phenomenon.'"

In the 1980s and early 1990s, Wayne Messmer handled the duty of singing the National Anthem. The moment that sticks in most fans' minds throughout the country (and that can still be viewed on YouTube) is Messmer singing before the 1991 NHL All-Star Game at the Chicago Stadium. The Blackhawks were contenders for the Stanley Cup, and the roar literally shook the old building.

Unfortunately, Messmer was shot during a robbery outside a restaurant in April 1994 and was unable to perform at the final six Hawks home games at the Stadium. For those games, the team used a recording of him singing instead.

When the Blackhawks moved from the Chicago Stadium to the United Center, however, the organization also changed National Anthem singers. Messmer performed the song for the last time at the first Blackhawks' home game at the U.C. on January 25, 1995.

In 1995 the Blackhawks opened up the position to a rotation of singers, and one gentleman who tried out has since earned the regular job of presenting "The Star-Spangled Banner" to United Center faithful: Jim Cornelison.

Cornelison started making regular appearances in 1996, but the classically trained opera singer won the permanent job in 2007. "It's really a different situation [from] anywhere else I've sung," Cornelison told NHL.com. "I've always had pregame jitters, and if I don't have jitters then I get jitters because [I] don't have jitters. I think that keeps [me] sharp when [I'm] nervous."

While there has been some discussion from national bloggers about the sanctity of the song, fans, players, and military personnel—active and veteran—who have attended a home Blackhawks game have almost universally agreed that the applause during the National Anthem is one of the best traditions in North American sports.

13 Tommy Ivan

Tommy Ivan was known as much for his style as he was for his substance. He was never seen in anything less than a well-cut suit and a bold handkerchief, but the quality he brought to both the bench and front office were among the best in the history of the game.

He was one of the smallest men ever associated with the Chicago Blackhawks, but he made one of the largest impacts on the history of the organization. Standing only 5'5", Ivan made an indelible mark on two franchises in the NHL—the Detroit Red Wings and Blackhawks—that ultimately led him to induction into the Hockey Hall of Fame.

Ivan's career got off to a rough start, though. As a 26-year-old playing in the minors, he suffered a cheekbone fracture that ended his playing career. After a few years trying his hand as a referee, he landed a job in the Red Wings organization as a minor league coach. His time in the minors with Detroit laid the foundation for one of the most impressive coaching tenures in NHL history.

Ivan was promoted to the head coach in Detroit in 1947 and also took over managing the organization's minor league teams. While coaching Detroit's minor league teams in Omaha and Indianapolis, he became familiar with numerous young players who would eventually leave incredible legacies in the world of professional hockey.

Terry Sawchuk, Ted Lindsay, Sid Abel, and Gordie Howe were a few of the youngsters promoted by Ivan while he was coaching the Red Wings. In the seven years Ivan coached in Detroit, the Red Wings finished first six times and won three Cups.

Yet all that winning wasn't enough. Ivan wanted to be a general manager, but Detroit's front office was managed by Jack Adams. Because the legendary Adams wasn't going anywhere, Ivan decided to end his relationship with Detroit.

The Blackhawks and Red Wings shared a number of things in common at this time in their histories. When Ivan began with both teams, each was in miserable shape. And they shared common ownership. In 1953–54, James D. Norris and Arthur

Hockey star Bobby Orr (right) holds a multimillion-dollar Blackhawks contract at the signing ceremony with general manager Tommy Ivan (left) on June 24, 1976, in Chicago.

Wirtz took control of the Chicago Blackhawks. Both had been major shareholders in the Detroit Red Wings organization, and one of their first moves as owners was signing Ivan away from the Wings.

Chicago was 17 years removed from their last Stanley Cup when Ivan took over the front office, but he immediately went about the work of changing the culture in Chicago. The Blackhawks were playing in front of pitiful crowds of 3,000–4,000 per night and had been finishing at or near the bottom of the standings on an annual basis.

In one of his first deals as Chicago's general manager, Ivan acquired 1955 Calder Trophy–winner Ed Litzenberger from Montreal. His remarkable eye for talent led to a quick injection of top talent into the Blackhawks organization, as Ivan brought in players such as Bobby and Dennis Hull, Stan Mikita, Pierre Pilote, and Ken Wharram.

In 1957–58 Ivan made the first of his remarkable trades to bring goalie depth into the system when he made a deal with his former mentor in Detroit, acquiring Glenn Hall and Ted Lindsay.

By 1959 Ivan had built the Blackhawks into a playoff team and, in 1961, the Blackhawks brought the Stanley Cup back to Chicago. In the 12 years following the Cup win, the Blackhawks went on to play in the Stanley Cup Finals four more times.

The stands were no longer empty, either. For 14 straight years, the Chicago Stadium was sold out when the Blackhawks played, and the packed stands at the Chicago Stadium were treated to some of the best talent in the history of the game.

The biggest demerit on Ivan's record was the trade that sent Phil Esposito to Boston in a blockbuster deal. As Ivan regularly remembered it later, though, he sent one of the players he received—Gillies Marotte—to Los Angeles for Gerry Desjardins. He later dealt another player acquired in that trade—Jack Norris— to Montreal with Bill White in exchange for Phil's younger brother, goalie Tony Esposito. Of course, Tony Esposito went on to a great Hall of Fame career in Chicago.

Ivan served as the general manager of the Blackhawks from 1954 to 1977, eventually handing the reins to Bob Pulford. When he stepped away from the Blackhawks' front office, though, he didn't walk away from the game completely. He moved on to play a critical role in the United States Olympic Hockey program, including serving as the chairman of the 1979–80 Olympic Hockey Festival. Ivan was an important part of the process that built Herb Brooks' 1980 U.S. Men's Ice Hockey Team that made us all believe in miracles.

Ivan was inducted into the Hockey Hall of Fame as a Builder in 1974.

14 Billy Reay

In a November 12, 1973, article for *Sports Illustrated*, an anonymous Blackhawks player described his coach's face when he wasn't happy with the team's play. He said, "When the coach looks like that, he doesn't need a lot of words to transmit his displeasure."

That player was talking about legendary Blackhawks coach Billy Reay, who still has more wins than any coach in Chicago history.

Many fans do not remember that Reay actually played in the NHL for 10 seasons, two in Detroit and eight in Montreal. In fact, he centered a line in Montreal with one of the greatest scorers ever, Maurice "Rocket" Richard, and was part of two Stanley Cup championship teams (1946, 1953). He is also credited as the first player to raise his arms and stick above his head in celebration after scoring a goal, something that's seen on a nightly basis in the game today.

He will always be remembered for his trademark fedora, which was always visible behind the bench, and for handling some of the more colorful players in the game at the time. Hired before the 1963–64 season, Reay took the pieces he was given by general manager Tommy Ivan and turned them into functioning, competitive teams for 13 years. During Reay's tenure, the Blackhawks finished first six times and made three appearances in the Stanley Cup Finals. In 12 of his 13 seasons, the Blackhawks qualified for the postseason.

While playing for Reay as their head coach in Chicago, Blackhawks players would regularly win the major leaguewide awards. Bobby Hull (one Ross, one Lady Byng, and two Hart Trophies), Stan Mikita (four Ross, two Lady Byng, and two Hart Trophies), Pierre Pilote (two Norris Trophies), and goalies Glenn Hall (one Vezina Trophy) and Tony Esposito (three Vezina Trophies) all won significant individual hardware under Reay's leadership.

As Blackhawks team historian Bob Verdi recalled in a February 2011 article for Blackhawks.com, Reay coached in an era when *coach* meant more than just the man with the clipboard. "He was a one-man show in those days. Coaches didn't have assistants or traveling secretaries or public relations types in tow. Reay handed out boarding passes at airports when the Blackhawks took commercial flights. He was in charge of per diem meal money. And he conducted business with quiet dignity, always dressed immaculately from fedora to the toe, forever aware that players dealt with family pressures, nagging injuries, and daily issues like anyone else."

However, the years passed and Reay, like Ivan, got older. During the 1977 season, only a few days before Christmas, Reay was relieved of his duties as the head coach of the Chicago

Blackhawks via a note slid under his hotel-room door. Like Ivan, who left the organization after the season, Reay was replaced by new head coach/GM Bob Pulford.

Reay's Blackhawks teams built a remarkable record of 516 wins, 335 losses, and 161 ties. Known as "X-Reay" to his players for the look referred to in the *Sports Illustrated* article, Reay was respected by his players but did not spend much time building rapport with the media outside of Chicago. Perhaps because he never put much stock in his relationship with the media, Reay is still (somehow) not in the Hockey Hall of Fame. His 542 total career wins (including two seasons in Toronto before coming to Chicago) still ranks 12th all-time; Joel Quenneville and Marc Crawford knocked him out of 10th during the 2010–11 season.

15 Bill Mosienko

In the game of hockey, being listed at 5'8" tall and only 160 pounds is normally considered a disadvantage. But for Bill Mosienko, it may have helped him.

After making his NHL debut late in the 1941–42 season, Mosienko received a medical exemption from military service that allowed him to stay home from World War II. However, that exemption also limited his travel—and kept him out of the United States.

Once he was able to travel to, and play in, the United States for the 1943–44 season, Mosienko was ready to become a superstar in the NHL. He exploded onto the scene with 70 points in his first full season and combined with linemates Doug Bentley and Clint Smith to establish an NHL-record 219 points as a line. Mosienko's

Bill Mosienko holds up three pucks to symbolize his NHL record for the fastest three goals by a single player, set against the New York Rangers on March 23, 1952.

team rookie record of 70 points stood for 37 years, until Denis Savard broke it in 1980–81.

Perhaps more impressive than his scoring record, Mosienko followed that performance with a number that may never be topped: zero. In 1944–45, Mosienko won the Lady Byng Memorial Trophy after being called for zero penalty minutes in 50 games.

With all the respect that the gentlemen of the game—such as Detroit's Pavel Datsyuk—receive today, the career numbers for

Mosienko seem to be a typo at first glance. In 14 years with the Blackhawks, Mosienko totaled only 121 penalty minutes. In fact, he had fewer than 10 penalty minutes in an entire season on five different occasions.

Mosienko remains one of the most respected players in the game's history. Because of his small stature and his status as one of the league's top scorers, Mosienko was frequently a target for physical play and was often injured. He almost never retaliated, though; he was involved in only one fight in his career.

Early in his career, Mosienko was one of three Hall of Famers on the famous Pony Line, with fellow diminutive forwards Doug and Max Bentley. Together, Mosienko and the Bentley brothers made up one of the most dangerous lines in NHL history—and none of them stood taller than 5'8".

Mosienko has one record that may stand forever. On March 23, 1952—Chicago's regular-season finale—the Blackhawks were playing the Rangers in New York in front of 3,254 fans. The Hawks were battling the Boston Bruins in the middle of the six-team league standings, while the Rangers were comfortably in last place.

Lady Byng Recipients

The Lady Byng Memorial Trophy is awarded by the Professional Hockey Writers Association to the "player adjudged to have exhibited the best type of sportsmanship and gentlemanly conduct combined with a high standard of playing ability." It was initially awarded in 1925.

The following Chicago Blackhawks have won the Lady Byng Memorial Trophy:

- Elwyn "Doc" Romnes: 1935–36
- Max Bentley: 1942–43
- Clint Smith: 1943–44
- Bill Mosienko: 1944–45
- Ken Wharram: 1963–64
- Bobby Hull: 1964–65
- Stan Mikita: 1966–67, 1967–68

That Rangers team allowed 219 goals that season—second-most in the league—but it was the three goals they allowed on March 23, 1952, that will be remembered most. On that night, Mosienko scored three goals...in 21 seconds! In the third period, Mosienko beat Rangers netminder Lorne Anderson three times and almost added a fourth in less than a minute in a 7–6 Blackhawks victory. Searching for Bill Mosienko videos on NHL.com or Google yields footage of the goals.

Gus Bodnar also set a record with three assists in 21 seconds that night.

Despite scoring at least 20 goals per season five times, the statistic that Mosienko is most remembered for is his 21-second hat trick. The symmetry in Mosienko's career is remarkable, too; he scored two goals in 21 seconds in his NHL debut.

Mosienko was voted into the Hockey Hall of Fame in 1965 after a spectacular career in Chicago. He scored 258 goals and added 282 assists in 711 NHL games. He ranks eighth in Blackhawks history in goals and 10th in points, with 540.

16 The Bentley Brothers

Long before the NHL came to know families like the Sedins, Staals, or Stastnys, the Blackhawks had the best pair of brothers to play the game—Doug and Max Bentley.

Doug signed with the Blackhawks before the 1939–40 season and amazed opponents and the media with his abilities. The following season, he was joined in Chicago by Max, who was four years his junior. The two partnered to make one of the best scoring duos in the NHL. From 1940 to 1947, the Bentleys were the best

The all-brother line of the Chicago Blackhawks. The Bentleys cut up on the ice as they prepare for their first appearance in Chicago as a unit on December 3, 1942. From left to right are Reggie Bentley, Max Bentley, and Doug Bentley.

thing going for the Blackhawks. Doug led the league in goals in consecutive years—1942–43 and 1943–44—before taking a year off during World War II to take care of his family's farm. Doug led the NHL in points with 73 for the 1942–43 season, and was a first-team All-Star three times (1943, 1944, and 1947).

In 1950 the *Herald American* newspaper named the top athletes in each sport in Chicago for the first half of the century. Doug Bentley was chosen as the best hockey player in the city, joining Luke Appling (baseball), Bronko Nagurski (football), Barney Ross (boxing), and Chick Evans (golf) as the best Chicago athletes. When the list was put together, Doug ranked second in NHL history with 204 goals.

Doug Bentley left the Blackhawks after 13 seasons and 546 games, having scored 217 goals and added 314 assists. He still ranks in the top 13 in Hawks history in goals, assists, and total points.

After posting 70 points in only 47 games in 1942–43, Max spent two years away from the game because of World War II. When he returned in the 1945–46 season, he hadn't lost a step, contributing 61 points in 47 games.

The younger brother would be remembered as the better of the Bentley brothers. Max won the Lady Byng Memorial Trophy in 1943, led the league in scoring in 1946 and 1947, and won the Hart Memorial Trophy in 1946. He was also a first-team All-Star in 1946.

When Max won the scoring championship in 1946, he and Doug became the first brothers to both win the scoring title in league history. The only other brothers to both win the scoring crown are Charlie and Roy Conacher and Henrik and Daniel Sedin.

Unlike his older brother, though, Max Bentley did not choose when he left Chicago. After leading the league in 1946–47, the Hawks abruptly traded him to the Toronto Maple Leafs only six games into the 1947–48 season. Max spent six years with the Leafs before one final season with the New York Rangers.

In 1998, when The *Hockey News* published their list of the top 100 NHL players of all time, both of the Bentley brothers were

The Pony Line

Between the 1945–46 and 1947–48 seasons, the Blackhawks featured the best line in the game, called "the Pony Line." The Pony Line consisted of Max and Doug Bentley with Bill Mosienko, three of the most lethal scorers in the league at the time. In an era where a player with 70 points was almost unheard of, these three totaled 416 points in a combined 440 games over a three-year stretch.

Why were they called the Pony Line? "The Black Hawks' publicity man, Joe Farrell, came up with the name," Mosienko told Stan Fischler for *Hockey's 100.* "The three of us were so small, and every time we'd go for the puck, we'd give it a little bounce."

honored to be among the greats named. Max ranked at No. 48, while Doug came in at 73. Both were elected into the Hockey Hall of Fame as well; Doug entered the Hall in 1964, and Max followed two years later.

17 The Rivalry with Detroit

"I used to come to Blackhawks games with my father. I loved it. I loved the camaraderie, the electricity of a big night in the city… in a way, everything I know about life, I learned from my father watching the Blackhawks. It can all be summed up in two words. Two simple words that ring over and over in my memory: Detroit sucks!"

That's part of the script read by Chicago suburbanite and Blackhawks fan Jeremy Piven in a television commercial promoting Hawks tickets from the early part of the 21st century. For many Blackhawks fans, the words from Piven ring true.

Indeed, the evolution of contempt between the Blackhawks and the Red Wings has taken generations. The roots of the rivalry began in the earliest days of the two organizations. Red Wings owner James E. Norris and Blackhawks owner Major McLaughlin hated each other, and Norris went as far as to try buying into a new league to diminish the Blackhawks' market share in Chicago. Norris also tried to lock the Blackhawks out of the Chicago Stadium. In fact, Norris owned the Chicago Stadium in 1936.

When McLaughlin died in 1944, in the midst of the NHL losing players and teams to World War II, the coffee baron's estate was forced to sell the franchise to a syndicate led by Bill Tobin. Tobin, who had been the team's coach in 1929–30 and 1931–32, served as the team president from 1944 to 1954. However, he had been close friends with Norris for decades and did a better job of serving the interests of Norris than the Blackhawks during his tenure.

From 1945 to 1958, the Blackhawks were a doormat in the NHL, serving as little more than a farm team for Detroit. During that 13-year stretch, the Blackhawks qualified for the playoffs twice.

Foreshadowing events that would take place 50 years later, the death of an owner would dramatically change the fortunes of the Blackhawks franchise and its relationship with Detroit. James E. Norris passed away, and his son, James D. Norris, and his original partner in purchasing the Wings, Arthur Wirtz, left the Detroit organization to run the Blackhawks. The turnaround was immediate and came at the direct expense of the Red Wings.

Wirtz and the younger Norris' first move as owners was to hire Tommy Ivan away from Detroit. Ivan's eye for talent and his knack for drafting exceptional players made an enormous impact on the Hawks right away. He also made the infamous trade for Ted Lindsay and Glenn Hall, which effected a seismic shift in the NHL for the next decade.

In 1961 the rivalry was as hot as it had ever been. Detroit was led by Gordie Howe; Chicago featured headliners Mikita and Hull. The regular season was dominated by Montreal and Toronto, but both the Hawks (the three seed) and Wings (the four seed) staged incredible upsets in the first round of the playoffs. They met in the Stanley Cup Finals, and the Blackhawks came away with their first championship in 23 years at the hands of their archrival. That championship served as sweet redemption for Norris, Wirtz, and, most especially, Hall.

The 1960s were dominated by the Blackhawks, who played in two more Stanley Cup Finals during the decade. Hull and Mikita were the decade's elite scoring duo, and Pilote won three straight Norris Trophies.

From 1967 to 1982 Detroit struggled and went through what has come to be known as the "Dead Wings" era. No team was hit harder by the initial round of NHL expansion than the Red Wings, who suddenly saw their ability to stockpile talent diminished. However, ownership continued to play a major role in the success of the two teams.

In 1982 Mike Ilitch purchased the Wings from Bruce Norris, ending 50 years of ownership by the Norris family. Ilitch would transform the culture in Detroit and end the concept of the Dead Wings.

In the early 1980s, though, two players came into the NHL who would change the dynamics of the rivalry and alter NHL history. Just as Howe and Hull had been two of the great names 20 years prior, Denis Savard and Steve Yzerman sparked revolutions on both rosters that would make both franchises fast, high-scoring, and competitive for the next decade.

The Red Wings began to turn their franchise around and started to find success, thanks to Ilitch's willingness to open the payroll to unprecedented levels. In the mid-1990s the Red Wings brought in veterans from Russia and all over the NHL in order to break their Stanley Cup drought. While Detroit was spending money to buy a winner, Chicago's management was adopting the opposite philosophy; superstars were leaving Chicago on an annual basis.

The rivalry may have hit an all-time low in 2001, when the Blackhawks were skating a team featuring Tony Amonte and a group of names fewer fans could pronounce than recognize. The Red Wings had sparked a new rivalry with the Colorado Avalanche, and the chanting of "Detroit sucks!" was spawned as much by envy as it was a taunt of the other team.

At many Blackhawks home games, Detroit fans outnumbered Chicago fans. The cynicism in Chicago had reached an all-time high; the Hawks ranked at the bottom of the league in attendance, and the Wings were winning championships.

The theme of ownership impacting the rivalry popped up again in 2007, when Bill Wirtz passed away. His estate handed control of the Hawks to his son, Rocky. On New Year's Day in 2009, Rocky's second year of ownership, the rivalry found a unique venue when the two teams played outdoors at Wrigley Field in Chicago in the Winter Classic. It was the first hockey game ever to be played at Wrigley Field, and it came after Chicago beat out New York City, the other finalist to be the host city for the historic game.

Two years after Rocky took over, the Blackhawks–Red Wings rivalry was on center stage when the baby-faced Hawks faced the veteran Red Wings in the 2009 Western Conference Finals. The Red Wings had won the Stanley Cup in 2008 and were too much for those Hawks to handle. The Blackhawks finally raised the Cup again in 2010, after claiming the Central Division Championship, adding fuel to the longtime rivalry.

The United Center and Joe Louis Arena are both special venues with some of the most passionate home fans in sports. Now that both teams are winning and have rosters featuring some of the best players on the planet, the Blackhawks–Red Wings rivalry may be entering a renaissance, with both teams being competitive for the first time since Hull and Howe were on the ice.

18 Dale Tallon

It may have been one of the least heralded trades in the history of the Blackhawks, but the player acquired had arguably the greatest impact on the franchise of anyone ever added in that manner.

On May 14, 1973, the Blackhawks traded Jerry Korab and Gary Smith to the Vancouver Canucks for defenseman Dale

Tallon. Tallon had been the second overall selection in the 1970 Draft by the Canucks, and had been a two-time All-Star for Vancouver before being dealt to Chicago. He wasn't a statistical juggernaut by any means, though he did lead Vancouver with 42 assists in his rookie season. He was a solid defenseman.

In five seasons with the Blackhawks, he scored 44 goals and added 112 assists. In what would prove to be an ironic move that foreshadowed his future with the organization, Tallon was traded for a second-round draft pick in 1978.

Tallon's playing career was plagued with injuries and was cut short after 10 seasons in the NHL. After retiring in 1980, the Quebec native made Chicago his home. He spent the next 18 years as a color analyst for the Blackhawks, providing depth to the radio and television broadcasts while some of the special players in the organization's history were wearing the Indian-head sweater.

Starting in 1998, however, Tallon's relationship with the franchise started to evolve. He served as the director of player personnel from 1998 to 2002, a role in which he handled a great deal of the pro and amateur scouting. In November 2003, Tallon was named the assistant general manager, working alongside Bob Pulford. On June 21, 2005, Tallon was named the eighth general manager in the history of the Chicago Blackhawks.

Charged with the unbelievable task of trying to resuscitate the Chicago franchise, Tallon went about the work of building a roster within the new confines of the collective bargaining agreement created after the 2004–05 labor dispute. In Tallon's first season as GM, the Blackhawks finished 14th out of 15 teams in the conference.

Slowly, Tallon started winning minor battles with ownership and started effectively recruiting aging veterans like Martin Lapointe and Nikolai Khabibulin to come to the Blackhawks. How did he convince fading stars to come to Chicago? Usually by offering something other teams wouldn't: either more years or more money. Sometimes it took both.

Over time, though, some of the players Tallon signed started to click. Martin Havlat was a solid forward in Chicago for a number of years. Tallon's background in player development also came into play, and he was able to turn average players that were, in his mind, peaking into draft picks and undervalued players via trades.

Everything changed for the Blackhawks in 2007. Tallon was given an opportunity no Blackhawks general manager had before him: the first overall pick in the NHL Draft. There were a number of good players in the 2007 Draft class, but Tallon was sold on a scorer from Buffalo named Patrick Kane.

When the 2007–08 season began, Tallon's first-round pick from the previous draft—Jonathan Toews—and Kane were on the NHL roster. Both dealt with the growing pains of being teenagers in the National Hockey League, they have both blossomed into two of the best players ever to play for the Hawks.

Over the course of his time as general manger in Chicago, Tallon built a roster through draft picks, trades, and free agency that steadily climbed from the cellar to the top of the Western Conference. In only the second year that Toews and Kane were in Chicago, the team that was scraping the floor in the Western Conference just three years prior was eliminated in the conference Finals.

Tallon was responsible for drafting, trading for, or signing every player on the ice in June 2010, when the Blackhawks accepted the Stanley Cup from the commissioner for the first time in 49 years. At that moment, though, Tallon was in Florida.

The Blackhawks relieved Tallon of his duties as general manager in July 2009, demoting him to a senior advisor position and promoting Stan Bowman to the GM role. In May, just weeks before the roster he built realized their ultimate goal, Tallon left the organization to accept the job as general manager of the Florida Panthers.

History will remember Tallon's time in the Blackhawks front office in many ways. Did he overpay players like Khabibulin, Cristobal Huet, and Brian Campbell? Yes. But did he have to overpay top free agents to come play for a team that had terrible attendance and was more than a decade removed from contending? Absolutely. Top players didn't even return phone calls from Chicago for years while Pulford was making the decisions, but Tallon took the necessary steps to advance the organization to a place where players like Marian Hossa actually wanted to come to Chicago.

He will also be remembered for making stellar trades. He acquired Patrick Sharp with Eric Meloche for Matt Ellison and a third-round pick in the 2006 Draft. He turned Brandon Bochenski into Kris Versteeg, Jim Vandermeer into Ben Eager, and Tuomo Ruutu into Andrew Ladd. The Stanley Cup wouldn't have come to Chicago if Sharp, Versteeg, Eager, and Ladd weren't on the roster.

Finally, Tallon will be remembered for being an excellent evaluator of talent. When many analysts thought Phil Kessel was more NHL-ready than Toews, Tallon took the player he wanted. When analysts thought James Van Riemsdyk had a more NHL-appropriate game than Kane, Tallon stuck with the guy he thought would be the best player for the team.

He didn't hit a home run with every draft pick (Jack Skille), but considering the value brought to the organization by players like Dustin Byfuglien (245th overall pick in 2003) and Troy Brouwer (214th overall pick in 2004), there is no denying Tallon's outstanding eye for skill and his ability to bring players up to the NHL level.

Tallon gave more years to the Blackhawks organization—as a player, broadcaster and, eventually, in the front office—than anyone other than an owner. He will forever be an incredibly vital part of Hawks history.

19 Captain Serious

The 2006 NHL Draft was loaded with talent.

A big defenseman, Erik Johnson, was universally graded as the top player in the class, but from there it was pretty wide open with forwards. Sitting third in the draft, the Blackhawks would have a tough decision to make.

In 2005 the Hawks had selected Jack Skille with the seventh overall pick and hoped he would become a standout NHL player before long. Having selected a wing early the previous year, most analysts believed the Hawks would have to choose between a few young centers: Nicklas Backstrom, Jordan Staal, Phil Kessel, and Jonathan Toews. When Staal went second to Pittsburgh, the Blackhawks quickly made their choice. It would be Toews, and the franchise would never be the same.

At 16, in 2005, Toews was the captain of the Canada West U-17 team that won the gold medal in the World U-17 Hockey Challenge. Toews led the tournament in scoring and was named its MVP.

In 2006 Toews had a very busy year. He led North Dakota to the Frozen Four before the Chicago Blackhawks selected him. Later that summer, Toews was the youngest player on Canada's U-20 team at the World Juniors that won another gold medal.

On a roster with other future NHL stars Travis Zajac, T.J. Oshie, and Drew Stafford, Toews led the Fighting Sioux of North Dakota back to the Frozen Four in 2007.

Over that summer, Toews again represented Canada in the World Juniors and again won a gold medal. This time, however, Toews led Canada in scoring and made the tournament's All-Star team. This was the tournament in which Toews became a legend

The Triple Gold Club

The International Ice Hockey Federation (IIHF) is the governing body that handles the World Championships and Olympics as an intermediate entity between leagues such as the KHL, NHL, and others.

Players have competed in a mix of international tournaments as long as hockey has been played, and the IIHF created an elite, exclusive group for the greatest international players in the history of hockey, not just the NHL.

The Triple Gold Club is made up of players who have won a gold medal at the World Championships and Winter Olympics and a Stanley Cup victory at some point in their hockey careers. According to the IIHF's website, more than 15,000 players have played in the Worlds, over 9,000 have played in the NHL, and over 4,000 have competed in the Olympics.

Only 25 have qualified for the Triple Gold Club. Here is the list of members, followed by the year each player qualified:
- Tomas Jonsson, Sweden—1994
- Mats Naslund, Sweden—1994
- Hakan Loob, Sweden—1994
- Valeri Kamensky, Soviet Union—1996
- Alexei Gusarov, Soviet Union—1996
- Peter Forsberg, Sweden—1996
- Vyacheslav Fetisov, Soviet Union—1997
- Igor Lirionov, Soviet Union—1997
- Alexander Moginly, Soviet Union—2000
- Vladimir Malakhov, Soviet Union—2000
- Rob Blake, Canada—2002
- Joe Sakic, Canada—2002
- Brendan Shanahan, Canada—2002
- Scott Niedermayer, Canada—2002
- Jaromir Jagr, Czech Republic—2005
- Jiri Slegr, Czech Republic—2005
- Nicklas Lidstrom, Sweden—2006
- Fredrik Modin, Sweden—2006
- Chris Pronger, Canada—2007
- Niklas Kronwall, Sweden—2008
- Henrik Zetterberg, Sweden—2008

- Mikael Samuelsson, Sweden—2008
- Eric Staal, Canada—2010
- Jonathan Toews, Canada—2010
- Patrice Bergeron, Canada—2011

When he won the Stanley Cup in 1996, Forsberg became the youngest player to achieve Triple Gold Club membership at 22 years, 325 days. Toews was just 22 years, 43 days old when he accepted the Cup from Gary Bettman. Toews added both the Olympic Gold and Stanley Cup win to his résumé within four months of each other and was awarded a gold pin by the IIHF before the Blackhawks' Stanley Cup parade through Chicago in June 2010.

Toews is also the youngest Canadian-born player ever to win gold at the World Juniors, Worlds, and Olympics.

on the international stage with three shootout goals against the United States in the semifinals.

His 2007 wasn't over yet, though. Toews then played for Canada in the World Championships, where he again won a gold medal. With this gold, Toews became the first Canadian to win gold at both the World Juniors and Worlds in the same year.

He was still 19 years old but was ready to leave college behind. On October 10, 2007, Toews made his NHL debut against the San Jose Sharks, and he didn't disappoint. Toews began his career with a 10-game point streak (five goals and five assists), the second-longest point streak to begin a career in NHL history.

At the end of the 2007–08 season Toews finally lost at something: he was the runner-up to teammate Patrick Kane for the Calder Trophy. Washington Capitals center Niklas Backstrom was third in the voting that year. Over the summer of 2008, Toews again represented Canada in the World Championships and won the silver.

On July 18, 2008, before the Blackhawks' fan convention and at just 20 years, 79 days old, Toews was named the third-youngest

captain in the history of the NHL and the youngest in the history
of the Blackhawks organization. Only Tampa's Vincent Lecavalier
and Pittsburgh's Sidney Crosby wore the *C* at a younger age than
Toews.

His first season as captain ended with an improbable run
to the Western Conference Finals, where the Hawks lost to
the Detroit Red Wings. Toews led the Hawks with 34 goals in
just his second NHL season. With Kane and Brian Campbell,
Toews was voted a starter in the 2009 NHL All-Star Game for
the first time.

That's already a great résumé. But during the 2009–10 season,
the achievements continued. In the 2010 Winter Olympics, Toews
led the tournament in assists and was named the Most Outstanding
Forward in the Games while leading Canada to the gold medal.
With the gold, Toews became the youngest Canadian player ever to
win golds in the World Juniors, Worlds, and Olympic Games. His
Stanley Cup championship with the Blackhawks in 2010 elevated
Toews to an elite class.

The IIHF has an exclusive club of their own known as the
Triple Gold Club, which was made up of 23 players who had won
a gold medal in the World Championships and Olympic Games
and a Stanley Cup in their careers. Names like Peter Forsberg, Joe
Sakic, Rob Blake, Scott Niedermayer, Nicklas Lidstrom, and Chris
Pronger were on this most incredible list of 23 players. Names that
were not on the Triple Gold list: Gretzky, Lemieux, either Hull, Orr,
Bourque, or Roy. Toews' name became the No. 24 on this most
exclusive list.

While leading the Blackhawks to their first Stanley Cup
victory in 49 years, Toews again established himself as one of the
greatest players in the game. He earned the Conn Smythe Trophy
as Most Valuable Player of the NHL postseason by posting an
incredible 29 points (seven goals, 22 assists) in 22 games. He is

the only player in the history of the Blackhawks to win the Conn Smythe Trophy.

Clearly the Blackhawks made the right choice at center on draft day.

20 The First Great Hawks Goalie

The long history of the Chicago Blackhawks is filled with superstar players. Indeed, the Blackhawks have a wonderful tradition of great goalies, including Hall of Famers Glenn Hall, Tony Esposito, and Ed Belfour.

But before the fans were thrilled by Hall or Hull or Savard or Kane, the original superstar in Chicago was Charlie Gardiner.

Born in Edinburgh, Scotland, in 1904, Gardiner was one of very few European players to make it in the NHL in the early years of the league. He emigrated to Winnipeg with his family as a seven-year-old, though, and grew up around the game.

In the second year the Blackhawks existed, the 1927–28 season, they brought Gardiner to the NHL as a backup for Hugh Lehman. It didn't take long for coach Barney Stanley to hand the reins at net to Gardiner. During his rookie season, Gardiner had three shutouts and kept a mediocre Blackhawks team in many games. Still, the Hawks finished in last place.

The following season saw Gardiner emerge as one of the top goalies in the league, racking up five shutouts and posting a phenomenal 1.85 goals-against average. Despite Gardiner's solid individual statistics, he led the league in losses; the Blackhawks won only seven games all season.

Gardiner revolutionized communication on the ice, and was the Blackhawks captain, and as Gardiner improved, so did the Hawks. In 1930–31, Gardiner was named to the NHL's first All-Star team with a league-best 12 shutouts and a 1.73 goals-against average. The next year, Gardiner was the first Hawks netminder to win the Vezina Trophy. Between 1928–29 and 1933–34, Gardiner played in every Hawks game over a six-year span, which was the longest streak among all NHL goalies.

Between the pipes, the Blackhawks had the best player in the league. And finally, in 1933–34, they put a team in front of him that could win. That year, Gardiner led the NHL again with 10 shutouts and won his second Vezina Trophy. It was the third time in seven seasons that Gardiner led the NHL in shutouts. The Hawks followed Gardiner's lead all the way to the Stanley Cup Finals, where they defeated the Detroit Red Wings for the first championship in the organization's history.

Gardiner's performance was incredible considering the circumstances. Toward the end of the season, he had been suffering from a chronic tonsil infection that doctors failed to diagnose. The disease had spread, causing Gardiner to have uremia convulsions. Even though he was playing through excruciating pain the entire postseason, Gardiner allowed only 12 goals in eight playoff games en route to winning the Cup. In the final game, he could barely stand on his skates and was getting weaker the longer the game progressed. As the team celebrated on the ice, Gardiner disappeared into the dressing room and collapsed.

Just a couple weeks after he fulfilled his dream of winning the Stanley Cup, Gardiner suffered a massive brain hemorrhage. He had surgery, but complications cost him his life on June 13, 1934. He was only 29 and undoubtedly had a lot of hockey left in him.

When the Hockey Hall of Fame opened its doors in 1945, Gardiner was among the inaugural class of inductees. He finished his seven-year NHL career with a 2.02 goals-against average in

316 regular-season games, including 42 shutouts. In his postseason career, he held Blackhawks opponents scoreless in five of 21 career starts, allowing an incredible 1.43 goals-against average.

Despite his career being cut tragically short, Gardiner is remembered as one of the great superstars of the early years of the NHL, and he is remembered as the first great Blackhawks player.

21 Stosh's Stick

When the Blackhawks won the Stanley Cup in 1961, every player in the NHL had at least one thing in common when they were on the ice: the blade of their stick was straight and flat. Thanks to a couple Hawks, that all changed.

In the mid-1960s, Stan Mikita was not only one of the best centers in the game but also ranked among the league's scoring leaders on an annual basis. History also remembers him as an innovator who revolutionized the equipment now considered standard in hockey at any level.

An urban legend claims that Mikita broke a stick blade late in a practice once, and when he shot a puck out of frustration with the broken blade, he was intrigued by the reaction he received from the puck. The crooked blade caused the puck to sail through the air in a way he had never seen before, and his interest was piqued.

As Mikita recalled in an interview for the NHL Network, he began experimenting with a stick blade that wasn't straight away from the rest of his teammates. He would fashion a curve, starting at the heel of the blade, that wasn't too dramatic because he still wanted to be effective in faceoffs. But while the puck was on the ice, the control provided by the curved blade was unparalleled. And the movement it created while the puck was in the air was ferocious.

One day, Mikita brought the personalized sticks to practice, and one teammate in particular was anxious to get his hands on one. Bobby Hull, who possessed one of the most lethal shots in the history of the sport, was fascinated by the things Mikita could do with the puck while using a curved blade. He told Mikita he wanted a few, and he started working on personalizing his own sticks as well. Soon Hull's stick blade had a similar curve to a banana, and his shot became scarier than before.

In 1966–67 Mikita and Hull were the top two scorers in the NHL, posting 97 and 80 points, respectively. Detroit's Norm Ullman ranked third that year, 10 points behind Hull. The following year, Mikita again led the NHL with 87 points while Hull's 75 points fell back to sixth in the NHL. The two had been dynamite without the advantage of a curved stick blade. Now they were even more explosive.

However, the league took notice of the sticks being used by the two players and others who had started to imitate them. After the 1967–68 season the NHL initiated new regulations for the amount a stick blade could be curved, with the new rule stating that the curve could not be more than half of one inch.

Players, including Mikita and Hull, continued to press the issue, though. After the 1968–69 campaign, the league relaxed their rule to curves being allowed to go as far as 1.5 inches. That appeared to be too much again, and 12 months later the rule was rewritten again.

While the rules continued to change, the league assigned an official to personally check stick blades and physically stamp them as being acceptable. Hull remembers getting his sticks stamped before playoff games in 1971 and immediately heading into the equipment room to massage the blade to have a more dramatic cut.

Stan Mikita on October 17, 1961…still using a straight-bladed stick.

The Scooter Line

A popular misconception about the astronomical numbers put up by Bobby Hull and Stan Mikita is that the two players skated together the entire time they were teammates in Chicago.

Mikita's production came as the center of the Scooter Line, with Ken Wharram and three other wings who replaced each other in the third position: Ted Lindsay, who was replaced by Ab McDonald, who was later replaced by Doug Mohns.

A search for the Scooter Line on YouTube reveals that the line was so well known and respected that it was featured during the 2010 playoffs in one of the NHL's great "History Will Be Made" commercials. And history was indeed made when the Scooter Line was on the ice together.

In total, the NHL altered the regulation dictating acceptable curve depth four consecutive years, leaving it at one-half inch until again revisiting the issue after the most recent lockout, when they relaxed the rule again.

When Hull left the Blackhawks to join the Winnipeg Jets of the newly formed WHA, he forced the league to allow a more generous curve than the NHL so he could continue using his "banana blade."

Other players have pressed their luck with the depth of their blade curve, the most famous of which was Los Angeles' Marty McSorley, who was called for a penalty because of his curve in Game 2 of the 1993 Stanley Cup Finals when Montreal coach Jacque Demers challenged his stick.

But for all the unique, personalized sticks that players use today, the innovator who placed the original curve into the blade of his hockey stick was Mikita.

22 Mush March

In overtime, the diminutive right wing skates in and scores an overtime, Stanley Cup–clinching goal. Sound familiar?

In 1934 a right who was well below six feet tall named Harold "Mush" March scored the goal of his life to win the Chicago Blackhawks their first ever Stanley Cup championship. In the second overtime of Game 4 (back then the Finals were best-of-five), March scored the Cup-winning goal to defeat the Detroit Red Wings. March's goal broke a scoreless game after 30:05 of extra play.

The similarities to Patrick Kane's goal in the Blackhawks' 2010 Cup victory are remarkable. In the book *The Stanley Cup* by John Devaney and Bert Goldblatt, March recalls that there was some confusion for him when he scored the game-winner. "I didn't realize it at the second, you know, that we'd won the Stanley Cup, but it was great," said March. "I rushed in and got the puck and then the fellows grabbed me and wheeled me on their shoulders all the way around the rink."

March was listed at 5'5" tall and 155 pounds when he scored the Cup-clinching goal in 1934; Kane was listed at 5'10" tall and 178 pounds when he scored his game-winner in Philadelphia in 2010.

Just as Kane made the jump straight from juniors to the NHL despite his size, March made the jump from the Regina Monarchs to the Blackhawks in 1928. However, when March made the leap it was a rare feat; today, making the leap is commonplace.

The Cup-winning goal is just one of March's famous goals. He scored the first-ever goal in Maple Leaf Gardens on November

12, 1931, and also scored a game-winning goal in the first round of the 1934 playoffs to eliminate Montreal. March was known as one of the better scorers of his era and had a knack for scoring clutch goals.

Four years after his overtime goal against Detroit, March helped the Hawks capture their second Stanley Cup, this time defeating the Toronto Maple Leafs. Despite being the underdog, the Blackhawks won Game 1 in Toronto. March suffered a groin injury in Game 1, though, and he missed Game 2. Toronto won the second game, but March came back for Game 3 and Game 4. Chicago won both of those games, and the Cup came back to Chicago for the second time in franchise history.

March played on a couple of famous lines during his time in Chicago. In the 1933–34 season, March teamed up with Doc Romnes and Paul Thompson to be one of the best scoring lines in the game. They skated together for five years and were the top line on both the 1934 and 1938 championship teams.

After the 1938 championship, Romnes and Thompson moved on. A couple seasons later, March played on a line with two future Hall of Famers—Max and Doug Bentley. In 1941–42 March was replaced on that line by Bill Mosienko. Skating on the second line in 1943–44, March suffered a bad knee injury against Detroit in the playoffs. He struggled to come back from the injury when the 1944–45 season began but could not, and he decided to retire.

In his career, March played 17 seasons—all with the Blackhawks—from 1928–29 through 1944–45. His career totaled 759 games played, and he scored 153 goals while being credited with 230 assists. He was the last living member of the 1934 Stanley Cup championship team before he passed away in 2002. March still ranks 14th in Blackhawks history in games played.

23 Rocky

An ESPN poll in 2004 rated the Chicago Blackhawks the worst franchise in professional sports. In 2007 ESPN analyst Scott Burnside offered the following indictment: "The feelings toward the team range from disinterested to disgusted. Owner Bill Wirtz refuses to air any of the team's home games on local television… so the only opportunity to see the team on television is when it travels…. One source connected to the team said the Blackhawks have lost a generation of fans."

In a 2010 interview with Brian Cazeneuve for *Sports Illustrated*, Bobby Hull said, "I was appalled at the kind of hockey that these great Chicago fans had to watch during that time. I was appalled that they couldn't bring someone in to entertain these people, bring them out of their seats. They were so used to it. That's what bothered me more than anything."

And in the same interview, Stan Mikita echoed Hull's sentiments. He said, "A lot of us, we stayed around the area, at least for a while after we retired, and we'd meet those people on the street who just wanted to ask, 'What's the matter with your team?' To watch the franchise just go down the way it did was very hard. I saw an article that said it had gone from being one of the most valuable franchises to the second-least valuable franchise."

One of the most historic teams in one of the great North American sports cities had disappeared. After 28 years in the playoffs and decades of sold-out games, the team was as close to last place in the standings as it was to the bottom of the league in attendance.

The dawn was coming, though. It was just a matter of time and circumstances until the opportunity came for the resurrection of the Chicago Blackhawks. There were signs of hope years before the turnaround began. In 2000 Rocky Wirtz told the *Chicago Sun-Times*, "It's something that we're not going to tolerate. Fans should expect better. And we're fans, as well." He continued, "It's like being a chef and having to eat your own food. The old saying is, 'The fish stinks from the head down,' so we're going to take responsibility for what's been put out there."

Less than nine months after Wirtz offered his analysis, that opportunity became a reality. In late September, just a couple weeks before the 2007–08 season began, William W. "Bill" Wirtz succumbed to a battle with cancer. The longtime team president left a gigantic void but also a golden chance to restore what was once a glorious franchise.

When Rocky was handed control of the organization, he immediately began fixing the many problems. He hired John McDonough and Jay Blunk, two marketing geniuses, away from the Chicago Cubs. They immediately sought out a deal to make sure home games would be on local radio and, in that first season, some would be on television in Chicago.

The changes came fast and furious and started to remind the great hockey fans in the city that a team played at the United Center.

And the optimism of the alumni changed as well. "The way this organization has been rebuilt is just tremendous," said Hull. "Rocky knew some things were wrong with the way the franchise was being run, and he didn't hesitate to fix them. The home games were finally broadcast on TV. The team became part of the community again. The players are treated first-class, because management knows the game is all about the players."

Under the guidance of Rocky Wirtz, the once-cinched purse strings were opened up, and the Hawks were suddenly a player in the free-agent market. With a foundation of quality talent built by GM Dale Tallon, the Blackhawks returned to the playoffs in only the second year of the Rocky era and surprised the hockey world by advancing all the way to the Western Conference Finals.

Rocky brought back former players who had been burned so badly by his father's regime that they wouldn't show their faces in Chicago. Where bridges were thought to be little more than ashes, the new Wirtz ownership group went out of their way to rebuild relationships with the likes of Hull, Mikita, Esposito, and even some of the more recent players, such as Jeremy Roenick, who were so turned off they vowed to never come back.

What might be the greatest testimony to the impact of Rocky's vision is the almost immediate proof that his questioning of his father's ideals was proven to be correct. He fought to get home games on television and started to sell tickets simultaneously. And he brought back Pat Foley, the voice of the Blackhawks to a generation of fans. Where his father didn't want to disrespect season-ticket holders by showing games on television, Rocky has built a waiting list by showing the people at home what they're missing at the United Center.

Under Rocky's management, season-ticket sales jumped from 3,400 to 14,000 in two years, and there are now almost 10,000 names on the waiting list.

The symmetry is similar to when Rocky's grandfather, Arthur Wirtz, moved from Detroit to Chicago. When Arthur Wirtz and his partner, James D. Norris, took over the Blackhawks in the late 1950s, they had a team with a strong defensive group led by Pierre Pilote and Moose Vasko and quickly added two elite young forwards in Hull and Mikita.

When Rocky Wirtz took over, he already had Duncan Keith and Brent Seabrook patrolling the blue line and added two young superstar forwards, Jonathan Toews and Patrick Kane.

It took nine years for Arthur to win the Stanley Cup, though. Rocky did it in three.

24 Doug Wilson

With the sixth overall pick in a fairly deep 1977 NHL Draft, the Blackhawks decided to pick a smooth-skating, offensive-minded defenseman from Ottawa named Doug Wilson.

Wilson had posted 79 points (25 goals, 54 assists) in only 43 games prior to the draft for the Ottawa 67's, and the Blackhawks hoped he could make the transition from juniors to the NHL effectively.

He made the leap from juniors straight to the NHL in his first training camp as a 20-year-old in the wake of one of the more tumultuous seasons in the long history of the Blackhawks. In 1976–77, longtime head coach Billy Reay was fired in the middle of the season, and the Blackhawks had two assistant coaches for the second half of the season: Stan Mikita and Bobby Orr.

After that season, legendary general manager Tommy Ivan was also relieved of his duties, and Bob Pulford took over both as GM and head coach. Pulford immediately inserted Wilson on a blue line with, among others, Bob Murray and Dale Tallon.

Wilson played in 77 games in his rookie season, scoring 14 goals and adding 20 assists; his 34 points comprised the second-highest total among Hawks defensemen that year. After being limited to 56 games in his sophomore season, Wilson finally exploded during the 1979–80 season. Bob Murray and Wilson combined to register 111 points in 1979–80, and the changing of the guard was beginning in Chicago.

Starting in the 1980–81 season, the Blackhawks put some of the better talent in the league on the ice for the next decade. And Wilson led from the rear. Remembered as having one of the hardest shots in the 1980s, when Wilson wound up at the blue line, opponents thought twice about getting in the way.

After the 1981–82 campaign, Wilson received leaguewide recognition when he was named the winner of the James Norris Memorial Trophy, given to the league's best defenseman. That season, Wilson scored 39 goals and added 46 assists, posting an astounding 85 points as a defenseman. Wilson established a record for most goals scored in a season by a defenseman that year. He also added 13 points in 15 playoff games that spring.

Playing on teams with Denis Savard, Steve Larmer, Darryl Sutter, Al Secord, Grant Mulvey, and Murray, the Blackhawks had some of the most impressive statistical decades in the NHL. Unfortunately, while the Hawks were able to dominate the old Norris Division during the decade, they were unable to break through the concrete ceiling (read: Wayne Gretzky's Edmonton Oilers) in the Western Conference.

Because of the Oilers' dominance, most of the Hawks players who were so great in the 1980s are still underappreciated to this day. Indeed, both Wilson and Larmer should be in the Hockey Hall of Fame.

Wilson played in seven All-Star Games with the Blackhawks and represented Canada in the 1984 Canada Cup. His 779 points rank fifth in the history of the Blackhawks but are the most by a defenseman in the history of the organization. He also ranks 12th overall in goals with 225 and third overall with 554 assists. Wilson's 23 game-winning goals rank him 15th in team history and are 10 more than any other defenseman to play for the Hawks.

Wilson made it as far as the Stanley Cup semifinals on four occasions: 1982, 1985, 1989, and 1990. However, he was traded to the expansion San Jose Sharks before the 1991–92 season, when the Blackhawks finally broke through and advanced to the Stanley Cup Finals, only to be swept by the Pittsburgh Penguins.

Norris Trophy Winners

The James Norris Memorial Trophy is given each year to the "defense player who demonstrates throughout the regular season the greatest all-round ability in the position." It was initially awarded after the 1953–54 season and is voted on by the Professional Hockey Writers Association.

The following Chicago Blackhawks have won the James Norris Memorial Trophy:

- Pierre Pilote: 1962–63, 1963–64, 1964–65
- Doug Wilson: 1981–82
- Chris Chelios: 1992–93, 1995–96
- Duncan Keith: 2009–10

When he retired in 1993, Wilson had the fifth-highest point total for a defenseman in the history of the NHL.

Off the ice, Wilson was a leader as well. In 1985 he was one of the vice presidents of the NHL Players' Association. When NHLPA president Bryan Trottier joined the Islanders' front office in 1992, Wilson was named the new president of the NHLPA. In the spring of 2003, he was named the general manager of the San Jose Sharks.

In fact, looking back at the first group of defenseman Wilson joined in the NHL, there were three future NHL general managers: Wilson, Murray, and Tallon.

25 Chris Chelios

On June 26, 1990, the Chicago Blackhawks acquired defenseman Chris Chelios in a trade that didn't sit well with many fans. He came to the Hawks from Montreal with a second-round draft pick in exchange for Denis Savard. Even though Chelios had won a Norris Trophy in Montreal and was a Chicago kid coming home, the deal moving Savard out of town wasn't popular with everyone at the Chicago Stadium. Once he stepped on the ice, though, he was everything the Blackhawks needed in a captain.

Before Chelios arrived, the Blackhawks hadn't played for the Stanley Cup since 1973. However, with Jeremy Roenick leading the scoring and Ed Belfour between the pipes, the Blackhawks returned to the Finals after the 1991–92 season. On that team, Chelios and Steve Larmer were alternate captains, with Dirk Graham wearing the C. Between 1995 and 1999, Chris Chelios was one of the most respected captains in the history of the organization.

Chelios represented the Blackhawks in seven All-Star Games. He also represented the USA in the 1996 World Cup of Hockey and was captain of the USA's team at the 1998 Olympics—as a member of the Blackhawks.

Also, he is one of only four players in Blackhawks history to win the Norris Trophy as the league's best defenseman. Only Chelios and Pilote have more than one Norris in a Chicago sweater.

Chelios is the Blackhawks' all-time leader with 1,495 penalty minutes. He ranks third in Blackhawks history in scoring among defensemen with 487 points. He scored 92 goals, 13 of which were game-winners, and scored .733 points per game as a member of the Hawks.

When the mandatory waiting period ends, Chelios will be a first-ballot Hall of Famer, and a large part of his credentials came in a Hawks sweater.

But that doesn't tell the entire story of Chelios. While playing with the Blackhawks, Chelios infamously told radio host Mike North that he would never play for the Detroit Red Wings. Of course that stance was thrown out the window in 1999 when he relented and accepted a deal with the Wings that brought Anders Eriksson and two first-round picks back to Chicago.

Fans' memories are short, and most only remember that Chelios went on to win some hardware with the hated Red Wings. He won two Stanley Cups while playing in Detroit, and each time he brought the Cup "home" to Chicago. To many fans, seeing Chelios and friends parading the Cup around Wrigley Field or somewhere else in the city was salt in a gaping wound. The fact that he played more seasons in Detroit (10) than he did in Chicago (9) still serves as a bitter pill for fans to swallow.

What many fans forget is that Chelios had the Red Wings on a no-trade list for most of his time in Chicago and only relented to the trade when management had flushed the organization so far down the toilet that Chelios, who was 37 when dealt, accepted a deal out of Chicago.

Larmer was dealt to Hartford for almost nothing early in the 1993–94 season. They gave away Roenick in August 1996. Belfour was dealt during the 1996–97 season for essentially nothing. So it was far from Chelios' fault that the team was a wreck when he left. Chelios shouldn't be blamed for the Blackhawks' failure to do anything with the two first-round picks they got from Detroit in the trade or Eriksson's five goals in 97 games in Chicago.

But he is.

Chelios moved his family out of Chicago's western suburbs and up to Detroit, where he has a number of business interests to this day. Before the 2010–11 season, he accepted a job in the front office in Detroit that further antagonized the Blackhawks faithful that had loved him for nine great years.

When it was announced that Chelios would be honored with a Heritage Night during the 2010–11 season, the crowd at the preseason game reacted with a mix of applause and booing. On the night he was honored, the reaction was split again. While thanking the organization and fans, Chelios addressed the fans directly.

"Come on, guys. Let bygones be bygones. I'm one of you," he told the sold-out United Center. "I'll always be one of you from Chicago, and I'm proud of the fact that I'm from Chicago."

And, despite working in Detroit's front office, Chelios is still a Blackhawks fan. He even flew from his Michigan home to the parade in the Chicago Loop after the Hawks won the Stanley Cup in 2010. He called it, "The greatest thing I've ever seen."

Chelios may never be applauded again by some fans in Chicago, but that doesn't take away from him being one of the best defensemen to ever represent the Indian-head sweater. He was a great captain, an All-Star, and an Olympian as a member of the Hawks. The only title he couldn't claim in his hometown? Champion.

26 Maggie

Former Blackhawks forward Cliff Koroll described his longtime friend and teammate Keith "Maggie" Magnuson in an interview published in *Blackhawks* magazine by saying, "He made up for his lack of natural ability and size with his aggressiveness and great attitude." What a perfectly appropriate way to describe one of the most beloved people ever associated with the Chicago Blackhawks franchise.

Koroll and Magnuson met in Saskatoon as kids and became childhood rivals while playing junior hockey. Magnuson eventually followed Koroll to the University of Denver, where Maggie captained Denver to consecutive NCAA championships in 1968 and 1969. He was also a two-time All-American at Denver.

In 1969 Magnuson left the West and moved to Chicago to add a physical presence to the blue line. With red hair that nearly matched the color of the sweater he wore and despite a few missing teeth, he was the unlikely face of the franchise for much of the 1970s.

Looking back at his NHL career, Magnuson's résumé seems to be a collection of contradictions.

- He never won a Stanley Cup.
- He appeared on the cover of *Sports Illustrated* late in the 1970 season.
- He represented the Blackhawks in two All-Star Games.
- In 589 career games, he scored only 14 goals.
- He is second behind Chris Chelios with 1,442 penalty minutes.
- His No. 3 is retired (shared with Pierre Pilote).

That's Maggie for you. He played all 11 seasons of his NHL career in the Indian-head sweater and represented it as well as anyone in the history of the franchise.

On the ice, he might not have skated as fast or shot the puck as hard as Bobby Hull or Stan Mikita. As a defenseman, he certainly wasn't as flashy as Doug Wilson. But anyone in the league would have wanted him on their team. If someone took a shot at one of Magnuson's teammates, Maggie would be sure to "introduce" himself the next time they shared the ice.

In 1971 *Time* magazine reported, "[W]hen trouble finds him or a teammate, Magnuson goes to work with fists, knees and elbows. No one is immune. The Detroit Red Wings' great Gordie Howe was one of Magnuson's childhood idols, but the very first time the 206 lb. Howe crashed head-on into the 185 lb. Magnuson, the youngster dropped his gloves and started swinging…. Mashing rivals into the boards like marshmallows, the feisty young defenseman was involved in so many brawls that he piled up a total of 213 minutes in penalties his rookie season, highest mark in the National Hockey League. Trouble was, he often got as good as he gave."

Off the ice, nobody made more stops at hospitals or charity gatherings than Magnuson. He believed in family, and he believed in the crest he wore on his chest, which is why he was one of the cofounders of the Blackhawks Alumni Association.

He was a wonderful leader. He replaced Mikita as the team's captain in 1976 and served in that capacity until 1979 when he retired. After playing, he coached the team from 1980 to 1982.

Unfortunately, Magnuson's life ended far too early. On December 15, 2003, the 56-year-old Magnuson was killed in an automobile accident in Ontario. He was on his way home from the funeral of another former NHL player, Keith McCreary, when the car carrying Maggie was involved in a three-car accident just south of Toronto. Former NHL player Rob Ramage was driving the vehicle, and he was later convicted of impaired driving causing death and dangerous driving causing death. He was sentenced to four years in prison.

When Maggie's name and number were lifted into the rafters at the United Center next to Pilote's in 2008, more stories were told in the stands about Maggie's confrontations than his playing abilities. The videos shown on the screen that night showed him fighting (and, in most cases, losing), but his heart and love for the Indian head was his outstanding legacy.

27 J.R.

Boston native Jeremy Roenick was drafted eighth overall in 1988 after his junior year in high school, and he made his NHL debut later that season. He pitched in 18 points in 20 games and was effective in the playoffs his rookie season.

Roenick's first full season in the NHL, 1989–90, saw him score 26 goals and register 40 assists as the Blackhawks improved 22 points in the standings. He was starting to establish himself as a legitimate scoring threat on an aging team that was going through some dramatic changes.

After that season, in part because of Roenick's emergence as a scorer, the Blackhawks traded longtime fan favorite Denis Savard to Montreal for Chris Chelios. Roenick backed up the faith (or penny-pinching) of management in 1990–91 by scoring 41 goals and 53 assists (94 points), and he was selected to play in the legendary 1991 All-Star Game at the Chicago Stadium.

The Hawks jumped another 18 points in the standings to win the Presidents' Trophy in 1990–91, with Roenick leading the team with 10 game-winning goals. He teamed up with Steve Larmer (who had 101 points that year) to give the Hawks one of the most potent offenses in the league.

The next season, 1991–92, was magical in Chicago. The Blackhawks advanced all the way to the Stanley Cup Finals. Roenick scored 103 points that year (53 goals, 50 assists) and was selected to play in his second All-Star Game.

He was then firmly established as one of the elite scoring forwards in the NHL. Roenick scored 22 points in 18 postseason games that year, but the Hawks were eventually swept in the Stanley Cup Finals by the Pittsburgh Penguins.

The two seasons that followed that campaign made Roenick a legend in Chicago and a leaguewide household name. Roenick had back-to-back 107-point seasons, matching Bobby Hull's incredible 107-point season in 1968–69.

Despite the team's successes of the early 1990s, this was a time filled with frustration for Hawks players and fans. The trade of Savard for Chelios ended up bringing another eventual Chicago legend home, but unloading one of the best players in franchise history wasn't the easiest trade to stomach.

Again in large part due to Roenick having established himself as the team's top scorer, the team moved another fan favorite, Steve Larmer, in a three-team deal that landed Larmer on the New York Rangers. Larmer hadn't missed a game in a Chicago uniform in over a decade, but management was beginning to show an unwillingness to keep a great core together. Larmer wanted to win the Cup, and the front office wasn't showing any signs of keeping the Hawks competitive.

Jeremy Roenick (right) and Blackhawks goalie Ed Belfour celebrate after the Blackhawks beat the Vancouver Canucks 2–0 to take a 2–0 lead in their best-of-seven series on May 23, 1995, in Chicago.

The 1993–94 season was Roenick's fourth All-Star Game, and he set career highs in power-play goals (24) and short-handed goals (five). He was +21 for the season and was clearly one of the top players in the league. But the Hawks fell back further in the standings.

It was in 1994 that Roenick took another step in his evolution as a legend: the video game *NHL '94* made Roenick a god.

In a classic scene in the movie *Swingers*, a game of *NHL '94* breaks out accompanied by multiple references to Roenick (including a fight between Roenick and Wayne Gretzky). Roenick was transcending the game and becoming a part of pop culture.

However, just as Roenick had replaced Savard and Larmer, an addition to the team started the erosion of Roenick's roster status on the Blackhawks: in 1993–94 another Bostonian, Tony Amonte, arrived in Chicago.

As was the case with many of the team's top players, Roenick wanted to receive appropriate compensation for the superstar numbers he was producing for the team. Unfortunately, ownership wasn't willing to make Roenick one of the highest-paid players in the game. After 524 games in Chicago, Roenick was traded to Phoenix on August 16, 1996.

When he left, Roenick ranked among the best forwards to ever wear the Indian-head sweater. He still ranks seventh in team history in goals (267), 11th in assists (329), eighth in points (596), and ninth in plus-minus (+117).

Roenick was also one of the most spectacular clutch players to ever play in Chicago. He ranks second in franchise history with 108 power-play goals, third with 19 short-handed goals, and fourth with 28 game-winning goals. He also played in 82 postseason games with Chicago, scoring 35 goals and adding 42 assists.

Not only was Roenick one of the best Blackhawks ever, but he is also one of the best American-born players to lace up skates in the NHL. In July 2009 *Hockey News* ranked Roenick eighth on their list "Top Ten American-Born Hockey Players," while ESPN rated Roenick in their top five in 2007. J.R. was inducted into the United States Hockey Hall of Fame in 2010.

Almost as impressive as his Hall of Fame credentials, Roenick's likeness in *NHL '94* was rated fourth on IGN's *Top Ten Athletes in Videogame History.*

Off the ice, there have been two aspects of Roenick's personality that have been consistent throughout his introduction to the hockey world. The first part of Roenick that made a mark on many Chicago fans was the level to which he gave back. Never one to shy away from an autograph request, Roenick was always personable with the fans in Chicago.

The other part of his personality was more explosive: Roenick was rarely far from controversy. During the 2004–05 lockout, Roenick infamously told the media that fans believing pro athletes were spoiled could "kiss my ass." There was also a legendary incident in which Roenick was allegedly one of the players on the U.S. Olympic Team who did substantial damage to a number of hotel rooms.

In the years since he left Chicago, Roenick has openly maintained hard feelings toward the organization. Even after he was honored with his own Heritage Night during the 2009–10 season, he publicly picked other former employers—San Jose and Philadelphia—to beat the Blackhawks during the 2010 playoffs.

And yet, despite the hard feelings he had no problem expressing throughout the playoffs, the real J.R. appeared moments after the Blackhawks were handed the Stanley Cup. Roenick broke down in tears on the air and said, "For the kid who was there in 1992 who was crying when I came off the ice in after we lost Game 4 at Chicago Stadium—you waited 18 years. I hope you have a big smile on your face. Congratulations."

When Dan Patrick, the host of NBC's coverage of the Finals, pressed Roenick about his state of mind, J.R. captured the emotional state of most Chicago fans at that moment and put the beginning of his great career into perspective with one brief statement: "It's the Chicago Blackhawks, man…. It's pretty unbelievable."

28 Pit Martin

In late 2008 Hall of Fame NHL linesman Matt Pavelich said of Hubert "Pit" Martin, "He wasn't like Stan Mikita or Bobby Clarke. He just did his job. He had real good hands and he never backed down from anyone. He was small, but he wasn't timid. He'd go right into the corners. I just remember him as a real nice guy."

The 5'8", 165-pound Martin was a quick, smooth-skating center who used speed and smarts to be an effective hockey player. And he was effective for a long time in Chicago.

There are two aspects to Martin's legacy in Chicago that are dramatically different: what was and what might have been.

Martin was a good two-way center who spent seven of his 11 years in Chicago flanked by Jim Pappin and Dennis Hull. The three developed wonderful chemistry, and Martin was always in the middle of it all.

After the Hawks finished in last place during the 1968–69 season, Martin publically called out the entire roster and the organization as a whole. In many ways, this was a precursor to Denis Savard's "Commit to the Indian" speech of almost 40 years later. "The problem in Chicago is a total lack of direction," Martin told then-reporter (and now official team historian) Bob Verdi. "There is no leadership from the owners, the general manager, or the coach. And when they're not concerned, the players aren't concerned."

He then moved on to the players, saying, "Then there's the matter of star conflict. The Hawks have one big star [Bobby Hull] and another fairly big star [Stan Mikita], and the club seems to be set up to make them happy. The rest of us simply don't matter."

When the Blackhawks jumped from last to first place in the standings the following year, Martin received the Bill Masterton Trophy, an award given to the most dedicated player in the league. He led by example that year, scoring 30 goals and adding 33 assists.

But Martin was rare in an era where players disagreeing with management usually came at the expense of their roster spots. He was a reporter's best friend in the 1970s, always biting on an open-ended question and providing comments to generate controversy.

While the team was fighting over money with Bobby Hull, Martin felt comfortable questioning why he wasn't getting paid either. After head coach Billy Reay said he believed Martin was worthy of All-Star consideration, he used that as ammunition to beg the obvious question: where's my money?

Because of the success enjoyed by the MPH Line—Martin, Jim Pappin, and Dennis Hull—all three began receiving leaguewide recognition. The world eventually saw the quality that Reay had

Masterton Trophy Winners

The Bill Masterton Memorial Trophy is awarded to the NHL player who best exemplifies the qualities of perseverance, sportsmanship, and dedication to the game as selected by the Professional Hockey Writers Association from a list of nominees presented by each team.

The following members of the Blackhawks have been awarded the Bill Masterton Memorial Trophy:
- Pit Martin: 1969–70
- Bryan Berard: 2003–04

praised, and Martin represented the Blackhawks in four consecutive All-Star Games between 1971 and 1974.

In his 11 years in Chicago, Martin played 740 games. The influence of the MPH Line is seen all over the Blackhawks' all-time records. Martin ranks seventh in team history with 627 points, one spot behind Dennis Hull. He also ranks sixth in team history with 34 game-winning goals, right behind Pappin's 35. Both Dennis Hull and Martin rank among the franchise's top 10 in goals as well, with Martin ranking 10th (243).

Martin also played in 80 postseason games in Chicago, posting 51 points. That mark ranks 13th in team history, and it again immediately follows another member of the MPH Line in the record books; Pappin ranks 12th with 52 career postseason points.

The second part of Martin's legacy that cannot be ignored is that, despite all of his great years with the Blackhawks, fans have to wonder what might have been. Martin will forever be the answer of a trivia question: who did the Blackhawks receive in one of the most lopsided trades in NHL history (the trade sending Phil Esposito, Ken Hodge, and Fred Stanfield to Boston)?

Unfortunately, Martin was killed in a snowmobiling accident in December 2008, just three months before the MPH Line was honored together with a Heritage Night at the United Center.

29 Major McLaughlin

$12,000.

On September 25, 1926, that was the entry fee paid by Major Frederic McLaughlin to own a franchise in the National Hockey League.

McLaughlin, who had inherited a successful coffee business, didn't stop there. With the Western Hockey League struggling financially, he paid $200,000 for the rights to the Portland Rosebuds. This purchase gave him a roster to move halfway across the country to Chicago. The name, though, wasn't something suitable for a hockey team in Chicago in McLaughlin's mind.

McLaughlin had served as a commander during World War I and found the name for his new investment on the battlefield. He had served in the 333rd Machine Gun Battalion of the 86th Division of the U.S. Army, a division that had referred to itself as the Black Hawks.

On November 17, 1926, the Chicago Blackhawks hosted the Toronto St. Pats at the Chicago Coliseum, a 4–1 Chicago victory.

Very little in McLaughlin's tenure as owner of the team was that cut-and-dry. His approach was similar to George Steinbrenner's with the New York Yankees over the next 18 seasons, as he went through 18 coaches. The original coach of the Blackhawks, Pete Muldoon, was fired after that first season, giving birth to the Curse of Muldoon.

The front-office bravado wasn't reserved for the coaching staff, though. McLaughlin moved the Blackhawks into the Chicago Stadium, where the Hawks again won their first game—a 3–1 victory over the Pittsburgh Pirates—on December 15, 1929. With a new stadium and a talented roster, McLaughlin had put together a winning team.

With Charlie Gardiner in net, the 1933–34 season brought the first Stanley Cup championship to Chicago.

After Gardiner's untimely passing over the summer of 1934, McLaughlin again messed with his lineup and, just four years later, the Hawks defeated the Toronto Maple Leafs for their second Stanley Cup victory in five seasons.

Irene Castle, an actress and dancer who was married to McLaughlin when he purchased the franchise, is credited with creating the Indian-head logo on the front of the Blackhawks sweaters.

McLaughlin is not only the original owner of the Blackhawks, but he could also be credited with starting the rivalry with Detroit. James Norris, the owner in Detroit, never got along with McLaughlin. Indeed, he went so far as to create a team in the American Association and then leased the Chicago Stadium in an attempt to kick McLaughlin and the Blackhawks out of the building. Conn Smythe, then the owner of the Maple Leafs, referred to McLaughlin as a "strange bird."

McLaughlin is also remembered as a strongly patriotic owner who went out of his way to have as many American-born players on his roster as possible; eight players (and the head coach) on the 1938 Stanley Cup championship team were born in the U.S.

The Blackhawks were shocked when McLaughlin succumbed to heart disease on December 17, 1944, leaving the franchise in need of new ownership.

Despite all of his eccentric nuances, McLaughlin was an innovator who built the NHL's presence in Chicago. In 1963 he was inducted into the NHL Hall of Fame as a builder.

30 Eddie the Eagle

Rodney Dangerfield might be the only person on Earth to get less respect than Ed Belfour. Belfour had a good career in high school, despite being cut. As a junior he made the team as a backup and impressed his coaches, and as a senior he led the team to a Zone 4 championship. Despite his success, not a single college offered him a scholarship, nor did he get drafted.

Belfour opted to play in the Manitoba Junior Hockey League but couldn't lock down a starting job there, either. He finally demanded the starting job and played his way into an All-Star nomination. Even though he was a backup to start the season, he was named the MJHL's top goaltender in 1984.

Despite the strong season, he still couldn't even land a tryout with an NHL team. So Belfour enrolled at the University of North Dakota; he was 21 by that time and too old to play in the juniors. Even though the coaches at UND were familiar with Belfour's skills, he had to walk on and started the year as their third-string netminder.

Again, Belfour forced his way into the lineup. In his one season with the Fighting Sioux, Belfour won 29 of his 34 starts and led UND to the 1987 NCAA Championship. Suddenly the NHL noticed Belfour, and he could hold out for the best offer.

Chicago received glowing reports from UND head coach John Marks, who was a former All-Star with the Hawks. In what would prove to be a stroke of painful irony, the best contract offer Belfour received was from the Blackhawks.

Belfour still couldn't get a roster spot in Chicago for the 1988–89 season and bounced back and forth between the Blackhawks and the minors. In a partial season, he went 4–12–3 in 23 games with the Hawks. After not receiving a guarantee of a roster spot in the fall of 1989, Belfour walked away from the minors and began a 33-game world tour that lasted nearly six months with the Canadian national team.

Not a single team was willing to draft him, but Ed Belfour wasted no time proving everyone wrong. Once he returned from the world tour, the desperate Blackhawks recalled Belfour for the 1990 playoffs. To say Belfour was impressive would be underselling his performance in the 1990 postseason; he went 4–2 with a 2.49 goals-against average and figured to have the inside track to be the starter the following season. And yet, when training camp opened

30-Win Goalies

Despite the Blackhawks' long history of great goaltenders, it has been surprisingly rare for a goalie to win 30 games in a season. In fact, when Corey Crawford eclipsed 30 wins in his rookie season, it was only the 17th time the number was achieved by a Hawks goalie.

Here is the complete list of Chicago Blackhawks 30-game winners:

- Ed Belfour—43 wins, 1990–91
- Ed Belfour—41 wins, 1992–93
- Tony Esposito—38 wins, 1969–70
- Ed Belfour—37 wins, 1993–94
- Tony Esposito—35 wins, 1970–71
- Glenn Hall—34 wins, 1965–66
- Glenn Hall—34 wins, 1963–64
- Tony Esposito—34 wins, 1973–74
- Tony Esposito—34 wins, 1974–75
- Corey Crawford—33 wins, 2010–11
- Jocelyn Thibault—33 wins, 2001–02
- Tony Esposito—32 wins, 1972–73
- Tony Esposito—31 wins, 1971–72
- Tony Esposito—31 wins, 1979–80
- Glenn Hall—31 wins, 1961–62
- Glenn Hall—30 wins, 1962–63
- Tony Esposito—30 wins, 1975–76

for the 1990–91 season, there were seven goalies fighting for a spot with the Blackhawks.

Despite the organization favoring Jimmy Waite for the job and another young goalie—Dominik Hašek— making a strong impression, Belfour again won the starting job and forced doubters to respect him. The 1990–91 campaign turned in by Belfour remains one of the most epic rookie seasons in the history of the NHL.

He led a Blackhawks team that was evolving into a young, fast team into the postseason with an NHL-rookie record 43 wins in 74 games and posted a strong 2.47 goals-against average. Belfour nearly swept the NHL's postseason awards that year.

In an astounding turn of events, the unorthodox Belfour was suddenly the toast of the NHL. He won the Calder Memorial Trophy, the Vezina Trophy, and the William M. Jennings Trophy. Belfour was also nominated for the Hart Memorial Trophy but lost to Brett Hull.

The following season the Blackhawks made a run all the way to the Stanley Cup Finals, only to be swept by the Pittsburgh Penguins. Even though Belfour had been so strong the year before, Hašek was pressing him for playing time; in only 20 games, Hašek played well enough to earn All-Rookie honors.

Because he was the starter and had played well enough to have a strong bargaining position, Belfour demanded respect from the organization. In August the Hawks traded Hašek to Buffalo.

Belfour continued to earn the respect of his peers, winning the Vezina Trophy for a second time after the 1992–93 season. He won the William M. Jennings Trophy for a third time in 1995, but at that point the relationship between the front office and Belfour was becoming contentious.

During the 1995–96 season, the Blackhawks again had a young netminder they liked in Jeff Hackett. The tension between the understandably self-conscious Belfour and his backup was again an issue, as the two feuded throughout the season.

At this point the Blackhawks and Belfour were at a standoff. Belfour had one year left on his contract, and the Hawks were beginning to tire of his unwillingness to share the ice with the many talented backups they had brought along during his tenure. It didn't help that Hašek was developing into an elite goalie in his own right for the Sabres.

The wheels fell off when Belfour and the Blackhawks got off to a slow start in 1996–97. While Hašek was on his way to the third of his six Vezina Trophies, the Blackhawks offered Belfour a contract extension that was turned down by the goalie. The standoff ended when he was traded to San Jose after 33 starts.

Like other Blackhawks who were dealt out of Chicago during the 1990s (Denis Savard and Steve Larmer, to name a couple), Belfour continued to play well and eventually won a Stanley Cup elsewhere.

When he left Chicago, Belfour ranked third in Blackhawks history in games played by a goalie (415) and wins (201), trailing only Hall of Famers Tony Esposito and Glenn Hall in both categories. Belfour also ranked fourth in shutouts (30) in the team's long history.

Belfour will enter the Hockey Hall of Fame in 2011.

31 Trading Phil

Before the 1969–70 season, the Blackhawks made one of the best personnel moves in the history of the National Hockey League when they claimed a young goalie from the Montreal Canadiens in the intraleague draft (what today would be considered waivers).

Tony Esposito went on to a Hall of Fame career with the Blackhawks, poetic justice considering Chicago's history with the Esposito family. One of the Blackhawks' top prospects in the early 1960s, Tony's older brother Phil got called up to join the Hawks during the 1963–64 season. The 21-year-old center was immediately placed next to icon Bobby Hull, and it didn't take long for him to make clear he was good enough to be in the NHL.

After scoring only three goals in 27 games as a rookie, Phil Esposito catapulted into the league leaders by registering 55 points during the 1964–65 season. In his first three full seasons, he posted 71 goals and 169 total points, one of the best marks for that period in the league. However, after the 1966–67 season, the Hawks decided to shake things up, changing the history of the NHL forever.

On May 15, 1967, the Blackhawks decided to trade Phil Esposito and two other players to the Boston Bruins in exchange for center Pit Martin and two other players. Martin had made his debut with the Detroit Red Wings during the 1961–62 season but didn't lock up a spot on an NHL roster until he was moved to Boston during the 1965–66 season. In 111 games with the Bruins in under two seasons, Martin scored 36 goals and tallied 69 points.

So how did the trade end up for the Blackhawks and Bruins? Martin had a nice career in Chicago, which included two seasons as the captain (1975–77). The two other players the Blackhawks received, defenseman Gilles Marotte and goalie Jack Norris, never amounted to much in the National Hockey League.

Marotte piled up more penalty minutes than points; he registered just 73 points while accumulating 294 minutes in the box in only 192 games with Chicago. Norris appeared in only 10 games with the Blackhawks, establishing a 3–3 career record in Chicago. Both Marotte and Norris were out of Chicago before the end of the 1969–70 season.

Boston, on the other hand, received three of the better players in their franchise history in a single trade. Esposito went on to become a Hall of Fame center on the great Boston teams of the 1970s. In six of his nine seasons in Boston, Esposito eclipsed 125 points for the season, with a career-best 152 coming in 1970–71. Before he was traded to the New York Rangers during the 1975–76 season, Esposito scored 459 goals and piled up 1,012 points in black and gold.

He was one of the most popular players of his generation and is still one of the most beloved athletes in Boston. Famous bumper stickers all over Boston read, *Jesus Saves, Espo Scores on the Rebound.*

Esposito won the Art Ross Trophy five times in Boston and the Hart Memorial Trophy on two occasions. He also won the Lester B. Pearson Award twice.

When he retired in 1981, Phil Esposito was second in NHL history in career points and goals behind only Gordie Howe and was third in the league's history in assists behind Howe and his former Chicago teammate Stan Mikita.

Perhaps the most memorable image of Esposito in Boston came after he had retired. In one of the most stirring ceremonies in the game's history, defenseman Ray Bourque, who was one of the best players in the game in his own right at the time and had been wearing Esposito's No. 7, "gave" the number back to Esposito in a ceremony. Bourque took off his sweater, revealing his new No. 77, and Esposito's name and No. 7 were raised into the rafters of the Boston Garden.

32 Jim Pappin

Over the years, one unfortunate hallmark of the Blackhawks organization has been the best players in the team's history finishing their careers with something other than the Indian head on their chest.

After 821 games and three consecutive Norris Trophies, Pierre Pilote fell into that category. His production had dipped to only 37 points (one goal) in 74 games during the 1967–68 season, and the organization decided to move on. And, at 37, his career was winding down.

Jim Pappin was unpopular with Toronto coach Punch Imlach, and despite posting numbers in the minors each year that warranted him skating in the NHL, Imlach demoted him at every opportunity. A lot of Pappin's struggles with management in Toronto were borne of his willingness to speak his mind.

Between his NHL debut during the 1963–64 season and the trade sending him to Chicago, Pappin played in only 223 NHL games. Despite scoring the Cup-clinching goal in 1967, Imlach couldn't get rid of him fast enough. So on May 23, 1968, the Blackhawks dealt their Hall of Fame defenseman to the Toronto Maple Leafs for Pappin, a former top prospect who had underwhelmed the Toronto organization.

Once he landed in Chicago, the minors were part of Pappin's past. He emerged quickly in his first season with the Blackhawks, skating with Pit Martin and Dennis Hull. He scored 30 goals and added 40 assists in 75 games that year and showed all the signs of the "can't-miss" prospect he had been labeled years before.

On February 16, 1972, Pappin established a franchise record for scoring the fastest two goals in team history when he beat the Philadelphia Flyers twice in six seconds. His best season came in 1972–73, when he scored 41 goals with 51 assists. He also tallied eight goals and seven assists in only 16 postseason games that year.

During his time in Chicago, Pappin was one of the most consistent scorers of his generation. Between 1968 and 1975, Pappin played 488 games and registered 444 points (216 goals, 228 assists). He recorded seven hat tricks in Chicago, and his 35 game-winning goals still rank fifth in the organization's history.

In 69 postseason contests with the Blackhawks, Pappin proved to be a great player as well. He scored 26 goals, five of which were game-winners, and added 26 assists in playoff games while playing with the Blackhawks.

Pappin is also the central figure in a wild story surrounding a 1967 Stanley Cup ring. He lost the ring he won with Toronto while swimming in Florida and thought it was gone forever. His father-in-law at the time felt bad enough that he purchased a replica ring for him that had all of the real stones included. In 2007, 40 years later, a treasure hunter found Pappin's ring off the coast of Clearwater, Florida.

After retiring from the game, Pappin served in the Blackhawks' front office as the director of U.S. scouting.

33 The Silver Jet

He played in 904 games for the Blackhawks, the sixth-most in franchise history.

He scored 298 goals for the Blackhawks, the fifth-most in franchise history.

He accounted for 640 total points for the Blackhawks, the sixth-most in franchise history.

And yet he's best known as a little brother.

Dennis Hull's nickname was "the Silver Jet" because his big brother, Bobby, was "the Golden Jet." While Bobby stole most of the headlines and set more records, Dennis was a phenomenal hockey player in his own right.

During their respective primes, many in the game openly wondered which Hull brother had the harder shot. The respect Dennis received from his peers earned him five All-Star Game nominations.

For eight fantastic seasons, Dennis skated with Pit Martin and Jim Pappin on the MPH Line, which was among the most productive lines in the game. His best season came in 1973, when he scored 39 goals and added 51 assists, leading Chicago to the Stanley Cup Finals.

That was a consistent theme throughout his career: Dennis Hull carried the Blackhawks in the postseason. In 97 career postseason games, he scored 33 goals and added 34 assists. During the

1973 playoff run, Hull posted 24 points (nine goals, 15 assists) in only 16 games.

The vote for the Conn Smythe Trophy was taken before Game 7 of the Finals, and the collected media selected one player each from Chicago and Montreal who would win the award as postseason Most Valuable Player, depending on which team won. If Chicago won Game 7, the award would go to Hull, who was leading the postseason in scoring. Montreal won the game, though, and the award went to Montreal netminder Ken Dryden.

As Hull remembered, he lost more than a couple trophies that day. "The winner of the Conn Smythe also received a new car. During the warm-up of an exhibition game against Montreal early the next season, Yvan Cournoyer called me to center ice. He said, 'I have a message from Ken Dryden. He says your car is running really good!'"

That humorous story is an example of how Dennis Hull is remembered best: as a comedian. Each of the Hulls—Dennis, Bobby, and even Brett—had a fun-loving and magnetic personality.

In 1998 Dennis Hull wrote a wonderfully funny book titled *The Third Best Hull (I Should Have Been Fourth but They Wouldn't Let My Sister Maxine Play)*. The book shares many fun anecdotes from his life as a player, brother of an icon, and uncle of a scoring champion. It also shares a number of his stories from a rivalry he had with Henri Richard, the lesser-known brother of Maurice "Rocket" Richard.

"Every game I played against Henri Richard," Hull writes, "he'd come up to behind me at some point and say, 'My brother's better than your brother.'"

Indeed, since his retirement, Dennis Hull has carved out a nice career as a public speaker and master of ceremonies, bringing his unique stories and brand of humor to audiences all over North America.

The MPH Line

Of all the groupings of players in the history of the Blackhawks that received a nickname, none were as dominant—or lived up to the nickname—better than the MPH Line.

Putting the line together was a huge roll of the dice by the organization. They traded a young scorer who had shown a lot of promise, Phil Esposito, to Boston for Pit Martin and dealt their longtime leader on the blue line, Pierre Pilote, to Toronto for Jim Pappin.

But when both of those deals were made, management had in mind putting Martin and Pappin with Bobby Hull. When Bobby held out for more money before the 1968–69 season, head coach Billy Reay decided to stick with the plan and skate a Hull on the line. Younger brother Dennis got the call, and the rest is history.

The three were together on a line that didn't need to be touched for seven seasons. Between 1968 and 1975, the MPH Line was among the best in the game on an annual basis. It led the Blackhawks to two Stanley Cup Finals and combined to score over 1,300 points.

In 1972–73, after Bobby Hull left for the WHA, the Blackhawks desperately needed a scoring punch to come from somewhere; Bobby was the best scorer in the game at the time and left an enormous void on the roster. To compensate for his brother's absence, Dennis and his mates on the MPH Line combined to set a franchise record by combining for 272 points in one season.

The following season, the Blackhawks hosted the NHL All-Star Game. All three members of the MPH Line were nominated to represent the team in that year's game, and the three chose to be introduced together rather than separately.

What made the line unique was that each of them was, individually, among the best in the league at his position. And when Martin took the ice between Pappin and Hull, the three clicked like very few lines in the history of the league.

Dennis also represented the Hawks—and Canada—in the legendary Summit Series in 1972. He almost didn't accept the invitation to represent his country in Moscow, however.

Because Bobby left the NHL to play in the new WHA, he was banned from playing for Canada in the tournament. Dennis planned to boycott his brother's exclusion from the roster by sitting out himself, but Bobby talked him into playing on behalf of them both. Dennis did not disappoint, scoring two goals and adding two assists in the four games.

When he walked away (after one season in Detroit), Dennis had played 13 seasons for the Chicago Blackhawks.

34 The First Cup

The 1933–34 NHL season featured a couple important firsts.

That season saw the first, albeit unofficial, All-Star Game played in Toronto to benefit Leafs forward Ace Bailey, who had been forced into retirement after an awful hit by Boston defenseman Eddie Shore.

The other important first occurred when the Blackhawks won the Stanley Cup.

The season also included a number of notable finales. Unfortunate circumstances meant Bailey would never play in the NHL again, and neither would Chicago's All-Star netminder Charlie Gardiner.

In 1934 there were nine teams in the National Hockey League that were split into two divisions. The Blackhawks were part of the smaller, four-team American Division with the Detroit Red Wings,

New York Rangers, and Boston Bruins. The Canadian Division's five teams were the Toronto Maple Leafs, Montreal Canadiens, Montreal Maroons, Ottawa Senators, and New York Americans.

Led by first-team All-Star defenseman Lionel Conacher (the "most celebrated all-around athlete in Canada" according to *Time* magazine in 1934) and Gardiner, that Blackhawks team defined the cliché, "defense wins championships." The Hawks were the lowest-scoring team in the league by far, scoring only 88 goals in 48 games; only one other team, the Canadiens (99), was held under 100 that season.

However, Chicago held their opponents to only 83 goals that year, also the lowest in the league; Detroit was the only other team to allow fewer than 100 that year (98). For his part in the effort, Gardiner was awarded his second Vezina Trophy after the season.

In that era, six of the nine teams qualified for the playoffs. The two division winners—Toronto and Detroit—received a bye in the first round while the two second-place and third-place teams played each other in the quarterfinals.

Chicago eliminated the Canadiens before defeating the Maroons in the semifinals. The Red Wings were forced to play the highest-scoring team in the league, the Leafs, and were able to eliminate them. So the two archrivals would fight for the Stanley Cup in the Finals that season.

The Blackhawks defeated the Wings in an epic best-of-five series that lasted four games. Gardiner allowed only two goals in the Hawks' three victories, including a shutout that lasted over 10 minutes into the second overtime. Tiny right wing Mush March won the Cup for Chicago with the fourth game's only goal at 10:05 in the second overtime period.

When his named was engraved on the Cup, Gardiner became the first—and last—goalie who was a captain to win the Cup. In 1948 the NHL changed rules to state that goaltenders could not serve as captain; only Vancouver's Robert Luongo has done so since (2008–09 and 2009–10), and he obviously didn't win the Cup in either of those seasons.

Gardiner never saw his name on the Cup, though. In fact, he did not even stay on the ice with his teammates to celebrate the championship. He was suffering from a migraine that was later found to be a brain hemorrhage. He died just a few weeks later.

35 The Madhouse on Madison

Despite the signage in the United Center laying claim to the nickname, "the Madhouse on Madison" was across the street. It was the Chicago Stadium, and it was built without a tenant. Paddy Harmon, a Chicago sports promoter, was sold on the idea of professional hockey working in Chicago but wasn't awarded a franchise by the NHL. Despite not getting the Chicago franchise from the NHL, Harmon built a state-of-the-art arena for the team to play in, and the project left him financially ruined.

Harmon paid $2.5 million out of his own pocket to begin the $9.5 million project, building a stadium twice the size of New York City's Madison Square Garden. The Blackhawks started playing at the Chicago Coliseum when they officially began operations and moved into the Chicago Stadium in December 1929.

On December 15, 1929, the Blackhawks defeated the Pittsburgh Pirates 3–1 in front of an astounding 14,212 fans. That crowd was 6,000 more than the Chicago Coliseum or Madison Square Garden could hold at the time for a hockey game. Indeed, when the doors opened, the Chicago Stadium was the largest sports arena in the world.

Chicago Stadium saw every Hall of Famer to ever wear the Indian-head sweater and 10 trips to the Stanley Cup Finals. Long before Michael Jordan made the crowd roar, it was Bobby Hull and Stan Mikita who brought the Chicago faithful to their feet on a regular basis.

If you talk to longtime season-ticket holders and regular fans who attended games at the Chicago Stadium, there are great stories ranging from the days when fans could smoke cigars at their seats to there being fires in stairwells that went unnoticed during games. The old barn was as unique as the teams that played in it.

The last regular-season and playoff games played by the Blackhawks at the Chicago Stadium were both against an Original Six opponent: the Toronto Maple Leafs. On April 14, 1994, the Hawks lost their regular-season finale 6–4. All of the players whose numbers had been retired at that point—Mikita, Bobby Hull, Glenn Hall, and Esposito—were in attendance.

In the playoffs that year, the Blackhawks faced the Leafs again in the first round. Chicago was eliminated in six games by Toronto, playing the final hockey game at the Stadium on April 28, a 1–0 loss.

Hockey and basketball weren't the only events to take place at one of the great original multisport venues in North America. In fact, the first event to take place at the Chicago Stadium was a boxing match between world light heavyweight Tommy Loughran and world middleweight champion Mickey Walker.

Some of the other great events to take place at the Stadium included Muhammad Ali winning the Golden Gloves tournament in 1960 and fights featuring some of the great names in boxing history: Sugar Ray Robinson, Jack Dempsey, Rocky Marciano, Joe Louis, and Floyd Patterson, among others. Political conventions and musical performances were also regulars at the stadium. Frank Sinatra, Elvis, the Rolling Stones, and KISS are some of the musical acts that performed there as well.

But the Chicago Stadium was—and forever will be—remembered as a sporting venue that was home to some of the greatest hockey and basketball players to ever play their respective games.

Fans will remember that the acoustics of the stadium were remarkable, and players will remember it as deafening. Every seat looked down at the action in a way that aimed all of the noise down on the center of the arena floor, making the Chicago Stadium the loudest building in the NHL.

A big part of the noise can be credited to the legendary 3,663-pipe Barton organ. The building would physically shake when the roar was at its peak, a shaking that could be felt in the dressing rooms (which were under the seats and down a flight of stairs from the ice surface).

However, the Stadium came with controversy, and that was part of the foundation of one of sport's great rivalries. One of the "friends" from whom Harmon borrowed money to build the arena was James E. Norris. When Harmon died in an automobile accident on July 22, 1930—not even a year after seeing his dream of professional hockey in the Chicago Stadium realized—the building's ownership fell into the hands of a group of creditors that covered the $7 million Harmon borrowed to finish the construction. Norris was at the front of the line.

Like Harmon, Norris had fallen short of Major Frederic McLaughlin's bid to own the NHL franchise in Chicago. Harmon and Norris tried to bring a second NHL team to Chicago, but McLaughlin would not provide the required consent for that to happen. So after Harmon's death, Norris founded the Chicago Shamrocks of the new American Hockey Association, a rogue league. Norris used his ownership stake in the Chicago Stadium and his position as the Blackhawks' landlord to try and kick the existing Chicago hockey team out of the building.

The move got the NHL's attention, and Norris was granted the right to own a team outside of Chicago. In the fall of 1933,

The Blackhawks hold a final farewell for the 65-year-old Chicago Stadium on April 14, 1994, during a pregame ceremony. Hall of Fame banners were lowered and given to Bobby Hull, Stan Mikita, Glenn Hall, and Tony Esposito.

Norris bought the Detroit Falcons and changed the name to the Red Wings. His contempt for McLaughlin wouldn't cease, and the birth of a great rivalry was born.

When the building closed for the final scheduled time on April 14, 1994, public-address announcer Harvey Wittenberg read the following address:

"Ladies and gentlemen, may I have your attention for one last message? This is a message from the Chicago Blackhawks to you, the Chicago Blackhawks fans.

"For 65 years here at the Chicago Stadium, ordinary, hard-working people known as the Blackhawk fans have come together to create an extraordinary atmosphere.

"You have devoted your emotions to the Blackhawks and have become an important part of the team. Your loud and affectionate praise [has] given us an advantage that is unmatched in professional sports play. You have affected the lives and lifted the performances of every hockey player ever to skate on the Stadium ice. We look upon you as ideal fans: hardworking, devoted assets. And we thank you for this.

"Here in the Chicago Stadium, performance is not just on the ice, the performance is everywhere: in the hallways, in the organ loft, the banners throughout the mezzanine and the balconies. Together we have created something exceptional. The Chicago Stadium experience has been truly special.

"As you leave tonight, we ask that you:

"Remember the great lady known as the Chicago Stadium—

"Remember how it was built to happen—

"Remember the championship banners swaying gently in the rafters—

"Remember the people you sat next to 10 years ago that are your friends today—

"Remember the organ loft and the press box and your favorite seat—

"Remember the stairs leading all the way to the second balcony—

"Remember your favorite great players whether they are Bobby Hull, Jeremy Roenick, Tony Esposito, Eddie Belfour, Stan Mikita, Denis Savard, Keith Magnuson, and Chris Chelios—

"Remember the feeling you have right now!

"On behalf of the Chicago Blackhawks, thank you for making all of this possible, and...

"REMEMBER THE ROAR!"

36 Bob Murray

Drafted with the 52nd overall pick in the 1974 Draft, Bob Murray was the type of defenseman that coaches dream about: smart, productive, and consistent.

He made his NHL debut as a 20-year-old in 1975–76, a season in which the Blackhawks did not qualify for the playoffs. That was the last time in his 15-year NHL career that Murray didn't get a taste of the postseason.

Like many of his great teammates in the 1980s, Murray's accomplishments are overlooked because of the great Edmonton teams of that decade. He was a two-time All-Star (1981 and 1983) and, while skating next to Doug Wilson, was part of one of the game's most dynamic defensive duos.

Murray experienced his greatest success in the NHL during the 1980–81 season. He was credited with a career-high 47 assists and totaled 60 points during the regular season. The following year, Murray was limited to 30 points in 45 games but added seven more points in 15 postseason contests.

The Blackhawks got close to the Stanley Cup Finals but were never able to get out of the Conference Finals during the 1980s; they played in the Conference Finals three times in four years starting in 1982. In total, Murray appeared in the Conference Finals six times in 15 years but never got a chance to play for the ultimate prize.

When he retired in 1990, Murray was one of only 17 defensemen in NHL history to play in more than 1,000 games. What separated Murray from the pack, however, was that he played all 1,008 of his games in the same sweater.

All-Time Assist Leaders

Being credited with an assist in hockey is sometimes a fickle event, determined in the old days by the game's officials and, now, with the help of video replay. Some of the top assist men in the league's history have played in Chicago, putting up impressive numbers along the way.
Here are the all-time top 10 assist men in Blackhawks history.

- Stan Mikita—926
- Denis Savard—719
- Doug Wilson—554
- Bobby Hull—549
- Steve Larmer—517
- Pierre Pilote—400
- Chris Chelios—395
- Pit Martin—384
- Bob Murray—382
- Dennis Hull—342

He is still the all-time leader in games played among Chicago defensemen, the only blue-liner to play in more than 1,000 games. He scored 132 goals and added 382 assists in his great Blackhawks career during the regular season. In the playoffs, Murray was clutch. He scored 19 goals and added 37 assists in 112 playoff games in his distinguished career. His 514 points still rank second in Chicago history for a defenseman behind only his partner, Wilson.

In 1991 the Blackhawks hired Murray as the director of player personnel. The organization eventually promoted him to general manager in July 1997, a position he filled for two years.

Murray joined the Anaheim organization in 2005 and, like many of his teammates in Chicago, won a Stanley Cup ring as a member of another organization; he was working under Brian Burke as the senior vice president of hockey operations when the Ducks won the Cup in 2007.

In 2008 Murray was named the general manager of the Anaheim Ducks, in the same division (and state) as Wilson, who serves in the same capacity in San Jose.

37 Stealing from Detroit

Center Forbes Kennedy played in 168 games for the Detroit Red Wings over four seasons, scoring 14 goals and 22 assists. In total, he racked up 300 penalty minutes during his Detroit career, playing in only four postseason contests.

After being traded to Chicago two years prior by Detroit, forward Johnny Wilson scored 23 goals and added 44 assists in 140 more games after the Blackhawks dealt him back to the Red Wings. He too only played in four postseason games for the Wings in his second stint in Detroit.

Goalie Hank Bassen won 33 games for Detroit over parts of six seasons with the Wings. In his best season with Detroit, he accumulated a 13–13–8 record and a .898 goals-against average.

Bill Preston never appeared in an NHL game.

What do these four players have to do with Chicago Blackhawks history? The Red Wings were going through some upheaval. After winning four Stanley Cups in the 1950s, the Wings were making sweeping changes. It began when Tommy Ivan left to become head coach and general manager in Chicago and continued as Detroit GM Jack Adams managed the Red Wings using the Sinatra approach: he did things his way.

During the 1956–57 season, future Hall of Fame forward Ted Lindsay had the vision to realize that the players in the NHL needed to organize if they wanted to received proper treatment from the league and teams. So he suggested there be a players' association and worked to form one. This infuriated Adams so much that he wanted Lindsay out of Detroit as soon as possible.

"The players needed an association," Lindsay said in McFarlane's *The Blackhawks*. "We needed a voice. We weren't interested in running hockey. We weren't asking for much. But back then a six-team league was a dictatorship. The owners would say 'Jump,' and we'd all start jumping."

Similarly, the Red Wings had a stockpile of young goalies and couldn't keep them all. When their reigning Calder Trophy–winner mouthed off at Adams after practice one day, he decided both needed to go. So in July 1957, Adams traded Lindsay and that goalie, Glenn Hall, to the Blackhawks for Kennedy, Wilson, Bassen, and Preston. The deal would prove to be a mistake of biblical proportions for the Red Wings.

Taking Terrible Ted away from the legendary line that, with Alex Delvecchio and Gordie Howe, had led the Wings to back-to-back Cups in 1954 and 1955 seriously hurt the production of the line going forward. In addition, Lindsay proved to be a valuable mentor to a couple young prospects coming up in Chicago—Bobby Hull and Stan Mikita.

Lindsay only skated three years in Chicago, with his best season coming in 1958–59, when he scored 22 goals in 70 games. He retired after the 1959–60 season, only to come back four years later for one last run in Detroit.

And Hall? He went on to a Hall of Fame career and is remembered as one of the most elite goalies to ever play the game.

Lindsay remembered the deal later in McFarlane's *The Blackhawks*: "In Detroit, Jack Adams was praying I'd have a bad season so he could hang me out. He hadn't spoken to me the last three years I was there. But I didn't play for Adams, I played hockey because I loved it…. As for Glenn Hall, I think he was thrown into the deal because he was a Ted Lindsay fan. For the next fifteen years, Hall was the best in the league."

This trade is one of the most lopsided deals in the history of the league and, unlike the trade that sent Phil Esposito to Boston, this one helped the Blackhawks.

38 No. 2

If it's possible to do almost nothing right and still win a championship, the Blackhawks did precisely that in 1938. The team had one first-team All-Star in left wing Paul Thompson, who scored 22 of the team's 97 total goals that year. Earl Seibert was named a second-team All-Star on the blue line, and center Cully Dahlstrom won the Calder Trophy as the league's best rookie. But it was hard to find much more worth noting during that season than those three awards.

Chicago scored the fewest goals in the league that year (97), and only the Montreal Maroons allowed more than the 139 goals scored by Blackhawks opponents. The Blackhawks had also won only 14 of their 48 games that year, earning a tie in only nine other contests. Yet they snuck into the playoffs because Detroit, somehow, was worse than the Hawks, winning only 12 games.

Even the Blackhawks doubted themselves! With the team's final three games of the regular season on the road, owner Major McLaughlin had all of the team's extra equipment shipped back to Chicago so they could start preparing it for the off-season.

Alex Levinsky was so convinced that even if the Hawks got into the playoffs the season would be over quickly that he emptied his apartment and sent his wife back to their home in Canada for the summer. He lived out of his car for the next month.

Even when the Hawks were winning that year, they appeared to be losing. In the third and final game of the quarterfinals against the Canadiens, Georges Mantha scored an awkward goal that looked like it would be enough, but Seibert tied the game late in the third period. The Hawks eventually clinched the series in overtime.

In the semifinal series against the New York Americans, the Blackhawks lost the first game 3–1. In Game 2 the dueling goaltenders both took a shutout late into the third period. It appeared that Nels Stewart had scored a game-winning goal in the closing moments of the third period, but the officials disallowed the goal, ruling Eddie Wiseman was in the crease. Seibert scored the series-clinching goal in overtime.

The Hawks went on to be the unlikely winners in another series, but nobody wanted to believe it was true. When Levinsky scored the go-ahead goal in New York, Americans fans held the goal judge's hand so he couldn't signal the goal was good.

During the series against the Americans, Blackhawks goalie Mike Karakas broke a toe and wasn't able to play in Game 1 of the Finals against the Toronto Maple Leafs. At that time, the rules covering the emergency replacement of an injured player were fairly loose, and the Hawks had hoped to use Dave Kerr of the New York Rangers. The commissioner's office objected, and the Hawks were forced to use a minor league goalie in the Americans organization, Alfie Moore.

The League wavered on whether or not they would allow the Hawks to use Moore for Game 1 until just hours before the game. When the league gave Chicago the OK, the team dispatched one of Moore's friends, forward Johnny Gottselig, to round up the goalie for that night's game.

He found Moore at a local bar, already having a "good time." "He'd had about 10 or a dozen drinks," Gottselig said, recalling the incident years later in an interview with John Devaney, author of *The Stanley Cup.* "We put some coffee into him and put him under the shower. By game time, he was in pretty good shape."

Before the first game of the Finals could get going, relying on a drunk minor league goalie was the least of the team's concerns. Chicago had major concerns about the playing surface, which led to a fistfight between Chicago coach Bill Stewart and Leafs owner Conn Smythe.

After the Blackhawks won Game 1 3–1, the league—prompted during the game by Smythe—ruled that Moore was not eligible to play in the series. Even so, they allowed the Hawks' victory to stand. For Game 2 the Hawks had to find another replacement, this time turning to another minor leaguer named Paul Goodman. Toronto crushed the Blackhawks 5–1.

Fitted with a custom steel-toed skate, Karakas was able to return for Game 3 of the series. The Blackhawks won the third game 2–1 and came home with a chance to clinch their second Cup in four years.

But even the commissioner's office doubted the Blackhawks. Frank Calder, the first president of the NHL, doubted the 1937–38 Blackhawks so much that, prior to the Cup Finals against the Toronto Maple Leafs, he had the Cup sent from Detroit— where the Red Wings had won it the previous season—to Toronto without even considering sending it to Chicago, even though the Hawks had an opportunity to win the series at home.

Moore and Goodman each only played in one NHL game apiece that year—Game 1 and Game 2 of the Finals, respectively— but each had his name engraved on the Cup. In fact, Moore only played in 21 regular-season games in his NHL career.

When the final horn sounded, the Blackhawks were winners but the Cup was in Canada. The Blackhawks set a record that year with eight American-born players on their roster, and Stewart was the first American-born head coach to win the Cup. (The second American-born coach to win the Cup wouldn't happen until 53 years later when Bob Johnson was on the bench for the Pittsburgh Penguins.)

It was fitting that the Hawks also set an attendance record for the Cup-clinching Game 4. The 18,497 people in attendance that night didn't know it at the time, but they were the last crowd to see the Stanley Cup won by the Blackhawks in the Chicago Stadium. Indeed, a Chicago team wouldn't clinch a championship in the Stadium again until the Bulls won the NBA title in 1992.

39 Commit to the Indian

In late January 2008 the Blackhawks were fighting for a playoff spot. They were without six injured forwards—including Jonathan Toews, Dave Bolland, Kris Versteeg, and Jason Williams—and were headed on a seven-game road trip after hosting the Columbus Blue Jackets.

The game was ugly on both sides, as the Jackets and Hawks combined to go 0–11 on the power play. Nikolai Khabibulin was good, allowing only one goal on 27 shots, 24 of which came in the first two periods.

But the Blackhawks offense was nowhere to be found. Despite putting 30 shots on net, the Hawks didn't generate anything of substance. The final score was 1–0 in favor of Columbus, and head coach Denis Savard didn't like the effort he saw.

In fact, Savard's postgame comments to the media were not only a spark for that team, but have become a rallying cry for fans since. "I'm really pissed off," he said. "We committed to them. Some of them, we commit to them for two years, three years… they've gotta commit to us…. They've gotta commit to the Indian. If they don't wanna commit to the Indian, then let's go upstairs; we'll get them out of here."

With impressionable youngsters like Toews, Versteeg, and Patrick Kane on his roster, the coach wasn't speaking to the microphones. His words were aimed at the ears in the locker room.

The Spin-O-Rama

Only the most elite skaters can pull it off, but when it's done well, any arena in the league is impressed.

Hockey players have always used a spin move to elude a defender, just as running backs do in football. But the move didn't reach leaguewide prominence or receive its nickname until it was done in Chicago.

When Denis Savard spun, it captivated most defenseman as much as it did the crowd. By the mid-1980s, the spin-o-rama had a name. The move became so popular that subsequent generations have wanted to perfect the move. In fact, the term *spin-o-rama* is so widely accepted now, it appears in official NHL rules. In Rule 24.2, which outlines legal procedure during a penalty shot, it reads: "The spin-o-rama type move, where the player completes a 360° turn as he approaches the goal, shall be permitted as this involves continuous motion."

Some players may have spun before Savard, and hundreds have since. But nobody performed the spin-o-rama like the man wearing No. 18 for Chicago.

He continued, "To gain an inch in this league you've got to want it and want to work. You might get a cut. You might get bruised. So what? Last time I checked, you're getting pretty good money to do it.

"And they don't want to do it. It's as simple as that. In this league, if you want to win, you've gotta pay a price. If you don't want to win, you'll be going like this [up-and-down waving hand motion]. Our message is pretty clear: we won't accept it."

Savard wanted the young ears of his players to hear his old-school, won't-accept-mailing-it-in sermon, and the Blackhawks' record from that point of the season to the end bears witness to its impact. From that date on, the Blackhawks went 17–11–4, even though they lost the first three games after the loss to Columbus.

Savard's career as a head coach didn't last very long, but the impact of this speech is still being felt at the United Center to this day.

40 So Long, Savoir Faire

In 1989–90 the Blackhawks had a fantastic season. Under new head coach Mike Keenan, the team stormed to the top of the Norris Division with 88 points. Behind Steve Thomas (team-high 40 goals), Steve Larmer (team-high 90 points), and Denis Savard (80 points in only 60 games), the Hawks had one of the most dynamic offenses in the league. They ended the season second in the Campbell Conference and had the veteran leadership in place to make a deep run through the playoffs.

They did precisely that, defeating the Minnesota North Stars 4–3 and then the St. Louis Blues 4–3 before an epic six-game series with the Edmonton Oilers. The Hawks lost the series to the Oilers, who outscored them 25–20 in the six games.

One of the surprises from that playoff run was a young net-minder who was called up for the playoffs. Ed Belfour posted a 4–2 record with an impressive 2.49 goals-against average in that postseason after not appearing in a regular-season game for the Hawks.

There was a feeling that something special was coming in the future for the Blackhawks. Then, on June 29, 1990, newly named general manager Keenan made his first bold move to shake up the roster. He dealt alternate captain Savard to the Montreal Canadiens for Chris Chelios and a second-round pick in the 1991 Draft (which was used to select left wing Mike Pomichter). The player coming back to Chicago had a fantastic résumé, but an icon was leaving.

Savard was the third overall player selected in the 1980 Draft (behind Doug Wickenheiser and Dave Babych), which was the highest the Blackhawks had selected in team history until Patrick

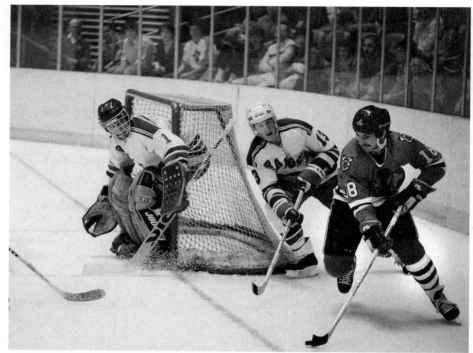

Denis Savard is chased by New York Ranger Bob Brooke as Brooke fruitlessly tries to stop him from scoring. Chicago won the game 5–3.

Kane was taken with the first overall pick 27 years later. He set the franchise record with 75 points in his rookie season.

In the decade Savard had spent in Chicago, he had established himself as the best scorer the franchise had seen since Bobby Hull and Stan Mikita. He scored over 100 points five times in the 1980s, with an incredible 131 in 1987–88 (still the franchise record). He set the team record for assists in a season with 87 in 1981–82 and tied the mark in the 1987–88 season. Moving Savard, who was just 29 years old at the time, was hard for any Hawks fan to stomach.

Chelios, though, was no slouch. Then 28, he had played six full seasons for the Habs and had served as their co-captain with legend

Guy Carbonneau in the 1989–90 season. In those six seasons, Chelios had scored 307 points (72 goals, 235 assists) in 390 games.

He was a member of the All-Rookie Team in 1985, finishing second in the Calder Trophy voting to some guy named Mario Lemieux. After the 1985–86 season, Chelios won his first Stanley Cup with Montreal. After the 1988–89 season Chelios won his first Norris Trophy.

How did the aftermath of the trade work out? Savard won the Stanley Cup with Montreal in 1993 and then spent less than two seasons with Tampa Bay before being dealt back to the Blackhawks for a sixth-round pick. In the four-plus seasons Savard spent away from the Windy City, he scored 242 points (96 goals, 146 assists) in 315 games. He was clearly not as productive as he had been in Chicago, where he had scored 1,013 points (351 goals, 662 assists) in just 736 games.

Chelios, on the other hand, took his game to another level. He won the Norris Trophy two more times, in 1993 and 1996, and served as the team's captain from 1995 to 1999. With young players like Belfour and Jeremy Roenick, he helped transition the Hawks from the high-flying teams of the 1980s into the 1990s and kept them competitive. The Hawks advanced to the Stanley Cup Finals once while Chelios was in Chicago, losing to Lemieux's Penguins in 1992.

Chelios played in seven All-Star Games as a member of the Blackhawks before being traded to Detroit in March 1999 for Anders Eriksson and two first-round draft picks.

When the trade went down, Hawks fans were stung by the loss of one of the most popular players in franchise history. But the return on the transaction was a player who is still held in the highest regard around the league and who will, some day soon, join Savard in the Hall of Fame.

41 WWW

For someone who was such a great advocate of the game of hockey and wonderful mediator between owners and players, the legacy of Hall of Fame owner William W. "Bill" Wirtz has become terribly tarnished in Chicago.

By the time he passed away, just days before the start of the 2007–08 season, he had become one of the most hated men in Chicago. Just months before his death, ESPN offered the following analysis of the state of the Blackhawks organization: "Even the put-downs have become caricatures; stories told and retold so often, they have become almost meaningless. The litany of problems facing the Chicago Blackhawks, on and off the ice, is so great, it appears to have created a kind of paralysis"

A 2004 poll conducted by *ESPN the Magazine* found the team to be the worst in all of sports, joining a list of periodicals including *Forbes* that had thrown the Blackhawks to the wolves. In fact, Wirtz's various nicknames—from "Dollar Bill" to "Billfold"— made regular appearances in the sports columns in Chicago.

In 2010, after the Cup returned to Chicago, Steve Rosenbloom still took this shot at the late owner of the team and his longtime right-hand man, Bob Pulford: "If you still weren't sure this wasn't your father's Hawks organ-I-zation when it won the Cup, then you figured it out when you saw that 404-gem ring worth an estimated $30,000. If Bob Pulford still was exchequer of the fiefdom for Billfold Wirtz, then Jonathan Toews would be showing off a Dutch Masters band."

Indeed, even his son (and successor as chairman of the Blackhawks) Rocky saw the problems with his father's approach. "I'd say, 'Dad, we're losing generations of fans by not televising home games,'" Rocky said in a 2010 *New York Times* piece by Richard Sandomir. "He said it wouldn't be fair to our fans with season tickets. But we'd gotten down to 3,400 season tickets, which meant maybe 1,500 to 1,700 fans. So we weren't televising home games for 1,700 people? Why bang your head against the wall?"

It isn't a revelation to say that the last 15 years of Bill Wirtz's ownership of the team were far from fan-friendly. His refusal to pay players well or pursue key players in trades or free agency, hurt the on-ice product, and his refusal to televise home games nearly destroyed the relationship between the team and the city that had passionately supported—loved—the team for 75 years.

But the story of Bill Wirtz should not be dismissed because of its final chapters. In fact, a case could be made that no owner has made as large an impact on the game in the post–Original Six

The $250,000 Coin Toss

In 1972 Bobby Hull left the Blackhawks in favor of the money in the new World Hockey Association. The WHA was chasing top players all over the NHL, and owners were starting to become scared that other stars would follow the Golden Jet's lead.

The Blackhawks had already lost one Hull, and they started to hear whispers that the WHA had their eyes on Bobby's little brother, Dennis, as well. So in 1973 the Hawks did for Dennis what they hadn't for Bobby. General manager Tommy Ivan called Dennis into his office and made him the offer of a lifetime: $1.5 million for 10 years. The 29-year-old quickly responded that he wanted $1.75 million, largely in disbelief that the team was making him such an offer.

Ivan, frustrated and angered by Hull's demands, went to owner Bill Wirtz and explained the situation. Wirtz's creative response was to make a wager with his star player. They would determine the total dollar amount of the deal with the flip of a coin.

Wirtz flipped a quarter in the air, and Hull called heads. When the coin came up heads, Wirtz agreed to give him $1.75 million over the 10 years. That would go down as the most expensive coin flip in the history of the organization.

era of the National Hockey League. NHL commissioner Gary Bettman said as much in his statement following Wirtz's passing. Bettman said, "His 41 years as president of the Blackhawks and 18 years as chairman of the board leave an incomparable legacy of contributions to the game and to the league. His strength, intelligence, character, and passion have been ingrained indelibly in the Blackhawks, in the league, and in me. Bill was a true icon and a great competitor."

Bill Wirtz became the president of the Blackhawks in 1966. For 18 years he served as the chairman of the board of governors and was a leading force behind the merger between the National Hockey League and World Hockey Association. This merger was an enormous move by the league to expand its operations to both coasts of North America, and Wirtz should be credited with being a guiding force in those negotiations.

He was also a strong supporter of his players in the early years. In 1972, when the WHA was emerging as a legitimate competitor of the NHL, Wirtz fought hard to allow NHL players to represent the league in the Summit Series against the Soviet Union. He was also responsible for establishing mutually acceptable arrangements covering the players and coaches, the tournament schedule, and the radio and television broadcasts.

If any owner had reason to boycott the inclusion of players at that time, it would have been Wirtz; he had just lost Bobby Hull to the WHA's Winnipeg Jets. But he still encouraged the league to allow players, including Chicago's Dennis Hull, to play in the tournament.

Dennis Hull remembered the charitable side of Wirtz well in McFarlane's *The Blackhawks*, saying, "He was extremely generous. I know Doug Jarrett wanted to buy a house one year and he went to see Mr. Wirtz. Bill said, 'How much do you need to buy the house?' Doug said, 'About forty grand.' So Bill gave him a $40,000 raise."

This generosity wasn't limited to his players. The entire Wirtz family has always been a strong supporter of hockey programs throughout the Chicago area. Since its establishment in 1993, Chicago Blackhawk Charities has donated millions of dollars to organizations all over Chicago, including the Amateur Hockey Association of Illinois. Bill Wirtz also served on the 1980 and 1984 Winter Olympic committees.

He always kept a sense of humor about how he was perceived, even signing his correspondence, "Dollar Bill."

His vision, along with that of Chicago Bulls chairman Jerry Reinsdorf, led to the building of the United Center as a state-of-the-art replacement for the Chicago Stadium. Because of his impact on the game at the professional and amateur levels, Wirtz was inducted into the Hockey Hall of Fame in 1976. He was also recognized with the Lester Patrick Award in 1978 and inducted into the U.S. Hockey Hall of Fame in 1985.

42 The Curse of Muldoon

Many casual sports fans assume the only team in Chicago that has dealt with curses is the Cubs. Unfortunately for the Blackhawks organization, they have some bad mojo in their past as well.

In 1917 Pete Muldoon became the first coach to bring the Stanley Cup to the United States. That championship was won in Seattle, but a few years later his wife's hometown came calling.

When the Blackhawks were founded in 1926, the first man to stand behind the bench was Muldoon. Already with more than a decade of coaching experience on his résumé, the

40-year-old Muldoon is remembered as a good teacher and an effective leader.

The first season for the Hawks was a relative success but apparently wasn't good enough for the franchise's original owner, Major Frederic McLaughlin. After a number of heated exchanges between Muldoon and McLaughlin, the coach submitted his resignation with two weeks remaining in the team's inaugural season. Effective after the final game, Muldoon had seen enough.

"Our worthy president wanted to run the club, the players, the referees, etc.," Muldoon said a couple weeks after the season. "He learned the game very quickly. In fact, after seeing his first game, he wrote me a letter telling me what players should and should not do."

Muldoon moved back to Seattle after resigning and died shortly after from a heart attack. McLaughlin passed away a few years later, and the team's new ownership started to experience financial problems. In need of something the newspapers would write about, an alleged curse was born as little more than a publicity stunt. In 1947 the team's publicist, Joe Farrell, concocted the story to create a buzz about the team in a city that was already well aware of the Billy Goat Curse that haunts the Cubs.

The legend, as created by Farrell, remembers Muldoon placing a curse on McLaughlin and the team as part of his departure: "Fire me, Major, and you'll never finish first. I'll put a curse on this team that will hoodoo it until the end of time."

Despite Stanley Cup victories in 1934, 1938, and 1961, the Blackhawks never finished first in the league or, later, their division.

As the years passed by, the legend continued to grow. In fact, when the Hawks finally finished first in 1967, coach Billy Reay exclaimed, "What happened to the curse of Muldoon?" as he was thrown into the showers by his excited team.

Indeed, one newspaper—the *Reading (PA) Eagle*—had the following headline the next day: "Black Hawks Win 1st Title and End 'Curse of Muldoon.'"

That same edition of the paper, dated March 13, 1967, quotes Stan Mikita also referring to the drought. Someone in the gathered media asked Mikita if the champagne was cold. "It ought to be," replied Mikita. "It's been on ice for 40 years."

That regular-season crown came in the final season of the original, six-team NHL. However, the Hawks weren't able to turn their regular-season success into a championship; they lost to the Toronto Maple Leafs in the semifinals.

After Chicago was eliminated by the Leafs, a writer from the *Toronto Globe and Mail* busted the curse. Jim Coleman, who was writing for the *Globe and Mail* 20 years prior, admitted that the story was a fabrication when he first printed it.

Despite all of the embellishments and exaggerations that came with the story over the years, it might have eventually come to hold weight. The Blackhawks organization did not win a regular-season division championship and Stanley Cup championship in the same season until 2010.

43 The Voice of the Hawks

On June 16, 2008, the Chicago Blackhawks brought a smile back to the faces of many longtime fans well before Patrick Kane was throwing his gloves in the air in Philadelphia.

"His voice is synonymous with Blackhawks hockey and it resonates loudly to our entire fan base," team president John McDonough said in a Blackhawks press release about the return of Pat Foley to the broadcast booth at the United Center.

Foley began lending his voice to Blackhawks broadcasts in 1981, and his infectious enthusiasm brought some of the greatest players in the franchise's long history home to fans for two decades. A Chicago native and Michigan State grad, Foley was as much a part of the fiber of the sports scene in Chicago as Harry Caray or Jack Brickhouse.

It's impossible to remember a great goal or incredible finish to a game without hearing Foley's voice. His exclamation when a Hawks player scores is legendary, and his excitement when a big save is made is equally contagious. Whether he was making "Baaaanermaan!" a household name or matter-of-factly stating, "Niemi says no," he is the voice of 30 years of Blackhawks history.

In 1991 Foley received an Emmy for Outstanding Achievement—Sports Program Live Series and was inducted into the Chicago Sports Hall of Fame in 2002, joining Brickhouse and Caray.

Why do Blackhawks fans love Pat Foley? Because he doesn't pull punches. When Alexander Karpovtsev was traded to the New York Islanders for a fourth-round pick on March 9, 2004, Foley relayed the news with one of the most epic two-minute rants in broadcast history. The rant is available on YouTube by searching for "Karpovtsev."

Unfortunately, there was a two-year break in the marriage between Foley and the Hawks. In May 2006 the Hawks cited "personal" reasons for taking their contract offer to Foley off the table. The team replaced him with John Wiedeman on radio and Dan Kelly Jr. for television, leaving Foley to take his talent to the AHL with the Chicago Wolves.

After two long seasons, Foley was brought back where he belongs, joining Eddie Olczyk for most games on Comcast SportsNet and WGN. Wiedeman has remained part of the broadcast team as the radio play-by-play man. In 2009 Foley and Eddie Olczyk were awarded Midwest Emmy Awards for Outstanding Achievement in Play-By-Play.

The return of Foley made an impact on the number of people viewing Hawks games on television "eee-mediately." According to the Blackhawks, "household ratings for Blackhawks games on

Comcast SportsNet have increased over 130 percent while contests on WGN-TV have increased over 85 percent since Foley and Olczyk were paired together at the start of the 2008–09 regular season. Comcast SportsNet's top five all-time rated broadcasts were recorded during the first [one game] and second rounds [four games] of the Blackhawks' run to the 2010 Stanley Cup, all of which had Foley and Olczyk with the call."

In December 2010 the Blackhawks extended the contracts of Foley and Olczyk through the 2013–14 season. The organization recognized Foley's contributions again when they announced this extension. "Blackhawks fans connect in a very special way with each and every broadcast.... We are fortunate to have one of the premier broadcast tandems in all of professional sports," said executive vice president Jay Blunk.

Indeed, Foley is one of, if not the best, play-by-play artists in the hockey world. From Denis Savard's 1,000[th] career point to Marian Hossa's incredible overtime game-winner against Nashville in the 2010 playoffs, Foley's voice continues to be the central component in the soundtrack of the Blackhawks.

44 Taking 88 at No. 1

Dale Tallon labeled the selection pretty well from the podium: "This historic pick."

On a June day in 2007, the Chicago Blackhawks made the first overall selection in the NHL Draft for the first time in the organization's long history. They had picked as high as third overall, including the selection of Jonathan Toews the previous summer, but never had Chicago been in the top spot.

Watching the coverage of the draft on TSN (which can be viewed on YouTube), the historical implications of this selection weren't lost on anyone. Before the Blackhawks representatives had even left their table on the floor in Columbus, the analysts made clear that it was a "crucial time" for the Blackhawks.

There were two players who were near the top of almost every predraft rankings. One was a bigger, more physically "ready" player. The other was a diminutive scorer.

Barely 18 years old, James Van Riemsdyk was a slender sniper headed to the college ranks. Listed at 6'3" and just a shade under 200 pounds, he had posted 25 points (13 goals, 12 assists) in only 12 games with the U.S. National U-18 Team in 2006–07 and made a favorable impression on many scouts.

In an article for *USA Today* on January 12, 2007, veteran NHL analyst Kevin Allen quoted *USA Hockey*'s Jim Johannson when breaking down Van Riemsdyk: "I think [he] will be a very solid player and is a safe draft pick. He can be a complete player—competes well on the puck and for his size can really go when he needs to."

Patrick Kane, on the other hand, stood a few inches under six feet tall and allegedly weighed 175 pounds. After looking at his numbers, though, the only questions anyone could ask were related to his size; in 58 games in juniors the previous year, Kane had scored 145 points (62 goals, 83 assists). He then added 31 points (10 goals, 21 assists) in only 16 postseason games.

Allen broke down Kane's game this way: "Although not explosive, Kane is considered a quick player with magical hands and a good game. Scouts say he has the opportunity to be an impact offensive player at the NHL, especially with the league opening up the game through its rules changes."

Both players were American-born—Van Riemsdyk from Middletown, New Jersey, and Kane from Buffalo, New York—making

2007 a rare year when both of the top two players were from the United States. And the Blackhawks could have either one. The Hawks made their historic choice, stating, "We proudly select, from the London Knights of the Ontario Hockey League, Patrick Kane."

The paths of the top two picks would cross again; Van Riemsdyk was the second overall selection by the Philadelphia Flyers.

Just moments after being selected, still wearing a red Blackhawks sweater bearing the No. 07 (for the year), Kane told TSN that his goals were simple. "That's my goal," said Kane. "To go into that camp and make the team…. Don't get me wrong. I'm going in to make the team right away."

Kane did make the team right away and answered his critics quickly. He scored 21 goals and added 51 assists en route to winning the 2007–08 Calder Memorial Trophy as the top rookie in the league. The runner-up? The teenage center playing next to him, Toews.

In the subsequent two seasons, Kane and Toews led the Blackhawks back into the playoffs for the first time in nearly a decade. Over his first two postseasons, Kane put up 42 points in only 38 games. None, however, were bigger than the final tally of the 2010 NHL season.

With Van Riemsdyk on the opposite end of the ice wearing the home orange sweater, Kane slipped the puck into the corner of the net—and history—to close out a storybook run for the Hawks. At only 22, Kane had justified the faith of Tallon three years prior when the Original Six franchise made him their first No. 1 overall selection.

Kaner

The Blackhawks have a great, colorful history filled with vertically challenged scoring stars. From Mush March to Bill Mosienko and Max and Doug Bentley to Pit Martin and Stan Mikita, there have been generations of great players in Chicago who weren't 5'10". In fact, at 6'1", Jeremy Roenick is literally a giant on the Blackhawks all-time leaderboard.

So when the Hawks opted to select Patrick Kane instead of James Van Riemsdyk in the 2007 NHL Draft, anyone with a sense for the franchise's history shouldn't have been surprised.

When Kane began his career on a line with Jonathan Toews, history should have indicated to Blackhawks fans that something special was going to happen. Mosienko and the Bentley brothers formed the legendary Pony Line. Martin was a member of the great MPH Line. And Mikita centered the famous Scooter Line.

Kane fits perfectly into the history of the Blackhawks. And his play has already added his name to the pantheon of great players in Blackhawks history.

When Kane scored 72 points in his rookie season, he became the first Blackhawks player to win the Calder Memorial Trophy—the league's top rookie honor—in 17 years; Ed Belfour won the award in 1991.

When Kane scored 88 points during the 2009–10 season, it was the highest single-season point total from a Blackhawks player in 16 years; Jeremy Roenick posted 107 in consecutive seasons, the more recent of which was the 1993–94 campaign.

When Kane scored a Stanley Cup–clinching goal in overtime in Philadelphia, he was the second Blackhawks forward to do so.

March won the 1934 Cup for Chicago with a goal in the second overtime period, defeating the Detroit Red Wings.

(Historical oddity: four of the 15 overtime Cup-clinching goals have been scored against former Blackhawks netminders, including Kane's against Michael Leighton. Glenn Hall in 1970, Dominik Hašek in 1999, and Ed Belfour in 2000 are the others. A fifth overtime Cup-winner was scored against the Blackhawks when Toe Blake beat Mike Karakas in 1944.)

The Blackhawks have been represented by Kane on the international stage as well. He has been an All-Star twice in his first four

Calder Memorial Trophy Winners

The Calder Memorial Trophy is the award given each year "to the player selected as the most proficient in his first year of competition in the NHL." The award is voted on by the Professional Hockey Writers Association.

The NHL started naming a Rookie of the Year after the 1932–33 season, but the trophy was named for Frank Calder, the president of the NHL from 1917 to 1943, after the 1936–37 season. It became the Calder Memorial Trophy after Calder's death in 1943.

Originally, the award carried one limitation: to be eligible for the award, a player could not have played any more than 25 games previously in any single season or have played in more than six games in each of two separate preceding seasons at any professional level. After Sergei Makarov won the award in 1990, an amendment was made to the criteria to win the trophy. Eligible players must be 26 years old or younger by September 15 of their rookie season.

The following Chicago Blackhawks have won the Calder Memorial Trophy:

- Cully Dahlstrom: 1937–38
- Ed Litzenberger: 1954–55
- Bill Hay: 1959–60
- Tony Esposito: 1969–70
- Steve Larmer: 1982–83
- Ed Belfour: 1990–91
- Patrick Kane: 2007–08

seasons (only three All-Star Games have been played), and he was a member of the 2010 United States Men's Olympic team. In six games with Team USA, Kane scored three goals and added two assists. However, the U.S. lost to three of Kane's Chicago teammates—Toews, Duncan Keith, and Brent Seabrook—in the gold medal game against Canada.

In 2011 Kane continued to etch his name into the Blackhawks record books. On March 4 Kane became the second-youngest player in the organization's history to play in 300 games, just behind Grant Mulvey. Ten days later, on March 14, Kane became the third-youngest player in Hawks history to score 100 goals, behind only Roenick and Bobby Hull. Not bad company.

However, something Kane has been forced to deal with that the great players in the past did not have to worry about is social media. The Blackhawks have a long list of colorful players, from Reg Fleming and Bobby Hull to Bob Probert and Theo Fleury. But the on- and off-ice issues that many of these players had to deal with stayed largely in the form of rumors or urban legend.

In the summer of 2009 Kane was arrested outside Buffalo after an incident with a cab driver. According to the police report, Kane and his cousin, James, were involved in an altercation over correct change, and the driver claimed that he was assaulted.

Kane pled not guilty, and the story eventually evaporated. He went on to have the best season of his career, ending with the dramatic goal in Philadelphia and the Cup coming back to Chicago. But the focus of social media and camera phones have stayed focused on the Hawks' young star.

To Kane's credit, he has continued to produce on the ice. He is quickly climbing the all-time scoring list in the franchise's history and is one of the most dangerous wings in the game today.

46 The Invisible End of 49 Years

Kirk Gibson hit the original "walk-off home run" against Dennis Eckersley in 1988; Eckersley then created the term after that game.

Michael Jordan's jumper over Craig Ehlo in 1989 announced the Bulls' arrival as a contender.

Adam Vinatieri hit a Super Bowl–winning field goal as the clock rolled to zeroes in 2002.

All had official, formal closure. Gibson hobbled around the bases, Jordan pumped his fist, and Vinatieri was mobbed by teammates. All of these moments had certainty that the game was over. But this wasn't the case for Patrick Kane.

With exactly 16 minutes remaining in overtime, Andrew Ladd lost a board battle, and the puck was kicked out, where Brian Campbell held it in the offensive zone. He skated backward toward the Stanley Cup Final logo on the blue line and dumped the puck to Kane against the boards.

Kane described the play in simple terms: "I threw a couple head fakes and took it to the net," he said. It was perhaps the most anticlimactic championship-winning event in professional sports history.

From just outside the circle, Kane shot the puck and everything except Kane was suddenly locked in slow motion. The Flyers were all looking around for the puck. Ladd, who was between the circles, started to assume a defensive posture. Kane skated right past Nick Boynton and flew down the ice, flipping his gloves in the air, leaving his stick behind and starting a one-man celebration.

"It was kind of an awkward celebration," Jonathan Toews said postgame. "We didn't know what to do. We were all standing around waiting for the official call."

Meanwhile, the Flyers, broadcasters, and fans in Philadelphia had no idea what was going on. On the Canadian broadcast, which is still available on YouTube, the camerawork and commentary capture the pandemonium perfectly. As the Blackhawks' drought is being declared over, CBC shows Flyers goalie Michael Leighton looking at the refs in disbelief as they all look for the puck.

While the shot was under review, a stunned Flyers bench joined the packed stands in watching the Blackhawks celebrate on the ice. Even many of the Hawks players admitted later that they weren't sure where the puck had gone. There was no horn. No flashing red light. Only a one-man parade celebrating his way down the ice, trying to sell the world on the reality that he had won the Stanley Cup for Chicago.

Kane's tally marked the 15th time in league history that the Cup had been won on an overtime goal and the first time since New Jersey's Jason Arnott eliminated the Dallas Stars in 2000.

In fact, it wasn't even the first time in Blackhawks history that the Cup was clinched on an overtime game-winner. When the Blackhawks won the Stanley Cup for the first time in 1934, Mush March scored in overtime to break a 0–0 tie with the Detroit Red Wings. But it was the first time in 49 years, one of the longest championship droughts in all of North American professional sports, that the Chicago Blackhawks were Stanley Cup champions.

Once the dust was settled, the players commented on the unbelievable win. "I think you envision this and hope for the best when you first come in," said Kane. "But everything we've been through, it's been obviously an unbelievable year. Very exciting. It's fun to be a part of it right now. Crazy game tonight. Just unbelievable, the result, though."

Toews agreed, saying, "Everything you go through, the tough times over a long season like we had this year, with such a great group of guys like we have in this locker room, nothing compares to that camaraderie and what you go through as a team. The pressure we were facing all season, to get to this point and win a Stanley Cup, we knew we could do it. We battled hard for each other. That's what makes this one so much better."

Brent Seabrook's words in the video montage prepared by the Blackhawks for Opening Night of the 2010–11 season have become immortal with Hawks fans when talking about one of the signature moments in NHL history: "You don't doubt a goal-scorer. When he knows the puck's in, he knows the puck's in."

After nearly five decades of watching high draft picks, superstars, and Hall of Famers fail to achieve that one goal, it was the highest pick in the franchise's history who broke through the concrete ceiling.

47 A Picture Worth a Million Words

The Stanley Cup is the hardest championship trophy to achieve in professional sports and the most coveted friend of hockey players of any age. When the Blackhawks won the Cup for the first time in 49 years, the well-documented celebrations that took place all over Chicago brought fans all over North America closer to the incredible trophy.

Part of the unique history of the Cup started in 1995, when the NHL allowed the Cup to travel the world to spend a day with players, coaches, and management of the championship team. During the summer of 2010, the Cup made a number of memorable stops.

It appeared at Wrigley Field for a game between the Cubs and White Sox. It was displayed during Chicago's Gay Pride Parade.

Jay Leno hosted the Cup on *The Tonight Show with Jay Leno*. Later in the summer, during a celebration that only Chicago and Boston could host, the Cup appeared at U.S. Cellular Field next to the Vince Lombardi Trophy from the 1985 Super Bowl–champion Bears, the Commissioner's Trophy from the 2005 World Series–champion White Sox, and the Larry O'Brien Trophy from one of the championship Bulls teams from the 1990s.

But the Cup saw the most action with fans. Whether it was in France with Cristobal Huet, Slovakia with Marian Hossa, western Canada with a handful of Hawks, or Hinsdale, Illinois, with Brent Sopel, most of the Blackhawks players made themselves—and the Cup—available for photos with fans. In fact, the organization hosted a number of private photo opportunities with the Cup

From left: the Lombardi Trophy, the Larry O'Brien Trophy, the Commissioner's Trophy, and the Stanley Cup. Chicago and Boston are the only cities to have won all four in the past 25 years. Here they sit on display at U.S. Cellular Field.

for season-ticket holders in early October, just as the Hawks were beginning the defense of their championship.

From hospitals to golf courses, thousands of Hawks fans lined up to have their photos taken with the Cup, and every picture came with a unique story and personal group of memories.

While it isn't guaranteed that the Cup will spend every summer wandering the Chicagoland area, fans can still have their photograph taken with the Stanley Cup during the season. The Cup is on display at the Hockey Hall of Fame in Toronto, where fans can have quality photographs taken. All Blackhawks fans should have their picture taken with the incredible trophy that has been won by the Hawks four times (and counting).

For more information on the Hockey Hall of Fame, visit HHOF.com. Also be sure to check out the *Stanley Cup Journal* at the Hall's website, which tracks the incredible journey of the Cup throughout the summer it spent with the Blackhawks organization.

48 Earl Seibert

Unfortunately, the outstanding playing career of Earl Seibert has been a footnote to one of the darkest moments in Blackhawks history. He placed a lot of blame on himself for the terrible end of Howie Morenz's career and his subsequent death, and Seibert's name will forever be linked to that awful series of events.

But history should remember Seibert as the first elite defenseman to wear the Indian-head sweater in Chicago, beginning a long line of Hall of Famers to patrol the blue line for the Blackhawks.

When he was acquired from the New York Rangers in a trade for Arthur Coulter on January 15, 1936, Seibert was already an

All-Star in the NHL. He was a punishing defenseman who was willing to block any shot and drop the gloves with anyone. Legend recalls that Seibert was the only defenseman of the era who Eddie Shore wouldn't fight.

He was selected onto the first or second NHL All-Star team in 10 consecutive seasons from 1935 to 1944 and added an offensive aspect to the game that was rare for a defenseman of that era. In 398 games as a member of the Blackhawks between his arrival and when he was eventually traded to Detroit in January 1945, Seibert scored 191 points (57 goals, 134 assists).

"Seibert had size, speed, and a gift for anticipation. He was, according to hockey old-timers, the equal of Boston's great star Eddie Shore in almost every way. What set them apart was, perhaps, flair, color, and controversy," McFarlane reported in *The Blackhawks*.

However, while Shore piled up penalty minutes (1,047 in 550 career games), Seibert was whistled for only 380 in his time with the Blackhawks. Indeed, despite the Morentz injury leaving a cloud over his career, Seibert is remembered mostly as a clean player. He was also the first player in the NHL to wear a helmet. After suffering a bad concussion in Springfield in the late 1920s, he was fitted with a helmet as a precautionary measure.

Seibert is also remembered for his hard-nosed negotiating skills. His multiple contract disputes with the Rangers ultimately led to him being traded to Chicago, and he later wound up in Detroit after a similar situation in Chicago.

Urban legend claims that Seibert had become the favorite player of the Blackhawks' original owner, Major McLaughlin. After the 1938 Stanley Cup championship, McLaughlin gifted partial ownership of the team to Seibert for his service to the franchise. After McLaughlin died, however, manager Bill Tobin denied the alleged deal, instead banishing him to the cellar-dwelling Wings.

This act of disrespect, coupled with the guilt associated with Morenz's death, made it hard for Seibert to stay associated with the game. He coached the Springfield Indians, owned by Shore, for five years before walking away from the game for good.

He was so turned off to the game that, in 1963, he did not attend his own Hall of Fame induction ceremony. His father, Oliver, was inducted two years prior, making the Seiberts the first father-son tandem to be in the Hall together. In 1998 Seibert ranked No. 72 on the *Hockey News'* list of its 100 greatest hockey players.

49 Rudy

In a 1963 *Sports Illustrated* article, Arlie Schardt wrote, "This sudden realization of the Black Hawks' long-latent power represents the flowering of five years of patient cultivation by Coach Rudy Pilous, who made the Hawks the smoothly functioning unit of interchangeable parts that they are today."

That is how he described the resurrection of the Blackhawks and credited Pilous' hard work and dedication to bringing a lifeless franchise back to prominence. Pilous was among a handful of individuals who were crucial to the success of the franchise in the 1960s and, as the head coach, was most visibly responsible for every win and loss.

Hired in January 1958, Pilous told *Sports Illustrated* five years later that "it seemed as crazy as winning the Irish Sweepstakes. Even at that, I had to think it over for a while, though, because this was the graveyard." He had been a longtime scout and minor leaguer, with only one year of head-coaching experience with St. Catharines of the OHA.

The graveyard Pilous referred to was the Chicago Stadium, where the Hawks were regularly booed and finished in fifth place of the six-team NHL. They were barely ahead of the Toronto Maple Leafs and, with 55 points, finished 14 points behind fourth-place Boston for the final playoff spot.

That 1957–58 team saw more new faces in Chicago than just Pilous, though. An 18-year-old Bobby Hull broke in that year, scoring 13 goals in 70 NHL games. The Blackhawks had acquired two players in a major trade the summer before as well, when GM Tommy Ivan dealt for veteran forward Ted Lindsay and young goalie Glenn Hall.

Coach Rudy Pilous (right) joins his players as they celebrate around the Stanley Cup in a Detroit hotel after their 5–1 victory over the Detroit Red Wings in the Stanley Cup Finals on April 16, 1961.

Chicago was putting pieces in place—including a late-season call-up the following season of another teenager named Mikita—but they still needed someone to lead the group. Pilous was perfect for the job.

In *The Blackhawks*, McFarlane wrote, "Pilous had more than coaching smarts. He had an abundance of personality. He loved the limelight and he knew how to entertain. Whenever Chicago played at the Montreal Forum, fans serenaded him with shouts of 'Pil-oo, Pil-oo.' He would egg them on, then doff his hat and flash them a smile."

He was an entertainer who certainly knew the game of hockey and got the best out of his team. But the smiling, engaging coach who provoked fans on the road was a far stretch from the man who worked his players. Hull and Mikita often complained that Pilous was "cold" and hurt team morale.

In Schardt's same 1963 *Sports Illustrated* article, he penned, "Pilous, the master of the soft sell, is a tall, trim 48-year-old who looks as jolly as the song leader in a German beer hall. But he also is a shrewd, alert man with an unusually acute instinct for commanding grown men in a combative, competitive profession. 'They're men,' he says simply. 'I don't know much about their personal lives. I never check up on them. They know what they have to do. I don't fraternize with them in a social way. I have to have their respect. I have to be humble and firm at the same time.'"

He was the man who put Vasko and Pilote together and had the vision to build the Scooter Line. While he may have clashed with some of his players and Ivan, he won. His record as head coach of the Blackhawks was 162–151–74. He still ranks third in Blackhawks history in wins behind only his successor, Billy Reay (516), and Bob Pulford (185).

After years as a doormat in the NHL, Pilous led the Blackhawks to the playoffs in all five of the full seasons he spent on the bench and twice appeared in the Stanley Cup Finals. In 1961 he was the coach who ended a 23-year drought when the Cup finally returned to Chicago.

His influence on the game was bigger than the six years he served on the Chicago bench, though. During his years as a coach in minor league hockey throughout Canada, especially in St. Catharines, more than 75 players coached by Pilous matriculated to the NHL.

Bobby Hull thought enough of Pilous as a coach that he fought for him to get the job with the new Winnipeg Jets of the WHA, who had just signed Hull away from Chicago, 11 years after he was fired by the Hawks. After one year on the bench, Pilous became the general manager in Winnipeg and built three Avco Cup winners in 1976, 1978, and 1979.

In 1985 Pilous was inducted into the Hockey Hall of Fame as a builder.

50 Big-Screen Blackhawks

"Tonight, 17,000 hockey fans have been taken hostage, but only one of them knows it." That's what the trailer for 1995's *Sudden Death* states is the premise of the Jean-Claude Van Damme action flick that centered around a bomb being set during a Stanley Cup Finals game between the Pittsburgh Penguins and the Chicago Blackhawks.

While *Sudden Death* doesn't hold down a spot in anyone's top 10 list of all-time-greatest action films, it is just one example of the exposure the Chicago Blackhawks have enjoyed in pop culture, even while the organization itself wasn't necessarily marketing itself.

While fans in Chicago couldn't watch home games on television, they could at least find a Blackhawks sweater in some classic films.

A great Chicago movie, *Running Scared* featured Gregory Hines and Billy Crystal as Chicago cops. Crystal briefly appears in the Blackhawks sweater in the film, which hit theaters in 1986.

The same year, Rob Lowe played a hockey prospect in *Youngblood.* Many fans don't remember that his father in the movie was played by former Hawks forward Eric Nesterenko.

More memorable to fans of both film and hockey is Chevy Chase's personalized Blackhawks sweater in 1989's *National Lampoon's Christmas Vacation.* The white CCM sweater bearing the name *GRISWOLD* and number 00 is still a top seller and can be seen at Blackhawks games in Chicago and even while the Hawks are on the road.

Even though Clark Griswold wore the sweater just long enough to explain to his wife that Cousin Eddie was emptying the RV's septic tank into the sewer while smoking a cigar in their front yard, the jersey has become a pop-culture icon.

Three years after the world celebrated Christmas with the Griswolds, Wayne Campbell and Garth Algar played a spirited game of street hockey. Wayne displayed soft hands in a personalized sweater, beating Garth with a backhand; clearly Garth wasn't representing his Tony Esposito sweater appropriately.

The sweaters worn by Mike Myers and Dana Carvey in 1992's *Wayne's World* weren't the only place the Blackhawks popped up in the film. The infamous "Foxy Lady" scene happens in the fictitious Stan Mikita's Doughnut Shop, a send-up of Tim Horton's.

When Myers and Carvey brought the Wayne and Garth characters back to *Saturday Night Live* early in 2011, Myers brought back his red Blackhawks sweater for the segment.

The list of Blackhawks appearances in film also includes a brief scene in 1996's *Swingers.* In the film, Trent (Vince Vaughn) takes part in a classic video-game battle between the Blackhawks and

L.A. Kings. Not only does he dominate with Jeremy Roenick, but when his opponent gets up to pay for the delivery food, he lifts the pause and proceeds to use Roenick to beat up Wayne Gretzky. The trash-talking about Gretzky and the Blackhawks is still some of Vaughn's most memorable work.

Vaughn, raised in the suburbs outside Chicago, travelled extensively with the Blackhawks during the 2010 Stanley Cup playoffs and was seen sitting on the glass many nights. In fact, Vaughn included the Blackhawks in 2011's *The Dilemma*, in which the characters played by Kevin James and Vaughn attend a Hawks game together.

Through the years, the Blackhawks' great sweater has made a number of memorable appearances in films, only building the already classic brand.

51 Secord

If there was ever a smooth criminal to wear the Indian-head sweater in Chicago, it was Al Secord. Secord was acquired in a trade that, at least for a few years, helped Hawks fans forget the Phil Esposito trade with Boston. Chicago traded defenseman Mike O'Connell to the Bruins for Secord on December 18, 1980, and added one of the most unique players of the coming decade to their roster.

While Secord became known for his fists, including some legendary fights against many of the big-name fighters of the 1980s, such as Bob Probert (which can still be found on YouTube), his role as an enforcer has masked how gifted a scorer Secord was for the Blackhawks.

In 80 games during the 1981–82 season, Secord became the first player in NHL history to score 40 goals and record more than 300 penalty minutes; he finished the year with 44 goals and 303 penalty minutes. No player has matched the feat since.

The following season the Party Line was formed with three young players—Secord, Denis Savard, and Steve Larmer—who each brought a unique skill set to the rink every night. Savard was the skilled skater, Larmer had smooth hands, and Secord was the muscle. But there was one thing all three had in common: they could finish.

In 1982–83, Larmer's first full season, Secord exploded to score 54 goals, which is tied with Bobby Hull's 1965–66 season for the second-highest total in the organization's history. The 98 goals over two years still comprise one of the highest totals in the history of the Blackhawks, putting Secord in a class with Hull and Jeremy Roenick.

But what most fans will remember are the fights. And, unfortunately, those epic bouts took their toll.

After his 54-goal season, Secord only played in 14 games in 1983–84 and struggled with injuries for two years. After scoring only 19 goals in 65 games over two seasons, Secord regained his scoring touch in 1985–86 and jumped back to 40 goals. He would never be able to play a full season again, though.

After injuries held him to 29 goals in 1986–87, the Blackhawks decided to trade him. Secord was dealt to Toronto with Eddie Olczyk in a five-player deal that brought Rick Vaive, Steve Thomas, and Bob McGill back to Chicago.

Secord spent two seasons away, with a trade from Toronto to Philadelphia in the middle of the 1988–89 season included, but came back to Chicago as a free agent before the 1989–90 season. That was his final NHL campaign, and he played in only 43 games and scored just 14 goals.

The Party Line

The Party Line made its debut when Steve Larmer joined the Blackhawks full-time for the 1982–83 season and continued in the tradition of the Pony Line and the Scooter Line before it as one of the most deadly trios in the league.

For four of the five seasons between 1982 and 1987, Larmer, Al Secord, and Denis Savard terrorized defenses with their puck-handling and chemistry. Injuries cost Savard and, especially, Secord games during the five-year stretch, but the production was still overwhelming.

In 1,087 combined games over those five years, the Party Line combined to score 551 goals and add 667 assists, to total 1,218 points.

The party broke up when Secord was dealt to the Toronto Maple Leafs in September 1987. Unfortunately, all three members of the Party Line were eventually dealt out of Chicago. While Secord and Savard ultimately finished their careers back in Chicago, Larmer did not.

During his time in Chicago, Secord scored 47 points (20 goals, 27 assists) in 68 playoff contests; he is still the Blackhawks' career leader in postseason penalty minutes with 266.

While he played in Chicago, Secord scored 213 goals and added 159 assists in 466 regular-season games. His 1,426 penalty minutes still rank third in the team's history behind only Chris Chelios and Keith Magnuson, but he also had 25 game-winning goals.

The record books and memories of most Hawks fans state that Savard and Larmer were among the best scorers in the NHL for a decade. But their scoring totals were made possible by not only the physical play but also the scoring ability of Secord.

Something noticeably missing from old clips of Secord is a helmet on his head. In the present world of the NHL, facing ever-present concussion concerns, Secord piled up his penalty minutes and conducted his business without a helmet.

A search for "Al Secord" on YouTube yields some classic fights against the likes of Probert, Marty McSorley, and some names current fans will recognize: Vancouver Canucks head coach Alain Vigneault and Philadelphia Flyers general manager Paul Holmgren.

52 The Winter Classic

Jamey Horan, vice president of public relations and player development for the NHL, introduced the 2009 Winter Classic at one of the press conferences before the event by saying, "The Winter Classic truly is an original. It's a great matchup between two Original Six teams. It's played at an original sports venue, one of the greatest in America—Wrigley Field. And it will be played under original conditions: outside, exposed to the elements."

It was a unique, amazing thing to see snow falling at the baseball stadium that had seen Babe Ruth hit home runs and Gale Sayers run for touchdowns. But what was more astounding was the fact that the game was being played in Chicago.

On May 29, 2008, the National Hockey League bought into the vision of Rocky Wirtz, John McDonough, and the rest of the Blackhawks' front office when it selected Chicago over New York City as the host of the 2009 Bridgestone NHL Winter Classic.

After all, the Blackhawks had qualified for the playoffs only once in the previous 10 seasons and were struggling to restore respectability as a franchise. The front office was admittedly hoping to land a major event like the Winter Classic to springboard the team back into national prominence.

An iced-over Wrigley Field during the first period of the 2009 NHL Winter Classic between the Detroit Red Wings and the Chicago Blackhawks. It was the first hockey game ever held at the Friendly Confines and came after Chicago beat out New York hockey for the honor of hosting the historic game.

Wirtz admitted that the team was just a couple short years removed from being near the bottom of the NHL in not only the standings but also attendance. Coming off the strong rookie seasons of Patrick Kane and Jonathan Toews, though, the Hawks were starting to fill the United Center and hoped to be competing for a playoff spot.

The springboard worked. The NHL received over 240,000 ticket requests for the game and packed 40,818 into one of the oldest arenas in North America.

Hockey operations placed the ice surface with the goals in the outfield behind first base and third base, creating interesting site lines from all over the stadium. A wonderful outdoor festival took place before the game, with outdoor ice skating and thousands of fans "playing through" their New Year's Day morning. The bars were packed like a summer day with the Cubs playing.

The only differences were the snow on the ground and temperature in the mid-20s; then again, if you've ever been to a Cubs Opening Day, there have been baseball games played in similar conditions.

When the two teams took the field, they were wearing new throwback sweaters specially made for the game. Chicago was wearing a sweater that was modeled after their 1936–37 uniforms, with a crest that resembled those from the 1937–38 Stanley Cup–championship team. Detroit wore a tribute sweater resembling the 1926–27 Detroit Cougars, the original Detroit team.

The game was exciting, as the Blackhawks stormed to a 3–1 lead at the end of the first period before a three-goal second period for Detroit pretty much wrapped up the game for the Red Wings. The final score was 6–4, but the score was the furthest thing from the memories of anyone who attended the game.

With a breeze coming off the lake at around 20 mph and a warm, rainy week before the game, there was a level of uncertainty about the quality of the ice surface. But a plummeting temperature the night before the game made for ideal conditions. The fans were freezing, but the hockey was excellent. Indeed, perhaps the best sign in the stands that day read, "Holy Cow It's Cold."

The most important realization of the event was that the league was buying into the Chicago Blackhawks organization that had been dormant for a decade. In the following months, the Blackhawks charged into the playoffs and eventually lost to the Red Wings, again, in the Western Conference Finals.

It took a great deal of foresight to put an emerging team on national television on New Year's Day in the league's marquee event, and the Blackhawks repaid the league's faith by putting on one of the great events in Chicago sports history.

The 2009 Winter Classic might have been the 701st contest between the two historic franchises, but it was one of the most memorable.

53 Troy Murray

The 1980 NHL Draft is remembered as one of the best in Blackhawks history, mostly because the team selected two of the best scorers in the team's history: Denis Savard and Steve Larmer. However, their sixth pick, in the third round of that year's draft, was equally impressive.

With the 57th overall selection, the Blackhawks picked a defensive center who had been a teammate of Mark Messier in juniors. And of the 132 players in that year's draft who made it to the NHL, the most underappreciated might be Troy Murray.

Like Larmer, Murray didn't make the immediate jump to Chicago that Savard had. In 1981, while still playing for North Dakota, Murray was the captain of the Canadian team that won gold at the World Junior Championships. The following spring, he led UND to the NCAA championship. After that roller-coaster year, the Blackhawks had seen enough to bring him to the NHL.

He made his debut on April 4, 1982, when the Minnesota North Stars visited the Chicago Stadium. After that, the Hawks had one of the better two-way forwards of the decade.

During the next nine seasons, Murray was a great player for the Blackhawks. Wearing the same sweater number as another respected leader of the team—Dale Tallon—Murray was a consistent scorer. He scored at least 20 goals for five straight seasons and crossed the 50-point plateau in six straight, with the best season of

Selke Winners

The Frank J. Selke Trophy is awarded each year to the forward who, in the opinion of the Professional Hockey Writers Association, plays the best defense. The award was initially given after the 1977–78 season.

The following players on the Chicago Blackhawks have been awarded the Frank J. Selke Trophy:

- Troy Murray: 1985–86
- Dirk Graham: 1990–91

his career coming in 1985–86. That year, Murray scored 45 goals and totaled 99 points and won the Selke Trophy as the league's best defensive forward.

Murray was a unique forward who was willing to block shots and kill penalties, but he also brought a smooth offensive game to the ice every night. He scored more short-handed goals, 17, than Savard during his time with the Hawks, a number that still ranks fifth in team history.

After the 1990–91 season, Murray moved on and was made the captain of the Winnipeg Jets. He only spent parts of two seasons with the Jets before being traded back to the Blackhawks. After being shuttled back and forth between Chicago and the AHL, the Blackhawks traded Murray to Ottawa. He was the only Sens player with a positive plus-minus in 15 games during the 1993–94 season. In 1995–96 Murray was part of the Stanley Cup–champion Colorado Avalanche.

He played 688 games in a Chicago sweater, scoring 197 goals and adding 291 assists. Murray still ranks ninth in team history with 29 game-winning goals as well. He also appeared in 86 playoff games with the Hawks, recording 15 goals and 25 assists.

His number wasn't the only thing Murray shared in common with Tallon. On November 14, 2003, Murray replaced Tallon as the color analyst for Blackhawks radio broadcasts on WGN Radio;

Tallon stepped aside to become the assistant general manager of the team.

Murray also carries strong parallels with current Blackhawks center Jonathan Toews. After being drafted, Murray stayed at the University of North Dakota. Both players took UND to the Frozen Four after being drafted and eventually wore No. 19 in Chicago. Much like Murray, Jonathan Toews is one of the best two-way forwards in the game.

54 Cliff Koroll

Before the 1969–70 season, the Blackhawks were dealt a tough blow. Forward Ken Wharram, who had scored 20 goals in each of the past seven seasons with the team and was coming off a 30-goal season, failed his physical. This wasn't scar tissue in a bad knee, though; Wharram was found to have pericarditis—an inflammation of the sac surrounding the heart—and was not cleared to play. While Wharram was being treated for the condition, he suffered a heart attack that ended his career.

What the organization and fans didn't know was that a young player just signed out of the University of Denver would replace Wharram immediately, and the offense wouldn't miss a beat. In fact, the Blackhawks would be the first team in NHL history to go from last to first in one season during the 1969–70 season.

That young forward was Cliff Koroll, who joined the Blackhawks with his lifelong sidekick, defenseman Keith Magnuson. The two had started playing hockey together as kids and played together at Denver. Now, they would play their professional careers in Chicago together as well.

During his rookie year, Koroll made his mark on the Hawks record books. He became the first Blackhawks rookie to register a hat trick on December 14, 1969, in a win against Philadelphia and was part of the six fastest goals scored in team history (9:13) when the Hawks blasted the Habs 10–2 at the end of the season. It didn't take long for Koroll to permanently replace Wharram as the right wing on a line with Stan Mikita.

Koroll was an outstanding two-way forward who spent a great deal of time killing penalties and skating against the top line of the Hawks' opponent, but he still managed to cross the 50-point plateau on four occasions.

He played all 11 of his seasons in the NHL with the Hawks, retiring in 1980. He appeared in 814 regular-season games, scoring 208 goals, and was credited with 254 assists. Koroll, like Steve Larmer, never missed the playoffs in 11 seasons with the Blackhawks and, in 85 postseason contests over his career, scored 19 goals and 29 assists.

Koroll's regular-season numbers are among the best in the organization's history. He ranks 11th in team history in games played, 16th in goals, and 18th in points. His 39 game-winning goals comprise the third-highest total in team history behind only Larmer and Denis Savard.

When he retired, Koroll's relationship with Magnuson continued. He was named an assistant coach in 1980, serving next to the team's new head coach: Maggie. Though Magnuson would remain on as the team's head coach only into 1982, Koroll spent seven seasons on the Chicago bench as an assistant before eventually walking away from coaching in favor of the business world in 1989.

One of the great legacies of the relationship between Koroll and Magnuson has been felt off the ice. Magnuson was a major factor in founding the Blackhawks Alumni Association, and Koroll was one of the inaugural members when the group began in 1987. In 2003, when Magnuson was tragically killed, Koroll took his best friend's place as the head of the group.

55 From Havlat to Huet to Hossa

To say the Blackhawks were "rebuilt" is selling short the work management had to do to make the team not only competitive but a champion. The mind-set of management at the turn of the century was financially driven, but the business model was self-defeating.

Under the "guidance" of Bob Pulford and Mike Smith, the team took more steps backward than toward competing. Smith contributed to a book on the business of sports in 2004 and wrote the following about the Hawks' financial philosophy: "In hockey, the business can be viewed as being on a pendulum. There was a time when it had swung in the direction of clubs and ownership; now it has swung in the direction of the players. We need a correction of that pendulum."

Smith was the general manager in Chicago for three years and, despite a history of drafting well with the Winnipeg Jets, his drafts in Chicago were annual disasters.

When Dale Tallon took over as GM, he was charged with changing the culture of the organization as much as he was asked to find players to make the team competitive.

The first real benchmark in the climb came in July 2006, when Tallon completed a three-team trade that ultimately landed forward Martin Havlat from Ottawa. Havlat was a restricted free agent who had informed the Senators that he would only sign a one-year deal in Ottawa so that he could explore unrestricted free agency—and get more money—the following summer.

Havlat was coming off an injury-plagued regular season but had been electric in the playoffs for the Sens, posting 13 points in only 10 postseason games. He was a talented 25-year-old who brought a scoring touch to a last-place team that wasn't on the roster.

Tallon signed Havlat to a three-year, $18 million deal. The deal raised a few eyebrows around the league, largely because the Blackhawks were a team that had spent the better part of 20 years developing a reputation for not paying players; the scenario that was forcing Havlat out of Ottawa had been an all-too-familiar chorus in Chicago over the previous decade. When Havlat signed, his deal was the richest annual salary ever given to a Blackhawks player.

Despite missing 26 games in his first season in Chicago, Havlat posted 57 points in 56 games and was named to the 2007 NHL All-Star Game.

With Havlat and Patrick Sharp beginning to show signs of life up front, and a young duo of Duncan Keith and Brent Seabrook developing on defense, the Blackhawks appeared to at least have a core that was climbing toward competitiveness. But convincing free agents to come to Chicago was still hard; after years of Pulford and Mike Keenan making life miserable for homegrown superstars, the reputation of the Blackhawks organization was a tough sell.

The unfortunate catalyst to the Blackhawks' return to prominence was the passing of their owner, Bill Wirtz. When his son, Rocky, took over the team in October 2007, he added marketing geniuses John McDonough and Jay Blunk from the Chicago Cubs and immediately changed the mind-set in the front office. Rocky understood that, in direct contrast to Smith's statement, the Blackhawks would have to spend money to make money—and compete.

After the Blackhawks jumped in the standings and barely missed the playoffs in 2007–08, Tallon was given freedom to spend what was then unprecedented in the history of the organization. At the same time, the team that had ranked among the worst in the NHL in attendance started to fill the United Center, and there was a buzz in Chicago about the young team.

With the team's two biggest needs being depth on the blue line and between the pipes, Tallon had to be aggressive again. On the first day of free agency in 2008, this time with the blessing of ownership, Tallon made a splash.

Despite reportedly receiving bigger offers from other teams, free-agent defenseman Brian Campbell signed an eight-year contract worth over $7 million per season with the Hawks. Likewise, free-agent netminder Cristobal Huet signed a four-year, $22.4 million deal with the Blackhawks to (in theory) remedy their issues in net.

These two contracts marked the biggest shopping spree in team history and sent shockwaves through the league. During the press conference announcing the two deals, Campbell confidently asserted that he had chosen Chicago because he believed the Blackhawks could win. That had been a foreign concept in Chicago for a decade.

Despite Huet not taking over the reins as the top goalie in Chicago—Nikolai Khabibulin found the fountain of youth and had a resurgent season—there was still an incredible impact on the ice. With Havlat and Campbell playing key roles, the Blackhawks jumped into the playoff picture and made an unlikely run to the Western Conference Finals.

With a young core in place, the Blackhawks had to make tough roster decisions for the first time in almost a full decade. Havlat's three-year deal was expired, and Khabibulin was leaving as well.

But because of the baby steps—and overpaying—that had happened in the previous four years, the Blackhawks were in a position to attract free agents. Havlat was the first major casualty of the rebuilding process, but his departure was a move allowed by a luxury earned by Tallon: free agents actually wanted to come to Chicago.

For the third time in his tenure, Tallon made a bold move and surprised the hockey world when he announced a long-term contract with superstar Marian Hossa. Unlike Havlat and Huet, Hossa was a bona fide star in the league and was coming off consecutive trips to the Stanley Cup Finals, albeit with different teams that had lost each time. He was one of the most complete players in the NHL and was the highest-profile free agent to sign in Chicago in a long, long time.

Obviously the building of the Blackhawks worked, and the team brought the Stanley Cup back to Chicago for the first time in 49 years.

The evolution of philosophy and roster quality can be linked back to three *H*s, though—Havlat, Huet, and Hossa. If Tallon hadn't overpaid and been aggressive when the team was in the cellar, the Cup might not have come back to Chicago at all.

56 OT Thriller

One of the defining moments in Blackhawks history served as redemption, both for one player and the entire team.

The Nashville Predators had played the Blackhawks tough, and the series was tied at 2–2 coming into a huge fifth game in Chicago. In the game, the Blackhawks blew a 3–1 lead, and the Predators went ahead 4–3 with two third-period goals by Martin Erat.

Marian Hossa appeared to be the goat in this critical game. After taking a bad five-minute boarding penalty for a hit on Predators defenseman Dan Hamhuis with only 63 seconds remaining in regulation, the Blackhawks were forced to pull their goalie to skate at even strength. "I tried to go for the puck," Hossa said. "The guy turned his back to me. You don't want to hit a player that way, but I couldn't stop my motion."

But thanks to Patrick Kane's heroics with seconds remaining, the Hawks received second life. Kane backhanded in a Jonathan

Toews rebound to tie the game with 13 seconds left in regulation. It was the first time in the history of the National Hockey League that a game—regular-season or playoff—had been tied with a short-handed goal with less than a minute remaining. "Sometimes you catch a break," Kane said about his goal. "Five-on-five with the goalie pulled, you're trying to do everything you can to score a goal."

But the Hawks would have to kill almost four minutes of penalty time in OT to stay alive in the series. With just seconds of penalty time left to kill, Brent Sopel took a lap around the offensive zone with the puck and dropped it off to Dave Bolland, who then returned the puck back to Sopel at the blue line. While Sopel circled the offensive zone, Hossa left the box and skated straight to the net. Sopel shot the puck.

After a couple deflections, the shot ended up right on Hossa's stick in front of a wide-open net. The easiest one-timer of Hossa's life won the game and sent the United Center into one of the loudest fits of hysteria the building had seen since Michael Jordan left. "When I saw the puck coming to me, I just tried to put it in," said Hossa afterward. "What a relief. A huge win."

The irony of the goal went deeper than Hossa scoring the game-winner after serving the major penalty. In the early part of the second period that night, Tomas Kopecky found himself in the box. When the Blackhawks killed that penalty—they killed all four power-play opportunities for Nashville that night—he was in position to score as well.

Kopecky came out of the penalty box and, when Hossa cleared the puck, Kopecky was in the right place at the right time. He flipped a backhand behind Predators goalie Pekka Rinne to give the Blackhawks the 3–1 lead with 16:24 remaining in the second stanza.

The game was over, and the devastation of the loss proved to be too much for Nashville. The Blackhawks took the momentum from the huge rally and eliminated the Predators in the next game.

57 Tony Amonte

Despite playing nearly as many games in another sweater, Tony Amonte will always be remembered as a Blackhawks forward. Or will he?

Amonte played 1,174 games in the NHL, 627 of which were wearing the Indian head on his chest. He is among the best scorers to ever play in Chicago, but it was a goal he scored in an international game with no NHL implications that may have defined Amonte's legacy.

His elite scoring touch represented the United States over an entire generation of events, from three consecutive World Junior Championships (1988–90), two World Championships (1991, 1993), and the 1998 and 2002 Winter Olympics. However, it was while Amonte was representing his country in 1996 that he made his mark.

Playing with Blackhawks teammate Chris Chelios on Team USA, Amonte scored the game-winning goal in an incredible gold medal–clinching game over Team Canada in the 1996 World Cup of Hockey tournament.

That goal, and the 900 points he scored in the NHL, built a résumé that earned the Hingham, Massachusetts, native a place in the United States Hockey Hall of Fame in 2010. Those 900 career points rank 11th among American-born players.

Drafted 68th overall in 1988 by the New York Rangers, Amonte made his NHL debut in the 1991 playoffs before scoring 35 goals and finishing third in voting for the Calder Trophy as a rookie. In three seasons in New York, Amonte scored 84 goals.

However, the majority of Amonte's NHL games, and memories, come from his time in Chicago. Amonte was traded to the

All-Time Goal Leaders

The Golden Jet is the gold standard for goal-scoring in Chicago, but some incredible scorers have worn the Indian-head sweater over the years.

In total, only 17 players have scored at least 200 goals as members of the Chicago Blackhawks in the team's history. Some scored their goals faster than others—Jeremy Roenick played 524 games in Chicago, while Eric Nesterenko took 1,013 games—but all of these 17 players were key to the history of the organization. Only one defenseman, Doug Wilson, accomplished the feat.

Here are the 17 players in Blackhawks history to score at least 200 goals while in Chicago.

- Bobby Hull—604
- Stan Mikita—541
- Steve Larmer—406
- Denis Savard—377
- Dennis Hull—298
- Tony Amonte—268
- Jeremy Roenick—267
- Bill Mosienko—258
- Kenny Wharram—252
- Pit Martin—243
- Eric Daze—226
- Doug Wilson—225
- Doug Bentley—217
- Jim Pappin—216
- Al Secord—213
- Cliff Koroll—208
- Eric Nesterenko—207

Blackhawks on March 21, 1994, with the rights to Matt Oates for Stéphane Matteau and Brian Noonan.

Between that trade and the 2001–02 campaign, Amonte was a shining star on some very mediocre Blackhawks rosters. In parts of nine NHL seasons, Amonte played in the playoffs five times;

however, his Hawks appeared in the postseason only once in the final five years he was in Chicago.

Amonte was one of the most lethal scorers in the NHL while he was in Chicago, scoring at least 30 goals in six straight years and crossing 40 goals on three occasions.

The Blackhawks were also represented in the All-Star Game by Amonte on five consecutive occasions between 1997 and 2001. He topped the 30-goal mark in eight seasons (six as a Blackhawk) and led the Blackhawks in scoring twice (1996–97, 1999–2000). He also went five seasons in Chicago without missing a game—410 games—from 1997–98 through 2001–02.

On September 20, 2000, Amonte was named the Blackhawks' captain. However, despite wearing the *C* that year, the Blackhawks did not bring him back when his contract expired at the end of the season, and he moved on to the Phoenix Coyotes.

In total, Amonte scored 541 points (268 goals, 273 assists) in 627 games with the Blackhawks. Those 541 points rank ninth in the history of the Blackhawks, and his 268 goals ranks sixth in team history.

He was also clutch, scoring 34 game-winning goals for Chicago; that number is tied with Jim Pappin and Eric Daze for sixth in franchise history. Amonte also scored 20 short-handed goals, which ranks second in the team's history.

58 Eric Nesterenko

It figures that one of the most unique personalities in Blackhawks history was born on Halloween. Eric Nesterenko was truly a character who always played by his own rules. He turned down a scholarship to the University of Michigan to sign with the Maple Leafs, only to become so unhappy about his playing time that he talked his way out of Toronto.

So during the summer of 1956, after 20 games in the WHL, the Leafs sold his rights to the bottom-dwelling Chicago Blackhawks. Chicago was coming off a season in which they totaled 50 points— exactly half as many as first-place Montreal. The leading scorer, Red Sullivan, had only 40 points in 63 games, and the team racked up 832 penalty minutes while scoring just 155 goals.

The 1956–57 season saw the Hawks tally only 47 points in the standings, but the winds of change were blowing in Chicago. That season, Nesterenko brought his bruising power-forward game to the Hawks and skated for a new head coach: Tommy Ivan. Under new ownership, the Blackhawks had signed Ivan away from Detroit, and the rebuild was in progress. Nesterenko scored eight goals in his first season in Chicago with 15 assists and 32 penalty minutes in 24 games.

The following season showed that both Nesterenko and the Hawks were starting to put things together. He scored 20 goals, accumulated 104 penalty minutes, and was joined in the lineup by an 18-year-old left wing named Bobby Hull. That season, Ivan (also the general manager) brought veteran Ted Lindsay and young goalie Glenn Hall over in a trade from Detroit, and the Blackhawks jumped out of the cellar.

Another important move that took place during the 1957–58 season was Ivan stepping away from the bench. He handed the team over to Rudy Pilous, who did a masterful job handling a talented young roster.

In 1958–59 another teenager came to Chicago: Stan Mikita. The pieces were now in place for Chicago to contend, and they did. Under Pilous' guidance, the Hawks jumped 14 points in the standings and into third place, qualifying for the postseason. Two years later, the Blackhawks won the Stanley Cup.

Nesterenko's style on the ice was unorthodox, and his training methods raised eyebrows. Yet 50 years later, his emphasis on conditioning and diet is the norm in all sports and at any level.

When his NHL career was finished in 1972, Nesterenko ranked second in the organization's history, having played in 1,013 games (he ranks third behind Mikita and Hull today). His 1,012 penalty minutes still rank ninth in the franchise's history as well, all part of a colorful career that also included 207 goals.

After he left the ice, Nesterenko became a renaissance man whose life developed into a winding list of odd jobs. He worked as a disc jockey, stockbroker, travel agent, college professor, and freelance writer, to name a few of the items on his résumé.

He even gave acting a shot, playing the father of the title character (played by Rob Lowe) in the movie *Youngblood*. His most successful venture, however, was as a ski instructor in Vail, Colorado.

Some of his fights are available on YouTube (including one against Bob Pulford), but the legend of Eric Nesterenko goes well beyond the ice.

59 The Best Backup in Blackhawks History

His 389 career wins rank 11th in NHL history. He has the highest career save percentage (.922) in the history of the NHL (for goalies with more than 100 games played). His goals-against average (2.20) ranks seventh all-time. His 81 shutouts rank sixth all time. But he wasn't good enough to stick around Chicago for more than 25 games.

Dominik "the Dominator" Hašek showed flashes of his great ability during a couple brief stretches with the Blackhawks in 1990–91 and 1991–92. He was good enough in only 20 games to be named to the NHL All-Rookie Team in 1992, and his performance in the Stanley Cup Finals in relief of then-starter Ed Belfour was honorable.

But that was the problem: Belfour was the starter, and he didn't like sharing the ice with anyone, especially not a young phenom. Belfour had every right to be selfish. He won the Vezina Trophy as the league's best goalie in 1991 and had been a clutch performer in the postseason for Chicago. And the organization couldn't hold on to two outstanding goalies forever.

And so, on August 17, 1992, the Blackhawks traded Hašek to the Buffalo Sabres for goalie prospect Stephane Beauregard and future considerations.

How did the trade turn out? Beauregard never skated in the NHL for the Blackhawks. The future considerations became a fourth-round draft pick.

And what became of Hašek? He won a record six Vezina Trophies as the game's best netminder. He's the only goalie in history to win more than one Hart Memorial Trophy as the league's most valuable player, and he won them in consecutive seasons (1996–97, 1997–98).

Hašek was also named to six All-Star Games and won the Lester B. Pearson Award twice and the William M. Jennings Trophy three times. Between 1992 and 2002, Hašek was considered by many to be the best goalie on the planet.

In the history of the Blackhawks organization, there have been some very good trades and some terrible ones. The trade sending Hašek to Buffalo goes down as not only one of the worst in Chicago's history but in the entire history of the NHL.

Belfour won the Vezina Trophy in 1993 and feuded with backups after Hašek's departure. He stayed in Chicago until he turned down a mediocre contract extension, leading ultimately to him being traded to San Jose during the 1996–97 season.

Chicago's record books remember Belfour well, but the hearts of many fans wonder what could have been if the organization had chosen to keep Hašek instead. Both may be Hall of Famers, but neither lifted the Stanley Cup while playing in Chicago.

60 Pat Stapleton

Pat Stapleton, known as "Whitey," joined the Blackhawks for the 1965–66 season after parts of two seasons with the Boston Bruins. The diminutive defenseman was paired with Bill White, and the two were arguably the best blue-line tandem in the league during their time together.

For eight years, Stapleton's leadership—and practical jokes—kept the Blackhawks in contention. For many, Stapleton is remembered as much for his sense of humor as he is for his abilities on the ice. And nobody was able to avoid Stapleton's jokes.

Wittenberg wrote in his *Tales from the Chicago Blackhawks* that, "Veteran referee Bill Friday was set to work the Hawks–North Stars game when he looked into his bag to discover his skates were gone after he had stepped out to get a cup of coffee before the game. He called on the trainers of both teams to find him a spare pair of skates in his size. Miraculously, the skates arrived in time, and even though they were not dusted for fingerprints, the handiwork of Chicago's No. 12 was evident."

There are also great stories about Stapleton and White sending teammates off on imaginary "snipe hunts," and once convincing rookie Keith Magnuson that he had been traded.

What wasn't a laughing matter, however, was the success of the Hawks while Stapleton was on the roster. The team won four consecutive West Division championships while he was in a Chicago sweater and played in two Stanley Cup Finals (1971, 1973). He was named an All-Star four times and is tied for the NHL record for defensemen with six assists in one period.

Blackhawk Pat Stapleton (No. 12) slides his stick in between that of Buffalo Sabre Gilbert Parreault and the puck during a December 15, 1971, game in Chicago.

The 75th Anniversary Team

On Opening Night of the 2000–01 season, the Blackhawks celebrated their 75th anniversary by naming a roster of all-time great players, as selected by the fans, to their 75th Anniversary Team.

The following individuals were named to that roster.
- Centers: Stan Mikita, Denis Savard, Jeremy Roenick
- Left Wings: Bobby Hull, Dennis Hull, Al Secord
- Right Wings: Harold "Mush" March, Steve Larmer, Tony Amonte
- Defensemen: Bill White, Pierre Pilote, Pat Stapleton, Keith Magnuson, Doug Wilson, Chris Chelios
- Goaltenders: Glenn Hall, Tony Esposito, Ed Belfour
- Coaches: Billy Reay, Bob Pulford, Mike Keenan

Stapleton played 545 games for the Blackhawks, scoring 41 goals and adding 286 assists (including what was then a record 50 assists by a defenseman in 1968–69). His 327 points still rank sixth in franchise history among defensemen; he also played some center while with the Hawks. He was a master of the poke check and was effective at advancing the puck up the ice.

In 1972 Stapleton and White skated together on Team Canada in the great Summit Series in which Canada upset Russia. He grabbed the puck after Paul Henderson scored the Series-winning goal. Stapleton was the captain of the Canadian team in the 1974 Summit Series, where he was credited with three assists in eight games.

He left the Blackhawks in 1973 and signed with the Chicago Cougars of the WHA as a player-coach, where he won the Dennis A. Murphy Trophy as that league's best defenseman.

61 Bill White

Tommy Ivan was known for making bold trades that, more often than not, worked out fairly well for the Blackhawks. On February 20, 1970, he made a deal that would help the team's blue line for the next seven years.

In a six-player deal between the Hawks and Los Angeles Kings, Ivan acquired goalie Gerry Desjardins, Bryan Campbell, and defenseman Bill White in exchange for Gilles Marotte, Jim Stanfield, and backup goalie Denis DeJordy. DeJordy had been a solid reserve for almost a decade in Chicago; he shared the Vezina Trophy with Glenn Hall in 1967. But the Hawks needed a defenseman, and White was their man.

Known as a prankster and outstanding stay-at-home defenseman, White was brought in while the Hawks were missing Pat Stapleton because of a knee injury. When Stapleton returned, White immediately joined him, and the two became one of the best tandems in the league.

In a December 20, 2010, article for Blackhawks.nhl.com, Bob Verdi wrote that White said, "I enjoyed L.A. but was really excited about going to Chicago." White continued, "The [Chicago] Stadium was an electric place. I loved playing there as a visitor. We had some great players there with the Blackhawks and a lot of characters like Dennis Hull and the original beatnik, Eric Nesterenko. Lots of laughs."

That first season that White was in Chicago was a special one. The Blackhawks had finished in last place in 1968–69 but charged all the way to the top of the standings the following year. That team featured some aging veterans, including Stan Mikita, but also had a lot of fresh faces. Keith Magnuson, Cliff Koroll, and Tony Esposito were a few of the young players making an impact that year. When the Hawks added White, the roster was set.

In 1971 the Blackhawks advanced all the way to the Stanley Cup Finals. In 1972 Stapleton and White skated together on Team Canada in the Summit Series. And in 1973 the Hawks again made it to the Cup Finals.

Despite not making his NHL debut until he was 28 years old, White played in six consecutive All-Star Games between 1969 and 1974 and was a second-team All-Star in three of his seasons with the Hawks. He played in 415 games as a member of the Hawks, scoring 30 goals and adding 149 assists. With Stapleton again by his side, White was one of the six defenseman named to the Blackhawks' 75th Anniversary Team.

But being a great defenseman for the Blackhawks isn't the only notable entry on White's résumé. Just a few days before Christmas in 1976, White was struggling with injuries and was near the end of his great career. The Blackhawks were struggling, and management was getting antsy. In what was one of the lesser moments in the organization's history, legendary coach Billy Reay was informed of his termination in a note that was slipped under his office door.

The team turned to White to replace the organization's longtime coach. Assisting White on that team were two of his former teammates, Stan Mikita and Bobby Orr. The first thing he did as head coach was name Keith Magnuson his new captain.

Magnuson had long been on the receiving end of Stapleton-White practical jokes, including being sent on a snipe hunt and being convinced on a few occasions that the Hawks had traded him. This time, though, White was serious about naming him the new captain of the team.

White told Verdi about it for the same piece. "A wonderful man, Maggie, with great spirit," White said. "I called him and asked to have dinner with Keith and his wife, Cindy. We had a nice meal, then I told Keith I wanted him to be our captain. He deserved it. He was very happy about it, I think. Then I got up and left him with the check. Why shouldn't he pay for dinner? He's our captain, right?"

The White-led Blackhawks won only 16 of the 46 games he coached, and White was fired after the Hawks lost in the first round of the playoffs.

Dirk

After a long, winding road to the NHL, it wasn't until he arrived in Chicago that Dirk Graham was finally able to display all of his hockey skills.

Drafted by the Vancouver Canucks 89th overall in the fifth round of the 1979 Draft, Graham never made it to the NHL as part of that organization. And despite having seasons in the minors in which he scored 88 and 105 points in 67 and 72 games, respectively, it took a mammoth 70-goal, 125-point performance in 78 games for the Minnesota North Stars to finally call him up for six games in the 1983–84 season.

Even after that incredible season, he went back to the minors again the following season and didn't "make it" into the NHL for good until the 1984–85 season. Despite posting 22 and 25 goals in his first two full seasons with Minnesota, the North Stars, like the Canucks, weren't sold on Graham. After 28 games in the 1987–88 season, they traded him to Chicago for Curt Fraser.

Graham immediately established himself as a smart, hard-nosed leader with the Blackhawks. He scored 17 goals in only 42 games in his first season in Chicago. In 1989 he replaced Hall of

Famer Denis Savard as the team's captain, a role he would define until the *C* was given to Chris Chelios in 1995.

During his first season as captain, Graham was fined $500 by the league for his role in a fight that broke out during warm-ups before a game against his former team, Minnesota. Later that season he suffered a cracked left kneecap in a game against Montreal that cost him the rest of the season and the beginning of the 1990 play-offs. The knee injury required off-season surgery and hindered his game for the rest of his career.

During his time in Chicago, Graham was quietly a solid offensive player. He also scored more than 20 goals in four of his seven full seasons in Chicago, with his best coming with 33 goals and 45 assists in the 1988–89 season. That year he set a team record that he still owns, scoring 10 short-handed goals in one season. He still owns the franchise record with 26 career short-handed goals.

But scoring isn't what Graham is remembered for; more than anything else, he was a leader. Despite the instability that was a hallmark of the years he spent in Chicago—with Savard, Larmer, and other greats leaving town and management making more news off the ice than on it—the one constant between 1988 and 1995 was Graham's leadership.

In 1991 Graham became the second—and last—Blackhawks player to win the Frank J. Selke Award as the league's best defensive forward. A couple months after winning that award, Graham scored a crucial short-handed goal for Canada at the Canada Cup in the final. In 1992 he was the captain in the Blackhawks' trip to the Stanley Cup Finals, where they were swept by the Penguins.

Despite the outcome of those Finals being negative, Graham had a memorable series. He shares the NHL record for most goals in one period of a Stanley Cup Finals game, set when he scored three in the first period against Pittsburgh in Game 4 as he desperately tried to keep the Hawks in the series. Those three goals were scored in only 9:57, which is the NHL record for the fastest hat trick in Finals history.

Ultimately, his physical play forced him to walk away after the strike-shortened 1995 season. He missed part of his final season when he sprained the same left knee that suffered the cracked kneecap five years prior.

The organization recognized his leadership, and he remained with the team as an assistant coach for the 1995–96 season before taking a year off. In 1998–99 he was the head coach of the team for only 59 games.

Part of Graham's legacy is also being the first African American captain in NHL history. Graham had one mixed-race parent, making him the first player of African American descent to be named an NHL captain; Calgary's Jarome Iginla has been largely (and falsely) credited as the first African American captain in 1993.

63 Sharpie

With the 95th selection in the 2001 Draft, the Philadelphia Flyers drafted a versatile forward from the University of Vermont that would win a Stanley Cup in Philadelphia. Unfortunately for the Flyers, Patrick Sharp wasn't wearing orange when he hoisted the Cup.

Sharp played two more years at Vermont before making his NHL debut with Philly during the 2002–03 season, eventually splitting time between the Flyers and their AHL affiliate, the Philadelphia Phantoms the following season. His numbers with the Phantoms were good (15 goals and 14 assists in 35 games), but he didn't stick in the NHL.

All-Time Postseason Scoring Leaders

In four Stanley Cup Championships and 11 Finals appearances, the Blackhawks have seen a lot of special postseason performances in the organization's history. Here are the top 10 postseason point producers in Blackhawks history (career):

- Stan Mikita—155 games played—150 points
- Denis Savard—131 games played—145 points
- Bobby Hull—116 games played—129 points
- Steve Larmer—107 games played—111 points
- Doug Wilson—95 games played—80 points
- Jeremy Roenick—82 games played—77 points
- Dennis Hull—97 games played—67 points
- Pierre Pilote—82 games played—60 points
- Thomas Lysiak—65 games played—56 points
- Bob Murray—112 games played—56 points

Here are the top 10 point producers from a single postseason in Blackhawks history:

- Denis Savard—1985—15 games played—29 points
- Jonathan Toews—2010—22 games played—29 points
- Patrick Kane—2010—22 games played—28 points
- Bobby Hull—1971—18 games played—25 points
- Dennis Hull—1973—16 games played—24 points
- Jeremy Roenick—1992—18 games played—22 points
- Steve Larmer—1985—15 games played—22 points
- Steve Larmer—1990—20 games played—22 points
- Denis Savard—1990—20 games played—22 points
- Patrick Sharp—2010—22 games played—22 points

While the NHL was locked out during the 2004–05 season, Sharp was a key member of one of the most impressive rosters in AHL history with the Phantoms. Sharp ranked second on the team with 23 goals, which was an impressive feat considering the number of future NHL stars on that team. Mike Richards, Jeff Carter, Joni Pitkanen, R.J. Umberger, and Dennis Seidenberg were just a few.

He then averaged one point per game—eight goals and 13 assists in 21 contests—as the Phantoms marched all the way to the Calder Cup (the AHL championship).

Despite being one of the more polished players on the Phantoms, the volume of young depth on that roster—Richards and Carter were both teenagers—ultimately made Sharp expendable in Philadelphia.

On December 5, 2005, the Flyers decided to "sell high" on Sharp, dealing him with Eric Meloche to the Blackhawks for Matt Ellison and a third-round pick in the 2006 Draft. He finished the 2005–06 season, his first full NHL campaign, with only 31 points.

The next year, Chicago fans started to see what Sharp could do as he scored 20 goals in 80 games for a bad last-place Blackhawks team. He was second on the Hawks behind Martin Havlat's 25 goals that season, but those two began creating a foundation for the coming years.

In 2007–08, everything changed in Chicago. Sharp led the team with 36 goals and started spending time on a line with a couple teenagers named Patrick Kane and Jonathan Toews. Kane later won the Calder Memorial Trophy as the league's top rookie that season, while Toews finished as the runner-up. Sharp had emerged as a bona fide scorer in the NHL, though, and the Blackhawks jumped to third place in the standings.

Over the next two seasons, the Blackhawks shocked the hockey world by advancing first to the Western Conference Finals and then to the ultimate prize, a moment of sweet redemption for both Sharp and another one of his teammates on that Phantoms team, Ben Eager.

When Sharp held the Stanley Cup above his head on the ice in Philadelphia, Ellison—the player the Flyers had received in the trade sending Sharp to Chicago—had just completed his second season in Russia. Ellison played only seven games in Philly over two seasons and registered only one point, an assist.

Sharp has scored at least 20 goals in each of his first five seasons in Chicago and at least 25 in each season since Kane and Toews joined the team. In 2010–11 Sharp and Toews became the first Chicago teammates to both score 30 goals in the same season since Tony Amonte and Steve Sullivan in 2000–01, a full decade earlier.

In 2010 Sharp added another great achievement to his Chicago career when he was named the Most Valuable Player in the All-Star Game. He wasn't even on the ballot for fan voting.

While history remembers a number of terrible trades in which future Hall of Famers left Chicago, when the career of Sharp is finished, the trade made in 2005 to bring him to the Blackhawks may ultimately be remembered as the best deal in the franchise's history.

64 Own a Sweater

The Chicago Blackhawks are blessed with one of the most historic uniforms in professional sports. Like the New York Yankees in baseball, very few aesthetic changes have taken place to the classic sweaters worn by the Hawks since they were first created.

And many fans of all professional sports and professional analysts alike consider the red Chicago Blackhawks sweater to be the best in sports. The Hawks made a list published in the *New York Daily News* in August 2009, and when the NHL announced the top 20 jerseys sold on NHL.com during the 2009–10 season, both Patrick Kane (No. 6) and Jonathan Toews (No. 8) made the list.

What makes hockey, specifically the NHL, different from baseball and basketball is that, like football, the stands are filled with fans wearing their team's jersey. Only an NFL game has a higher percentage of fans in jerseys for a game than an NHL contest.

Every fan should have a Blackhawks sweater. However, there are a number of thoughts to consider before making this all-important purchase. After all, you don't want to spend money on something that may be in poor taste. First off, hockey has a long history of alternate third jerseys. Throughout their history, the Blackhawks have had some memorable alternate sweaters, from the horizontal stripes of the early 1990s to the current retro style, similar to the sweaters worn for the 2009 Winter Classic.

Fans have a mixed perspective on the alternate sweaters, but there is one clear belief: do not get an alternate sweater with a name and number sewn onto it representing a player who didn't wear that version of the jersey. Don't buy a black alternate sweater with Hull and No. 9 on the back; don't buy a Winter Classic sweater with Savard and No. 18 on the back. If the player never wore that model of jersey, why would you?

As an aside on this idea, there's the concept of patches on the sweater. The trifecta of bad form is the black alternate sweater with Bobby Hull's name and number on it, also bearing a Stanley Cup Finals or Champions patch. It is possible to like a player who was a member of the championship team, making the patch appropriate; it is also fully acceptable to have a traditional red sweater with a great player from the team's past without the 2010 championship patches sewn on.

Similarly, while there may be some humor involved, don't personalize a sweater with a catch phrase. We've all seen the *CHAMPS 61* and *DETROIT SUX* sweaters, but those are truthfully a waste of money. It's easier—and cheaper—to simply pick out your favorite player. Past or present, it isn't hard to find a suitable jersey for your collection and game-day wardrobe.

Frankly, if Michael Jordan will wear a Jonathan Toews sweater during the Stanley Cup Finals, why shouldn't we?

There is, however, the one exception: Clark W. Griswold. It is fine to purchase the GRISWOLD 00 sweater seen in *National*

Lampoon's Christmas Vacation. However, any thoughts of purchasing a Griswold sweater should conform to our first point. Chevy Chase never wore a red sweater, much less any incarnations of the alternate jerseys. Owning one is a questionable move at best.

At the end of the day, however, what makes owning a Blackhawks jersey an exciting part of any fan's expression of love for the team is that the style, name, patches, etc. are all a personal choice for the owner.

Sweaters rarely, if ever, lose their value to a fan. At any game at the United Center, fans wearing names like Wilson, Larmer, Hull, Magnuson, Chelios, Amonte, and Byfuglien are still seen, even though those players are long gone. What is important is that the player's name that the sweater bears is a favorite of the individual wearing it.

65 The Habs and the Have-Nots

The 1964–65 Blackhawks were an interesting cast of characters. The Hawks tied with the first-place Detroit Red Wings for the most goals scored during the season (224) and allowed the third-fewest goals in the league (176).

Stan Mikita led the league in scoring, capturing the Art Ross Trophy. Bobby Hull missed nine games with a knee injury but still managed to win the Lady Byng and Hart Memorial Trophies, and Pierre Pilote won the Norris Trophy while ranking eighth in the league with 59 points.

Before the season, the Hawks made a fairly major trade, sending Ab McDonald, and Reg Fleming to Boston for Doug Mohns. Dennis Hull, Doug Jarrett, and Ken Hodge made their NHL debuts that year as well. In his second NHL season, Phil Esposito was among the team leaders with 23 goals. Mohns, Mikita, and Ken Wharram joined together to form the legendary Scooter Line starting this season and combined to score 65 goals, with Mohns playing in only 49 games.

Yet, despite the collection of stars on the roster, the Hawks finished in third place, 11 points behind the Red Wings. In the first round of the playoffs, the Hawks defeated the Red Wings in a great seven-game series. Chicago came back and won Game 6 and Game 7 to eliminate the top-rated Wings, moving into a Finals series against Montreal.

The 1965 Finals were unique; this was the only Finals series between 1955 and 2003 in which each game was won by the home team.

Mark Kram reported the following in a May 10, 1965, *Sports Illustrated* article: "Still, the biggest factor in the Canadiens' cup victory, despite some fine individual performances, some spectacular skating and a lethal power play, was 'home ice.' Montreal had one more game at home than Chicago.... The inability of the teams to win away from home (only two were won on foreign ice in 20 playoff games) provoked much discussion. There were many explanations, but obviously one of the reasons was the treatment of the ice. In Chicago it was soft—a fact that proved a disadvantage to Montreal. 'The ice was too slow in Chicago,' said Jean Beliveau, 'and it took the edge off our game.' In Montreal the ice was hard, too fast for a team like Chicago, which tries to outmuscle the opposition."

The Habs' goalie tandem of Gump Worsley and Charlie Hodge combined to shut out the Blackhawks in Game 2, Game 5, and Game 7, and the Canadiens won the Cup.

Time magazine reported at the time that, "Jean Beliveau started the rout with a goal after 14 sec. of play, and the Canadiens added the other three before the first period ended. After that, it was back to the brawl. In seven games—17½ hrs. of playing time—players from both teams spent 5 hrs. 29 min. in the penalty box."

Another historical aspect of this season's Finals was the initial appearance of a playoff MVP award—the Conn Smythe Trophy. It was awarded to Montreal captain Jean Beliveau, who scored eight goals and added eight assists in that season's playoffs.

The Canadiens broke the Toronto Maple Leafs' streak of three consecutive Cups with the win and went on to win six of the next nine titles. Coach Toe Blake won his sixth of eight championships in 1965.

66 Here Come the Hawks

Long before the Fratellis became the unofficial authors of a theme song for the Blackhawks, "Here Come the Hawks!" was the song associated with the franchise.

Originally written by J. Swayzee and produced by the Dick Marx Orchestra and Choir in 1968, it is still a featured part of Hawks home games and video montages played at the United Center. Marx's only son is 1980s pop musician Richard Marx.

In recent seasons, a new song has emerged at the United Center, however, that has become synonymous with the Blackhawks.

Released in August 2006, the Fratellis single "Chelsea Dagger" received little hype in the United States beyond coming in at No. 77 on *Rolling Stone* magazine's *100 Best Songs of 2007* list.

A couple years later, though, it began getting regular play after Blackhawks players scored a goal, and the response from the crowd was unmistakably positive. Soon, "Chelsea Dagger" replaced some of the personalized songs played for specific players and has become a fixture during Hawks home games.

During the 2010 playoffs, the song reached a new level of cultural phenomenon when it became the central piece of feature news stories on television stations all over North America. The Vancouver Canucks were filmed listening to it and reacting and, to a man, each one's reaction was something close to, "It makes me sick" or, "I hate that song."

During the Stanley Cup Finals, a number of international media members were seen downloading the song on iTunes during the first game of the series.

67 Close but No Cigar...Again

In 1938 the Blackhawks won the Stanley Cup with arguably the worst team to ever accomplish the feat.

In 1967, the final year of the Original Six division, the opposite was true. The Blackhawks won 41 of 70 games and piled up a league-leading 94 points, 17 ahead of second-place Montreal. Stan Mikita led the league with 97 points, and Bobby Hull led the league with 52 goals. Ken Wharram finished with 65 points, tied with Gordie Howe for fourth in the NHL, and youngster Phil Esposito was just behind them with 61 points.

How good was the Blackhawks offense? Their top six goal scorers—Bobby Hull, Mikita, Wharram, Dennis Hull, Doug Mohns, and Esposito—combined to score 189 goals. That was more than the entire Boston Bruins (182) and New York Rangers (189) teams that year! Meanwhile the Hawks' goalie tandem of Glenn Hall and Denis DeJordy led the league in fewest goals allowed.

Indeed, four of the six players on the first team of NHL All-Stars were from Chicago, and Hall was on the second team despite leading the league in goals against. Hull, Wharram, Mikita, and Pierre Pilote were all first-team All-Stars, ahead of the likes of Tim Horton, Bobby Orr (who was a rookie that year), and Howe.

The Blackhawks also nearly swept the league's individual honors that year. As a team they won the Prince of Wales Trophy for having the best record. Mikita won the Art Ross, Lady Byng, and Hart Trophies, and Hall and DeJordy shared the Vezina Trophy. Chicago was the team to beat.

Unfortunately, the Toronto Maple Leafs didn't get the memo that this was the Hawks' year. Terry Sawchuk, Toronto's goalie, dominated the top offense in the league. After allowing five goals in the first game of the playoffs, he allowed only nine in the next five games. The Leafs were led offensively by a couple names that weren't familiar to Chicago fans yet—Jim Pappin and Bob Pulford.

In *The Blackhawks*, McFarlane wrote, "[Pulford] remembers Leaf goalie Terry Sawchuck's performance in [Game 5] at the Stadium as 'the greatest display of goaltending I ever saw. No one could have been better than Sawchuck was in that game against the Hawks.'

"Toronto was completely outplayed—except in goal—and outshot 49–31…. When the Leafs skated off with a 4–2 victory that afternoon, it was apparent the series was all but over." The Blackhawks lost to the Leafs in six games in the first round of the playoffs that year. One of the best regular-season teams of the Original Six era did not even get a chance to play for the Stanley Cup. Toronto went on to defeat Montreal in the Finals.

The stunning upset was sweet retribution, albeit 29 years later, for the Leafs' loss to the Hawks in the 1938 Finals. That year, the Blackhawks had the worst offense in the league, and Toronto was the prohibitive favorite.

While Toronto and Chicago had now exchanged surprising postseason victories, the two were also linked for their futility after this postseason. The Blackhawks didn't win the Stanley Cup again until 2010, while the 1967 championship is still the last time Toronto won hockey's ultimate prize.

68 Edzo

It wasn't easy for the Blackhawks to bring Eddie "Edzo" Olczyk home. He had been the youngest player on the 1984 U.S. Olympic Team, earning a place on that roster before his 17th birthday, and was ranked the third-best forward in the 1984 Draft class by the *Hockey News* when the Blackhawks selected him. Considering the top forward in that draft was Mario Lemieux, Olczyk was in elite company as a teenager.

General manager Bob Pulford had to trade up three places in the draft, sending goalie Bob Janecyk, the sixth overall pick; a third-round pick; and a swap of fourth-round picks to Los Angeles to get into position to bring Olczyk back to his hometown. Pulford also had to agree to send future considerations to the New Jersey Devils to guarantee Olczyk wouldn't be picked second overall behind Lemieux.

The youngest U.S.-born player selected in the first round of the NHL Draft by his hometown team, Eddie Olczyk made his NHL debut as an 18-year-old in 1984. Wittenberg wrote in *Tales from the Chicago Blackhawks*, "The toughest debut for a hometown player probably belongs to Olczyk. The pressure of being a No. 1 draft pick and third overall was a lot in 1984." Settling onto a line with Troy Murray and Curt Fraser appropriately nicknamed the

The Clydesdales

From 1984 to 1987, the Blackhawks had one of the biggest lines in hockey. With Troy Murray between Eddie Olczyk and Curt Fraser, the Hawks had three players on the same line who were all over 200 pounds. This was the Clydesdale Line.

During the three seasons the Clydesdale Line was together, each of the three enjoyed some of the best seasons of their respective careers. Olczyk scored 65 goals and was credited with 115 assists in 228 games during those three seasons. Fraser scored 79 goals, was credited with 89 assists, and piled up 375 penalty minutes. And Murray led the way, scoring 99 goals and adding 137 assists in those three years. In 1985–86, Murray enjoyed his best season in the NHL, totaling 99 points and winning the Selke Trophy as the league's best defensive forward.

But the sum of the parts was greater the three as individuals.

Clydesdales Line, Olczyk made an immediate impact on the team, scoring a goal in his first game. He posted 20 goals and 50 points in his rookie season.

His production jumped to 29 goals and 70 points in his sophomore campaign, but the pressure of playing in front of his hometown crowd was a double-edged sword. His popularity with sponsors, the media, and the fans made him an easy target for opponents and, on occasion, teammates' envy. His third season saw a decline in production, as Olczyk posted only 16 goals and 51 points.

On September 3, 1987, after only three seasons with the Hawks, Olczyk was traded for the first time in his NHL career (he would be traded four more times in the next 10 years). He was sent to Toronto with aging All-Star Al Secord in a trade that brought Rick Vaive, Steve Thomas, and Bob McGill back to Chicago.

For the next decade, Olczyk spent time with the Leafs, Winnipeg Jets, New York Rangers, Los Angeles Kings, and Pittsburgh Penguins before returning to Chicago for the 1998–99 and 1999–2000 seasons to end his career. In 1994, with former Chicago teammate Steve Larmer, Olczyk was part of the Stanley Cup–champion New York Rangers. Unfortunately, because of a hand injury limiting him to only 37 games that season, he did not have his name engraved on the Cup until after the fact.

In total, Olczyk played 1,031 regular-season games—scoring 342 goals—and 57 postseason games in his NHL career. While a member of the Blackhawks, he played in 322 games, scoring 77 goals and adding 132 assists.

After his playing career ended, Edzo (also nicknamed "Eddie O.") moved initially to the booth. He was the color analyst for Pittsburgh games until, in the summer of 2003, he was named the head coach of the Penguins. He served in that capacity until he was fired after an 8–17–6 start to the 2005–06 season. Olczyk was Sidney Crosby's first head coach in the NHL.

Starting with the 2006–07 season, Olczyk was again brought back to Chicago, this time as the color analyst for Blackhawks games on Comcast SportsNet Chicago and WGN. He also works as a primary color analyst and studio host for NBC on national telecasts, which included the 2010 Winter Olympics in Vancouver.

69 J.R. Gets Traded

On August 16, 1996, the Blackhawks traded Jeremy Roenick to the Phoenix Coyotes for the second time. The separation made a Donald Trump divorce seem like a high school breakup. And there are so many "what if?" questions surrounding the trade that many Blackhawks fans still don't want to think about it.

Roenick was an elite superstar in Chicago in the early 1990s. He played in the NHL All-Star Game four consecutive years (1991–94) and had strung together three of the highest single-season point totals in the organization's history: 103 in 1991–92 and consecutive 107-point seasons in 1992–93 and 1993–94.

When the work stoppage claimed the first half of the 1994–95 NHL season, the dynamics in Chicago continued to change. Despite being the face of the franchise—and only 25 years old—Roenick was about to follow Denis Savard and Steve Larmer out the door.

In the summer of 1995 the Blackhawks and Winnipeg Jets worked out a trade that would have sent Roenick to Manitoba in exchange for another superstar, Keith Tkachuk. At that time, Tkachuk was holding out for more money, and the Jets were in no position to offer him more; they were in dire straits financially and couldn't afford to pay Tkachuk his market value. Rather than lose their top player for nothing in free agency, the Jets decided to be proactive and worked out a deal that would swap two of the best scorers in the game.

However, when then-Jets owner Barry Shenkarow heard through the grapevine that Roenick allegedly didn't want to move to Canada, he backed out of the deal. This drew the ire of Hawks owner Bill Wirtz and general manager Bob Pulford and a dramatic move from Chicago as a direct response.

By September of that year, Tkachuk reached a point as a free agent that allowed other teams to extend an offer sheet to him. The bold slap-in-the-face response from Wirtz and Pulford was a five-year, $17.5 million offer sheet. This put the pressure on Winnipeg to either match the offer or walk away from the face of their franchise for nothing. Winnipeg matched the offer and was put into further financial trouble.

While the Tkachuk move was not the entire reason for the ultimate demise of the Jets, his deal may have been the final nail in the coffin. In December 1995 the Jets were sold to a group of investors led by Jerry Colangelo, and the franchise was set to be moved to Phoenix during the following summer.

Meanwhile, the relationship between Roenick and Chicago management continued to go south. During the summer of 1996, Roenick was in the same free-agent position that Tkachuk was the previous summer. After not being able to work out a deal with their best player, the Blackhawks' front office decided they would be better off dealing him. On August 16, 1996, Roenick was traded to…Phoenix.

The ownership, location, and logo may have been different, but the Blackhawks ultimately traded Roenick to the same team to which they thought they had traded him the year before. This time, however, the Blackhawks did not receive a superstar in return. Alexei Zhamnov, Craig Mills, and a first-round draft pick were all the Hawks received for one of the elite scorers in the game. In a stroke of powerful irony, Roenick began that season centering a line with Tkachuk.

When he left Chicago, Roenick had posted an incredible 596 points—including 267 goals—in only 524 games. The response to the trade was instant hatred for the front office in Chicago. In a brief story in the *Chicago Tribune* the following day announcing the details of the trade, author Rich Strom wrote, "In the process, [Zhamnov] became one of the most unwelcome Hawks, simply because he was the main man received by the Hawks in Friday's trade for fan favorite Jeremy Roenick…. Welcome to Chicago, Alexei."

To his credit, Zhamnov's Chicago career wasn't terrible. In 528 games he scored 140 goals, including 22 game-winners, and totaled 424 points. He represented the Blackhawks in one All-Star Game, during the 2001–02 season. But he wasn't Roenick.

Mills, then a 19-year-old wing who had been drafted in the fifth round two years earlier, appeared in 27 games over two years for the Blackhawks. He tallied three assists and 36 penalty minutes in a Chicago sweater.

The player the Blackhawks selected with the first-round pick they received in the deal, Ty Jones, was a bigger bust than Mills. The 16th overall pick in the 1997 Draft, Jones played in a total of eight games for the Blackhawks and was credited with 12 penalty minutes.

After Roenick left Chicago, he played another 839 games in the NHL. He added 246 goals and 374 assists to his already impressive résumé and played in five more All-Star Games.

It might not have been as bad as the Phil Esposito trade, but this was one of the worst public-relations disasters in the history of the franchise.

70 No. 2 and No. 7

The 2004–05 season is a ghost in the record books. A work stoppage cost the game an entire season, and it couldn't have come at a worse time for the Blackhawks. The organization was low on talent and were skating before crowds that were, on many occasions, largely in favor of road teams.

During the 2005–06 season, one in which the Blackhawks finished 14th in the Western Conference with only 65 points, the team took a chance and promoted two young defensemen. At only 22, Duncan Keith was three years removed from being a second-round selection by the Blackhawks in the 2002 Draft. And at just 20, Brent Seabrook made his debut two years after being selected 14th overall in the 2003 Draft.

That first campaign wasn't easy. Keith finished his rookie season with a -11 rating while he ranked second among NHL rookie blueliners with a team-best 23:25 average ice time. Seabrook finished at +5 for the campaign, and his 32 points were the second-highest among all Hawks defensemen that season. Seabrook's first two career NHL goals both came in overtime.

Over the coming seasons, No. 2 and No. 7 became locked at the hip on the Blackhawks depth chart. Keith's smooth skating and Seabrook's physical force were the perfect match, and the chemistry between the two developed quickly.

In the long history of the Blackhawks, there have been many great tandems on the blue line, from Pierre Pilote and Moose Vasko to Bob Murray and Doug Wilson. Keith and Seabrook were establishing themselves as one of the elite pairs in the game.

On October 8, 2008, the Blackhawks named Keith as one of their alternate captains. He was named a member of the 2008 and 2011 All-Star Games, and the two continued to establish their niche in Chicago—and earn the respect of their peers.

The elite status of the pair was confirmed during the 2009–10 season. On December 2, 2009, Keith took the stage at the United Center with Patrick Kane and Jonathan Toews when the organization announced long-term extensions with the three young stars. Keith's contract would be the largest in club history, a 13-year deal worth $72 million.

Despite stiff competition from throughout the league, both Blackhawks defensemen were selected to represent Canada in the 2010 Winter Olympics in Vancouver. Despite spending most of the Olympic games being separated by Canadian (and Detroit Red Wings) coach Mike Babcock, they were important parts of Canada's gold medal–winning effort.

This wasn't the first time Seabrook had found success in international play. He represented Canada in the 2003 World Under-18 Championships in Russia, where he won gold. He was also a member of two Canadian teams at the World Junior Championships, winning silver in 2004 and gold in 2005. Keith's prior international experience was limited to a silver at the 2008 World Championships, also with Canada.

When the two returned to Chicago with their hardware, they took their game to another level. Keith and Seabrook combined to post 99 points during the 2009–10 regular season and then combined to add 28 points in the Hawks' 22 playoff games. After the two added a Stanley Cup championship to their gold medal year, Keith was named the Norris Trophy winner as the league's top defenseman.

On February 28, 2011, the Blackhawks locked up Seabrook for five more years.

Keith already ranks among the best scoring defensemen in the organization's history, ranking seventh in points. Seabrook will likely join him in the top 10 soon, as the duo chases the nearly 1,300 points posted by Murray and Wilson.

71 The Wild West

The 1970–71 season began with a big change for the Blackhawks. The NHL moved them to the West Division, which the Blackhawks won fairly easily. They were, however, the only Original Six team in that division and featured one of the best offensive teams in the league.

Bobby Hull had another solid season, finishing fifth in the league with 96 points. Unfortunately, two of the four players ahead of him—Phil Esposito and Ken Hodge—were former teammates playing in Boston.

This was the second season that Phil's brother, Tony, protected the net in Chicago. He burst onto the scene in 1969–70 with 38 wins and followed that up with 35 victories and six shutouts.

In the playoffs that year, the Hawks easily swept the Philadelphia Flyers before eliminating the New York Rangers in seven games. They would face the Montreal Canadiens in the Stanley Cup Finals.

The Habs, led by Jean Beliveau's 76 points, finished third in the East Division behind the Bruins and Rangers. Their road to the Finals began with a seven-game series against the high-powered Bruins, who featured the top four scorers in the league that year. But this was to be Beliveau's final season, and he would not allow his team to go away easily.

In the second round, the Canadiens met another team that had pulled off an improbable first-round upset, the Minnesota North Stars. Montreal took six games to advance to the Finals, where Chicago was waiting.

The series was dominated by the home teams, as the host handled business in each of the first six games. In the seventh and deciding game, the Blackhawks took a two-goal lead, and the Cup appeared to be headed back to Chicago for the first time in 10 years.

But just moments after a Hull shot hit the crossbar, a missile off the stick of Jacques Lemaire from center ice beat Esposito to get Montreal on the board. Then Henri Richard took advantage of an uncharacteristic Eric Nesterenko turnover to tie the game late in the second period. Early in the third, Richard caught the Hawks in a bad line change and gave Montreal the lead.

In the closing moments, the Hawks made a furious attempt to tie the game, but Montreal rookie goalie Ken Dryden did not allow the puck to pass. Dryden had only played in six NHL games before that postseason but carried the Canadiens to the promised land with an incredible run of great play. He became a national hero for his efforts that postseason.

During the Finals, the Canadiens offense was led by Frank and Pete Mahovlich, who scored nine goals in the seven games. Only one game—a 5–2 Canadiens victory in Game 4—was decided by more than two goals in the series.

It was only the second time in Stanley Cup Finals history that a road team won Game 7; the only previous occurrence came in Detroit in 1945, when the Leafs clinched the Cup with a 2–1 win over the Red Wings.

The Hawks returned to the Finals only one more time in the following 21 years, losing to Montreal again in 1973.

72 Bobby Bounces

On June 27, 1972, the unthinkable happened. Bobby Hull, coming off his fifth 50-goal season, was in Minneapolis to sign a contract. And it wasn't with the Chicago Blackhawks.

Today, the story reads like laughable fiction. The World Hockey Association, which was desperately vying to become a viable rival to the National Hockey League, was trying to fast-forward the respect-earning process by throwing a lot of money at some NHL All-Stars. But nobody thought the infant league could steal the biggest name in the NHL away from Chicago...right?

With Hull's contract expiring after the 1971–72 season, the WHA started to formulate an action plan to win the star. This is where the story gets even more surreal. The owners of the WHA met in Vancouver to decide which franchise would make the pitch to Hull. This process consisted of names being drawn from a hat—literally! Ben Hatskin, owner of the Winnipeg Jets, won the lottery that day.

It appeared even Hull and his agent doubted that the new league could pull off the blockbuster deal. After asking the Blackhawks for

The Million Dollar Line

When Bill Hay joined the Blackhawks in 1959–60, he centered a line with the great Bobby Hull and Murray Balfour. In that first season that the three were together, they combined to score 75 goals and were nicknamed "the Million Dollar Line."

Over the five seasons that they were together, the three lived up to the nickname. On the 1960–61 championship team, they combined for 63 goals, and all three were among the top four on the team in points (Stan Mikita was third, ahead of Balfour).

In 1961–62, despite Balfour being limited to 49 games, they combined for 76 goals—50 of which came from Hull. The last year they were effective together was 1962–63, when they combined for just 53 goals.

Balfour was legendary for his poker playing, leading to a rumor that he made enough money gambling during the Stanley Cup season of 1960–61 that he allegedly never cashed a single paycheck from the Blackhawks.

$250,000 per season—and being turned down—the superstar's agent forwarded his demands to the WHA. The demands were simple: Hull wanted a five-year deal worth $250,000 per season, and a $1 million signing bonus up front.

In 1972 these terms were laughable. When the final offer was made in February 1972, every other owner in the WHA was on board to pitch in $100,000, and Hull could stay with the Jets as an executive for another $100,000 per season after his five-year deal expired. The deal was worth over $2 million total. These were terms the Blackhawks would not—and could not—match.

The Blackhawks front office thought there was no way Hull would go to the WHA. They were wrong. Hull later said, "If I told you that the big contract had nothing to do with my signing [with Winnipeg], I'd be lying. It made the future secure for my family. Then there were some things that disenchanted me in the NHL, and the way the Hawks handled their attempts to sign me. They just didn't think I'd consider jumping."

At the last minute, Chicago came to the table with an offer meeting Hull's initial demands of $1 million over five years. But it was too little too late.

Hull's move was not only bold but cost him his chance to be part of arguably the greatest international hockey tournament of all time—the 1972 Summit Series between Canada and the Soviet Union.

Canadian hockey officials and the NHL Players' Association wanted both Bobby and Dennis Hull to be on the roster, and Bill Wirtz's intimate involvement with the tournament and fighting to allow NHL players to take part could have opened a door for him to play.

But Campbell was so put off by his pending departure that he took dramatic action to keep Bobby Hull off Canada's team. He, with the blessing of the NHL's governors, told the NHLPA that if Hull played, the contracts of players named to Canada's team would no longer be guaranteed by their NHL clubs if they were injured. That pressure was too much for the Players' Association to take, and they removed Hull from the roster.

"To the governors, [Hull] was a defector and his presence on the roster would only add credibility to the rival league. They were beginning to realize it had been a huge mistake to let him get away," McFarlane wrote in *The Blackhawks*.

The impact on the Blackhawks team wasn't as dramatic as one might imagine. The Blackhawks won the West Division that year with an eight-point lead on the Philadelphia Flyers and Minnesota North Stars. Despite not having a single player on the NHL's first All-Star team, the Hawks advanced all the way to the Stanley Cup Finals, where they lost to the Montreal Canadiens in six games.

Hull was the WHA MVP in 1973 and 1975 and enjoyed ridiculous success in his first six seasons in the new league. He didn't play in the NHL again until the Jets joined the league in 1979.

73 Meet You in St. Louis

The two greatest, longest-standing rivalries in the Western Conference are between three teams, and the ties between the three are undeniable.

When Major McLaughlin passed away, two former owners of the Detroit Red Wings—James D. Norris and Arthur Wirtz—stepped up and purchased the Blackhawks. The two had interests all over professional sports, one of which was ownership of the St. Louis Arena.

The NHL decided to expand in 1967, and the influential pair of owners in Chicago did what influential owners in sports do: they "helped guide the decision-making process." In an effort to unload the decrepit arena, Wirtz and Norris convinced the league to put a team in St. Louis rather than Baltimore.

That move immediately haunted the Blackhawks organization when, in the expansion draft, the new St. Louis Blues selected Glenn Hall. With rookie head coach Scotty Bowman behind the bench in the team's first year and Hall splitting the goalie duties with veteran (and also Hall of Famer) Jacques Plante, the Blues quickly jumped from nonexistence to contention. In only their second season, the Blues won the Western Division, and the tandem of Hall and Plante won the Vezina Trophy.

Part of the league's expansion was a rule that an expansion team had to play in the Stanley Cup Finals. In the three years this rule was in place, the Blues took advantage each time. However, the Blues were swept out of the Finals by the Canadiens in 1968 and 1969 and by the Bruins in 1970.

But the following season, things changed. Just as the Chicago Cubs and St. Louis Cardinals share a division, the Blues and

Blackhawks became division rivals. Since 1970 the two have been heated division rivals.

The Blackhawks have faced the Blues in the playoffs more times since 1970—10—than they have any other organization. During the fast, physical 1980s, the two teams met five times (1980, 1982, 1983, 1988, and 1989), and Chicago won four of the five matchups.

While the scant 300-mile distance between the two cities led to a great deal of contempt, a trade made by St. Louis in 1988 made the rivalry personal to any longtime Blackhawks fan. On March 7, 1988, the Blues traded Rob Ramage and Rick Wamsley to the Calgary Flames for Steve Bozak and a 23-year-old forward whose last name happened to be Hull.

Brett Hull, the son of Blackhawks legend Bobby, was now playing for one of Chicago's most hated rivals. It didn't help the situation that rumors claimed Chicago could have had the young star but passed on the opportunity.

In eight of his 11 seasons in St. Louis, Hull scored at least 40 goals—and many of them came at the expense of the Blackhawks. Watching him score an unprecedented 228 goals in 231 games between the 1989–90 and 1991–92 seasons was especially hard for Hawks fans.

The 1990s saw the rivalry really heat up, as the Blackhawks and Blues fought for the top of the division on an annual basis. While Jeremy Roenick and Chris Chelios were playing for Chicago, Hull and Adam Oates were skating on the famed Hull and Oates Line in St. Louis. Three times in the first four seasons of the decade—1990, 1992, and 1993—the two teams met in the playoffs, with the first two series going seven and six games, respectively.

But perhaps no moment in the rivalry is as memorable as March 17, 1991. It all sparked after Glen Featherstone took offense to a Roenick hit, and from there all hell broke loose. With the two teams battling for the Presidents' Trophy, six players on each team were ejected for fighting in what has been dubbed the "St. Patrick's Day Massacre Game." After the game, the NHL suspended the Blues' Scott Stevens for two games and levied $10,000 fines and 10-game suspensions on Mike Peluso of the Hawks and Kelly Chase of the Blues.

The teams have also shared a head coach: Joel Quenneville. Between 1996 and 2004, Quenneville won more games than any head coach in the history of the Blues, and he took over behind the bench in Chicago in 2008. Obviously in 2010, Quenneville brought the Stanley Cup back to Chicago.

Since 1993 the two teams have only met once in the postseason (2002), but the rivalry remains one of the most physical in the league.

In the beginning, the relationship between Joel "Q" Quenneville and the Chicago Blackhawks was intriguing. As TSN's Darren Dreger wrote about the hire on September 26, 2008, "With Scotty Bowman hired by Chicago this summer to act as a Senior Advisor, Quenneville's addition brings another respected hockey mind into the Blackhawks organization, although some see his new part-time job as a nice insurance policy for Chicago in the event the team struggles and a coaching change is required."

Despite then-GM Dale Tallon denying there was anything more to the Quenneville hire, the perception of many media members became reality after only four games in the 2008–09 season, when the organization replaced Denis Savard with Quenneville. On October 16, 2008, Quenneville was named the 37th head coach of the Chicago Blackhawks.

Blackhawks coach Joel Quenneville hoists the Stanley Cup after they beat the Philadelphia Flyers in Game 6 of the NHL Stanley Cup Finals in Philadelphia on June 9, 2010. Quenneville has been a real boon to the team, and the Hawks gave him a three-year contract extension in September 2010.

In his first season in Chicago, Quenneville led a young team on an unpredicted run to the Western Conference Finals, and in just his first full season behind the bench, the Hawks won the Stanley Cup.

But looking back at Quenneville's history, none of the team's success under his guidance should be surprising. He was drafted in the second round (21st overall) in 1978 by the Toronto Maple Leafs. In 13 seasons as a defenseman in the NHL, *Q* scored 54 goals and added 136 assists. He was also whistled for 705 penalty minutes in 803 games with the Leafs, Colorado Rockies, New Jersey Devils, Hartford Whalers, and Washington Capitals.

He was an assistant coach with the Quebec Nordiques/Colorado Avalanche organization for two and a half seasons—including their 1995 Stanley Cup championship—on one of the most acclaimed benches in league history: Marc Crawford, Jacques Lemaire, and Quenneville have all coached over 1,000 games in the NHL.

In 1996 Quenneville accepted the head-coaching job in St. Louis, where he spent the next seven and a half seasons. He is the all-time leader in wins by a head coach in the history of the Blues organization with a 307–191–95 record (technically 307–191–77 with 18 overtime losses). After the 2004–05 season, he took over as the head coach in Colorado for three years. Only once in Quenneville's coaching career did a team he coached at the end of the season not qualify for the playoffs. He won the Jack Adams Trophy as the league's top coach in 2000 while with the Blues and coached the North American All-Stars in the 2001 NHL All-Star Game.

For all of the success he enjoyed with Colorado and St. Louis, though, it has been in Chicago that he has made his mark. His mustache has made him a fan favorite, joining Mike Ditka on the list of champion coaches in Chicago with a 'stache.

In February 2011 Quenneville missed a few games after being admitted to a suburban Chicago hospital with an ulcer. He returned to the bench, and the Blackhawks eventually qualified for the 2011 postseason.

Quenneville is one of only two men in NHL history to have coached in 1,000 and played in more than 800 games and one of only four men in NHL history to coach the Blackhawks to a Stanley Cup championship.

75 The Million-Dollar Man

In 1957 the Toronto Maple Leafs added a young left wing to their lineup named Frank Mahovlich. He scored 20 goals that year, winning the Calder Trophy. The game came easily to him, and the

Leafs were on their way to one of the great stretches of hockey in the Original Six era.

Mahovlich established a Leafs record by scoring 48 goals in 1960–61, a record that stood for 21 years. The following year, his 71 points led the Leafs during the regular season, and he added 12 points in 12 postseason games as the Leafs captured the Stanley Cup.

He was a superstar in the league, and any team would have loved to have Mahovlich on their roster. Some, apparently, more than others.

Mahovlich and Leafs coach Punch Imlach feuded publically for years. When his contract came up for renewal after the 1962 Cup win, the cold war between Imlach and Mahovlich reached a level that appeared to be beyond repair. The unhappy star claimed that the team had presented him with a lowball offer, and he wanted out of Toronto.

That year, the NHL's All-Star Game opened the season. There was an elaborate party before the game—much as there is today—with all of the owners and management celebrating the new season together. In 1962 the game was played in Toronto.

The night before the game, Blackhawks owner "Big Jim" Norris went out for cocktails with the three new owners of the Leafs—Harold Ballard, Stafford Smythe, and John Bassett. After a spirited evening, the talk turned to the business of the game, and Norris expressed interest in Mahovlich.

With beverages flowing, Norris offered the Leafs ownership group $1 million for their star winger. As legend recalls, the offer shocked Ballard.

In *The Blackhawks*, McFarlane says, "When midnight rolled around, Norris made Ballard an offer.

"'I hear you fellows are having trouble signing the big kid Mahovlich,' he began. 'I'd pay a lot of money to have that kind of problem.'

"'How much money?' Ballard asked.

"'I'd give you a million dollars for him,' Norris countered.

"Ballard almost dropped his drink. 'A million? For a hockey player? Jim, for a million, you've got him. He's yours.'

"The two men shook hands on a deal that took them mere seconds to consummate. Norris stood up and peeled ten $100 bills from a roll in his pocket. He handed them to Ballard.

"'A down payment,' he said. 'I'll get the rest of the money to you tomorrow morning.'"

As you might guess, the next day the beverages wore off, and the Leafs woke up to the reality that they had just sold their best player to a rival team. They quickly rounded up a deal to satisfy Mahovlich's demands, and Ballard had to tell Norris the deal was off.

The Leafs returned Norris' $1,000 "deposit," and backed out of what could have been one of the biggest blockbuster moves of the decade.

Toronto went on to win three of the next five Stanley Cups, and Mahovlich continued to put up Hall of Fame numbers.

76 Mike Keenan

Jeremy Roenick described the early part of his career playing for Mike Keenan to Mike Morrreale of NHL.com, saying, "He once grabbed me by my throat when we were playing in Kalamazoo and said, 'If you don't finish your check, if you don't hit that guy next time, you'll never play a game for me again in the NHL.' I was so scared I almost cried on the bench."

Bowman Owned Chicago

Despite being part of the Blackhawks organization now, there aren't many coaches who personally contributed to the demise of the Blackhawks more in the last 40 years than Scotty Bowman.

Beginning his coaching career in St. Louis in 1967–68, Bowman went on to win 1,248 regular-season games and nine Stanley Cup championships in his historic career. His teams qualified for the playoffs 28 times in 30 years, and some of his best work came at Chicago's expense.

Certainly the final nine years of his career in Detroit are fresh in the minds of Blackhawks fans. Bowman's Red Wings won three Stanley Cups and made the playoffs in each of his nine seasons in Detroit. The Wings also won six Central Division crowns in those nine years, burying the Blackhawks along the way.

But many Blackhawks fans don't realize that, of the four times a Bowman-coached team eliminated the Hawks from the postseason, none of those feats was accomplished in Detroit.

In 1992, the last time the Blackhawks appeared in the Stanley Cup Finals before 2010, Bowman was behind the bench in Pittsburgh. The Penguins swept the Blackhawks that year.

In 1973, the Blackhawks' last Stanley Cup Finals appearance before 1992, it was Bowman behind the Montreal bench when they defeated the Blackhawks. In each of the Hawks' last two Finals appearances before 2010, it was Bowman taking home the ultimate prize.

Between those two Finals eliminations, Bowman advanced in the postseason at the Blackhawks' expense two other times. His Canadiens eliminated the Hawks in the quarterfinals in 1976, and the Bowman-led Buffalo Sabres eliminated the Hawks in the quarterfinals in 1980.

He continued, "For fear of my career, I went on the ice and starting hurling my body at everything I could possibly get at, skating as hard as I could…. Mike taught me a style of game that I adopted. He taught me to play with passion and grit. Away from the rink, he was also there when I had off-ice problems, so Mike

Keenan was that guy who really put that in me and I carried it on for a long time."

His demeanor wasn't always a favorite of his players. In 1997 Ed Swift wrote in a *Sports Illustrated* piece, "Three times he has guided—some would say browbeaten—a team to the best record in hockey." *Browbeating, choking, badgering,* and *breaking* are all words that have been used to describe Keenan's approach to the bench. One other word cannot be ignored when describing him, either: *winning*.

Keenan never played in the NHL. He began coaching in the minors in 1979 and eventually led the Buffalo Sabres' minor league team in Rochester to the 1983 Calder Cup. In 1984 he was named the head coach of an underwhelming Philadelphia Flyers team that was losing icon Bobby Clarke to retirement. Despite that, from 1984 to 1987 Keenan's Flyers teams had the second-best record in hockey behind the Edmonton Oilers dynasty.

When the Flyers fired Keenan after a first-round exit from the 1988 playoffs, he was immediately hired by the Blackhawks. The following four years were some of the most exciting—and tumultuous—seasons in the history of the organization.

He immediately feuded with stars, especially the team's captain, Denis Savard. When Savard was injured, Keenan named Dirk Graham the interim captain and later gave Graham the title permanently. His heated exchanges with other stars, including Roenick, were well known. But Keenan could afford to tell his players exactly what he wanted from them; he was his own boss.

Keenan also served as general manager from 1990 to 1993 and was responsible for trades that sent some of the best players of the era out of town. He traded Troy Murray, Wayne Presley, Doug Wilson and, perhaps most famously, Savard to Montreal for Chris Chelios.

After the Hawks were swept by the Penguins in the 1992 Finals, he was forced to hand the coaching job to his protégé, Darryl Sutter, and focus only on the GM job.

The Blackhawks won two division titles and qualified for the postseason in all four seasons under Keenan's leadership, and his 153 wins as head coach still ranks fourth in franchise history behind only Billy Reay, Bob Pulford, and Rudy Pilous.

In total, he has one of the most exceptional coaching résumés in NHL history. He ranks fifth all-time in wins as an NHL coach. His biggest victory came as the coach of the 1994 New York Rangers team that, unlike the 1992 Blackhawks, ended their Stanley Cup drought.

77 Attend the Convention

In 2008 the Blackhawks created one of the most unique opportunities in the entire National Hockey League for fans to interact with each other.

In late July of that year, the Hawks hosted the first Blackhawks Convention, modeled after the Cubs Convention, John McDonough and Jay Blunk's successful fan fest for Chicago Cubs fans, which has been running for more than 30 years.

In each of the first three years of the Blackhawks Convention, more than 10,000 fans attended the weekend at the Hilton Chicago. The convention is a wonderful opportunity to participate in question-and-answer sessions with media personalities and favorite players from the past and present as well as to get cherished autographs or photos with players.

The convention, which begins on a Friday night each year with exciting opening ceremonies, brings the crowd to a boil that hockey usually doesn't experience in the middle of the summer. With the introduction of each player and some of the Hall of Famers who are

Jonathan Toews kisses the Stanley Cup during the 2010 Blackhawks Convention at the Hilton Chicago on July 30, 2010.

still with the organization, the fans are able to show their appreciation for the stars away from the rink.

However, the convention has been the center of some important moments in Blackhawks history as well. Jonathan Toews was named the youngest captain in the organization's history at the convention in 2008. Fans were introduced to Marian Hossa for the first time at the convention in 2009. And the Stanley Cup itself made an appearance at the Convention in 2010.

Beyond those revolutionary moments, fans have been thrilled to listen to great stories from the past as recalled by former Blackhawks such as Bobby Hull, Stan Mikita, Tony Esposito, and Denis Savard. They have also been able to voice their opinions and ask questions of team management, including general manager Stan Bowman, owner Rocky Wirtz, and team president John McDonough.

There are also some great opportunities for kids (and adults) to try their best to be a hockey player like their heroes. There have been goaltender simulators, radar guns to measure amateur slap-shot velocity, and other fun ways for fans to test their skills.

One of the most popular features of the convention, however, is the merchandise, and there are hundreds of unique ways fans can spend their money on Blackhawks memorabilia. Dozens of vendors pack one of the exhibit halls in the hotel with great items for fans of all ages, and there is the annual Locker Room Sale, featuring live and silent auctions of one-of-a-kind items from players, including game-used equipment.

Arguably the best feature of the convention isn't something money can buy or the hosts can provide. Spending time with 10,000 other passionate Blackhawks fans makes for wonderful storytelling, reminiscing, and discussion. On Friday or Saturday night, it is commonplace for fans to learn more about the team's history while having a beverage and befriending complete strangers.

Overall, this is the greatest mouthpiece for fans to thank the organization for their efforts and for the organization to return the thanks to the fans that love them so much.

Attending a Blackhawks Convention should certainly be near the top of any Hawks fan's to-do list.

78 The Worst MVP Ever

When most Blackhawks fans think of impactful goalies who didn't spend much time with the team, the name Antti Niemi comes to mind. After all, he only spent one full season with the Hawks and brought the first Stanley Cup in 49 years to the Windy City.

But in 1952, the Blackhawks acquired a 25-year-old netminder who hadn't been able to convince the Toronto Maple Leafs that he could be their No. 1 man between the pipes. In five short years, Al Rollins emerged as one of the top goalies the franchise had ever seen.

He brought a Vezina Trophy and Stanley Cup championship ring with him to Chicago from the 1951 season, but Chicago wasn't the same pedigree as Toronto in 1952.

Right away, Rollins stepped into a disorganized group and kept the Hawks afloat in the 1952–53 season. For the first time since 1946, the Blackhawks qualified for the playoffs, and Rollins was the runner-up for the Hart Trophy (to Detroit's Gordie Howe). However, despite being the runner-up for the league's most valuable player award, Rollins didn't earn a first- or second-team All-Star nomination. Coincidentally, a young goalie named Glenn Hall made his debut that year in Detroit.

The following season, Rollins put together one of the most unique seasons in the history of the NHL. During the 1953–54 season, the Blackhawks were a biblical disaster. They posted only 31 points—37 fewer than the fifth-place New York Rangers and 43 points out of the playoffs—and their record may have been the least hideous part of their statistical record. They scored 19 fewer goals than any other team in the league and allowed 60 goals more than the second-worst total in the league in only 70 games!

Rollins played in 66 of the Blackhawks' 70 games and predictably had the worst numbers in the game. His 3.23 goals-against average was 0.63 goals per game worse than the next-lowest number, and his record (12–47–7) was awful.

Yet Rollins' performance on the ice behind a pathetic roster earned the respect of his peers, opposing coaches, and the media. Despite his miserable numbers, Rollins was selected to play in the

NHL All-Star Game and, when the season ended, won the Hart Memorial Trophy as the league's most valuable player.

Over the next three years, though, Rollins' numbers continued to appear mediocre despite the talent in front of him slowly improving. In 1954–55, he followed his Hart Trophy–winning season with only nine wins in 44 games and finished those three campaigns with a 42–96–34 record.

In the summer of 1957 the Blackhawks made a trade that changed the history of not only their organization but the league as a whole. It also pushed Rollins out of a job. Glenn Hall and Ted Lindsay were traded to Chicago by Detroit, and Rollins found himself on the road to the minors in Calgary. The trade placed a future Hall of Famer between the pipes in Chicago and effectively ended Rollins' career just three short seasons after he won the Hart.

His legacy gets lost among some of the bigger names in net for Chicago, especially the man who ultimately replaced him, but Rollins was one of the more respected players of the 1950s. It is doubtful that a player with a résumé as hideous as Rollins' was in 1954 will ever again receive consideration for a postseason award as prestigious as the Hart.

79 Howie Morenz Passes

Howie Morenz has been referred to as hockey's first legitimate superstar. Morenz was already a star in Canada before joining the Montreal Canadiens. In fact, he was so popular on his junior team that he almost turned down the chance to play with the Habs.

Playing center for the Stratford Midgets, Morenz was the best player in the Ontario Hockey Association. He led the junior league

Lysiak Sits

In 1983 Hawks center Tom Lysiak received the longest penalty for a tripping infraction in NHL history.

During a 6–1 Blackhawks victory against the Hartford Whalers on October 30, 1983, Lysiak had been kicked out of the faceoff circle by linesman Ron Foyt on a number of occasions. After one such occasion, Lysiak decided to exact some revenge.

The faceoff was won by the Whalers, and the puck was played to Hartford wing Sylvain Turgeon, who was against the boards near Foyt. Rather than playing the puck or Turgeon, Lysiak instead took the legs of the unsuspecting linesman out from under him. Foyt wasn't hurt, but the league took notice.

A rule had been put into place just the season before that was meant to crack down on referee abuse. With that rule as a statute, referee Dave Newell handed Lysiak a 20-game suspension. Lysiak and the NHL Players' Association immediately took the case to court, winning a 10-day restraining order blocking his suspension. Just two seasons prior, Philadelphia's Paul Holmgren was suspended only five games and fined $500 for punching a referee in the chest during a game.

Ultimately the suspension was upheld, and Lysiak was limited to 54 games that season.

in assists and points in 1920–21 before graduating to the senior league, where he was also the league leader in goals, assists, and points in 1921–22 and 1922–23.

After being heavily recruited by the Canadiens during the 1922–23 campaign, Morenz signed a three-year contract to leave Stratford and move on to Montreal. When news of his signing went public, all of Stratford began begging him to stay.

Morenz tried to back out of his deal with the Canadiens, but additional pressure—and the threat that he would be locked out of professional hockey if he didn't play in Montreal—eventually convinced him that it was time to leave Stratford.

He played 11 years for the Canadiens and was the best scorer in the game. On December 23, 1933, Morenz became the NHL's career leader with 249 goals. Less than two weeks later, though, Morenz suffered a major ankle injury.

When Morenz returned from the ankle injury a month later, he didn't have the same speed on the ice that had, in many ways, defined his game. When he struggled to produce late in the year, the fans in Montreal began booing him. Trade rumors started, and Morenz tried to ignore them during the 1934 playoffs. However, there was truth behind the rumors: Montreal traded Morenz to the Blackhawks on October 3, 1934, in a six-player deal that has gone down as the biggest blockbuster deal in the early years of the league.

Morenz had a decent first season in Chicago, posting 34 points in 48 games, but was held off the score sheet in the playoffs in 1935. He continued to struggle in Chicago as the following season began and was traded to the New York Rangers after 23 games in the 1935–36 season.

In total, Morenz played 71 games for Chicago, scoring 12 goals with 37 assists. Nothing about his time in Chicago was remarkable.

It was the end of his career that left an overwhelming impact on the Blackhawks, Canadiens, and the NHL. After finishing the 1935–36 season in New York, Morenz returned to Montreal. He was contributing again, occasionally showing flashes of the brilliance he had shown the fans in Montreal for a decade. But on January 28, 1937, everything changed.

Chasing a puck in the first period of a game against the Blackhawks in Montreal, Morenz lost an edge and crashed into the boards. Chicago defenseman Earl Seibert, who was pursuing him on the play, crashed on top of Morenz, snapping his left leg in a gruesome injury. He was helped off the ice and taken to the hospital, where it was found that his leg had four separate fractures. His hockey career was over.

While in the hospital, Morenz began struggling with depression and suffered a nervous breakdown. In early March doctors determined that Morenz had suffered a heart attack. He collapsed on the floor and died moments before his wife and coach arrived to visit him in the hospital on March 8, 1937.

Morenz's death, at only 34, devastated the hockey world. The Habs and Maroons wore black armbands during their game the following night after Morenz's wife insisted the game be played, despite both teams wanting to cancel. On March 10 more than 50,000 people stood in line to pay their respects to Morenz, whose casket lay in state at the home of the Canadiens, the Montreal Forum.

He was one of the game's first superstars, and his terrible injury and subsequent death linked the Blackhawks and Canadiens in one of the darkest chapters in NHL history.

80 The Historic Beginning of a Historic Season

For the first time in over a decade, the Blackhawks were entering a season with expectations. In 2008–09, a franchise that hadn't seen a sold-out United Center, much less the playoffs, in almost a decade was suddenly trendy. They jumped into the playoffs, finishing fourth in the Western Conference and making a surprising run all the way to the Conference Finals.

With their young core group all returning, the summer figured to provide little drama. The biggest free-agent concern on the roster was Martin Havlat, but most of the key players would be back. Certainly GM Stan Bowman wouldn't do anything too crazy…. And then Marian Hossa showed up.

The Blackhawks were the dark-horse favorite to make a deep run in the postseason, if not make the Stanley Cup Finals. Because of their history, nobody wanted to use the word *favorite* in Chicago, but there was a buzz. Season-ticket sales had jumped from 3,400 to over 12,000 the year before, and suddenly the Bulls weren't the hot ticket at the United Center, for the first time—ever.

After bringing out every Chicago dignitary and Blackhawks hero throughout the previous season's playoffs—from recently acquired Bears quarterback Jay Cutler to Bob Probert and Bobby Hull—the Hawks had to take their marketing game up to another level when they opened the doors for the 2009–10 season.

So, on Opening Night, they started what would become one of the most magical seasons in the franchise's long history by doing something that had never happened before. Once the public-address announcer had formally introduced each member of the roster and the coaching staff, there were a few more gentlemen who needed to join the team.

In full uniform, out skated Denis Savard. Then Tony Esposito joined him on the line with the current team. Then Stan Mikita skated out to a thunderous ovation. But when Bobby Hull, in full dress, skated out and took his place with Mikita, Esposito, Savard, Kane, and Toews on the ice for the National Anthem, the crowd exploded with an ovation the building hadn't felt since Michael Jordan retired (the second time).

Never before had those four Hall of Famers been on the same ice. And, considering the history between Hull and the organization, seeing him skate out again with the Indian-head crest on his chest brought tears to the eyes of many longtime fans. Symbolically, the team was putting to rest all of the negativity that had clouded the previous four decades of its history in one grand gesture.

The game that night lived up to the incredible hype provided by the pregame ceremony. A tedious, scoreless third period followed a second that included five goals, and regulation ended with the game knotted at 3–3. The contest didn't end until Andrew Ladd broke the stalemate in the ninth round of a shootout—the longest shootout in the franchise's history.

An exhausting night with a roller coaster of emotions was the perfect beginning to what would become such a memorable campaign for the Blackhawks. But, for many fans, seeing the four great Hall of Famers on the ice with the current team signified what was to come: history.

81 An Epic Celebration

If the $30,000 championship rings the organization gave every player weren't over-the-top enough, the ceremony before the 2010–11 home opener was one more step into legend.

From the red carpet walked on by members of the current team and some of the organization's greatest players to a video playing while photos were projected on the ice surface, everything that led up to the entrance of captain Jonathan Toews and the Stanley Cup on that night was both overwhelming and perfect.

A team that accomplished what Hall of Fame players couldn't for 49 years deserved the tears of all 22,000-plus people. The night was both bittersweet and powerfully celebratory at the same time.

It opened with stirring music and a video tribute that reminded fans of two things: the incredible season that was and the reality that the team on the ice that night was not the same as the one that celebrated in Philadelphia.

Images of Brent Sopel, Dustin Byfuglien, Andrew Ladd, Kris Versteeg, Antti Niemi, John Madden, Ben Eager, Adam Burish, and Cristobal Huet flashed across the screen, faces and names that would not represent the Blackhawks in the new season.

Also gracing the screen were images of Dave Bolland scoring short-handed goals, Marian Hossa's incredible overtime game-winner against Nashville, and Patrick Kane's Cup-clinching skate-off goal in Philadelphia.

Once the stage was set and emotions were running wild, the Blackhawks front office was introduced, including owner Rocky Wirtz.

Then the players were introduced, beginning with the new faces. As the holdovers from the championship team skated onto the ice, the crescendo built until captain Jonathan Toews entered the arena with the Stanley Cup between his hands.

Flashbulbs exploded like lightning followed by thunderous cheering that registered decibel readings the building may never hear again. Tears were swallowed by thanks for the years of waiting coming to an end.

Wirtz addressed a packed house and received a reception worthy of a man who helped end a 49-year championship drought. When Rocky took over the team after his father passed away, every step taken was to ensure that the Chicago Blackhawks were fighting to be a successful franchise.

"Three years ago we began a journey to make the Chicago Blackhawks relevant again and return the proud franchise to its rightful place at the top of the National Hockey League," said Wirtz. "Every player who was a member of our team, whether here tonight or elsewhere, will forever be etched in our memories, our history and, of course, Lord Stanley's Cup."

The crowd chanted "Rocky! Rocky!" as his remarks came to a close, and the rhetorical questions were asked in the 300 level of the United Center: Did you ever think you would hear a Wirtz talk about committing to staying on top? and Did you ever think a Wirtz would say, "Let's raise the banner"?

When members of the 1961 team rolled out the new banner and presented it to the remaining members of the 2010 championship team, it brought Wirtz's comments full-circle; there was a connection with history in the organization now, and they were committed to winning again.

Names like Mikita and Hull and Pilote, all in the Hall of Fame, were on hand to present the new banner to Toews, Kane, Keith, and the current group of champions.

Slowly, the banner was skated the length of the ice, passing the Cup at the center of the arena before reaching the lines that would take it into the rafters.

Troy Brouwer admitted later that a few players needed a tissue after the banner assumed its position next to the other three on the Blackhawks' side of the United Center rafters.

As the league's commissioner looked on, one of the original franchises in the league's history made an aesthetically powerful statement that professional hockey in Chicago was not only back but would never be the same again. The striking departure from the previous regime wasn't lost on a single veteran fan that night.

82 The U.C.

When Harvey Wittenberg told fans departing the Chicago Stadium for the last time to remember the roar, they did so by taking it with them to the new building—the United Center.

While the U.C. is certainly a significantly more modern facility than the old barn, the new building proved it can handle the noise during the 2010 Stanley Cup Finals when, during the National Anthem before Game 2, the crowd was recorded at 122 decibels. That topped the 121 decibels reading from Game 1's National Anthem performance.

It all began at the U.C. when the lockout ended on January 25, 1995. The Blackhawks lost to the Edmonton Oilers—a result all too familiar over the previous 15 years at the Stadium—in the first

The Circus Trip

During the 1984–85 season, the Bulls and Blackhawks were sent on an extended road trip during the month of November because Ringling Bros. Barnum and Bailey's Circus was coming to the Chicago Stadium.

Every year since, two of the highest-profile teams in their respective leagues have been kicked out of their home in favor of lions, elephants, and clowns. Today, this annual venture is known as the "Circus Trip."

Over the first 25 years of the Circus Trip, the Blackhawks have had a winning record only three times. They have been winless on six occasions and three times have accumulated zero points during the trip, which is usually five or six games and two weeks in length. Oddly enough, one of the three winless trips came in 1992, a season after which the Hawks played in the Stanley Cup Finals.

NHL games at the U.C., as Joe Murphy scored the first Blackhawks goal in their new home.

The following season, the Blackhawks set a new full-season record for the NHL by averaging 20,415 fans per game. Early in the building's existence, the seats were packed on a nightly basis. Unfortunately, the Blackhawks did not enjoy similar success to the building's other tenant—the Bulls—and the decline of the team in the late 1990s led to many empty seats.

Indeed, in 2006–07, the Blackhawks officially bottomed out, averaging only 12,727 paying customers per night. When rivals like the Red Wings came to town, there were nights when fans for the visiting team outnumbered the hometown fans in the building.

Thanks to solid drafting, free-agent acquisitions, and a new-found marketing approach (meaning any marketing), the team climbed to averaging over 16,800 per game in 2007–08 and have led the league in average attendance each year since the 2008–09 season, actually averaging at least 104 percent of capacity over that stretch. It took time, but the roar returned.

Improvements to the structure have accompanied the growing hockey attendance. The 300-level concourse, which initially featured only small televisions by each entryway, now has large video boards above the concession stands.

The team also cut out part of the 300-level seats over the summers of 2009 and 2010, adding bar areas from which fans with standing-room tickets can enjoy the game in the four corners of the arena.

While the U.C. hasn't built the same history as the old Madhouse on Madison, it is still one of the loudest arenas in the NHL. Unless a person stands in front of you, there isn't an obstructed view of the ice anywhere in the building. And the food is classic Chicago.

Here are some other fun facts from the Blackhawks' time at the United Center:

- Tony Amonte scored the first hat trick in the U.C. on February 22, 1996, against St. Louis.
- The Blackhawks set an indoor attendance record for the franchise on February 15, 1997, when 22,817 fans came to see Wayne Gretzky and the New York Rangers.
- On March 19, 1998, Denis Savard became the fifth former Blackhawks player—and first at the United Center—to have his number retired by the franchise.
- On October 12, 2000, the team unveiled the Blackhawks statue titled "Badge of Honor" in honor of the franchise's 75th season in the NHL. In the fall of 2011, a new statue honoring Stan Mikita and Bobby Hull will join this great monument.

83 Roll to Rockford

Something absolutely every Blackhawks fan should do is drive 90 miles. For a lot of professional sports teams, the future faces of the franchise are developing their talents in a different state, if not a different time zone. In hockey, many times it's even a different country. But for Blackhawks fans, all you have to do is drive 90 miles west to Rockford to see the IceHogs skate.

Since 2007 the Rockford IceHogs have been the highest-level minor league affiliate of the Chicago Blackhawks, playing in the American Hockey League. However, many fans don't realize how close they are to seeing tomorrow's stars for incredibly affordable prices.

On the ice, the great game of hockey is still played. The players aren't as experienced or as well paid as the players you'll see at the United Center, but they're just a phone call away from the red sweater. One of the great advantages the Blackhawks enjoy by having their AHL affiliate so close is, if a player comes down with the flu on a home-game day (like Patrick Sharp did before Opening Night in 2010), a replacement can be in Chicago within a couple hours if needed.

Some of the names familiar to Blackhawks fans that have come through Rockford include Cam Barker, David Bolland, Troy Brouwer, Dustin Byfuglien, Corey Crawford, Jake Dowell, Niklas Hjalmarsson, Antti Niemi, Jack Skille, and Kris Versteeg.

For relative pennies next to the cost of tickets at the United Center, you can watch great hockey players and see, in many cases, the boys who will eventually be men in the National Hockey League some day. The atmosphere at games isn't nearly as professional as the approach on Madison Street, and the entertainment is great for kids of all ages. In fact, if you hang around the lobby of the MetroCentre for a while after the game, you might even score an elusive autograph from one of tomorrow's heroes.

Parking is available in a garage across the street from the stadium (which has a walkway from the second level of the MetroCentre) or in a number of lots in the surrounding blocks, and there are a number of watering holes in the vicinity that are worthy of a few hard-earned dollars before a game.

For more information on attending an IceHogs game in Rockford, there are a number of resources. 1) Consult the team's website, www.IceHogs.com. There, fans can get directions to the game, view the team's statistics and schedule, and buy tickets to the game of their choice. 2) Call or email the team directly. For special requests—perhaps a name on the scoreboard for a birthday—the team can be reached by phone at (815) 986-6465 or by email at IceHogs@IceHogs.com. 3) Go to the window at the box office. The MetroCentre is located at 300 Elm Street in Rockford, Illinois.

Fans will find an electric, hockey-loving environment and names they'll soon see playing for the Blackhawks. And it's only 90 miles from the United Center.

84 The Masked Man

Jacque Plante is remembered as one of the great goaltenders in the history of the National Hockey League.

Plante was an innovator between the pipes in many ways. He handled the puck more than any netminder of his time. During his

11 seasons with the Montreal Canadiens, between 1953 and 1963, he won six Stanley Cups, including five straight. His sweater has been retired by the Habs, and he was inducted into the Hockey Hall of Fame in 1978.

But it was on November 7, 1959, that he made perhaps the biggest start of his career.

Early in the 1959 season, Plante missed a handful of games because of a sinusitis operation. Because he also had asthma, he began wearing a crude, homemade mask made of fiberglass during practices. During games, however, goalies did not wear masks at that time; Plante only wore the mask to protect himself outside of game action. Facing the Rangers in New York on November 1, that changed.

Plante's nose was broken early in the first period by Andy Bathgate, the Rangers' hardest-shooting forward. The shot reportedly cut his face badly, and Plante required stitches. After a delay of over 20 minutes, Plante was allowed to return to the ice, but he was wearing one of his masks.

"Jacques came back to the bench and told Toe, 'I'm ready to go back in, but I have to wear my mask,'" remembered Hall of Famer Jean Beliveau.

Though Montreal coach Toe Blake didn't like Plante wearing the mask, the Canadiens won the game 3–1 that night. Blake did not want Plante to continue wearing the mask, but the goalie was firm in his stance. "If I don't wear the mask, I'm not playing," Plante told the Montreal media.

A few days later, Plante made history when he started an NHL game at the Montreal Forum against the Blackhawks wearing a mask. That night the Habs and Hawks skated to a 2–2 tie, and the Habs didn't lose for 18 games after Plante started wearing the mask. Plante won the Vezina Tophy after the 1958–59 season and was selected to the NHL's All-Star first team, all while wearing a mask.

It's nearly impossible to imagine goalies playing without masks today, but it was a foreign idea in 1959.

When asked about Plante's mask on the 50th anniversary of its first appearance in a game, the *Montreal Gazette*'s Red Fisher told NHL.com that it caused a stir. "When he came out with the mask, you could feel and hear the buzz of the crowd," Fisher recalled.

In 1972 Plante wrote the book *Goaltending*, which was published in both English and French. In the book, he describes in great detail the process of becoming a goalie from game-day preparation, off-ice exercises, and how to appropriately select equipment.

Yet it wasn't for his puck handling, teaching, or writing that Plante made his biggest impact on the game. History will remember that it was against the Chicago Blackhawks, in Montreal, that Plante started his first game wearing a mask.

Since Plante started that game on November 7, 1959, masks have become part of the most basic safety equipment in hockey. Indeed, the mask has evolved into the on-ice personality of modern goalies, bearing elaborate, custom artwork created for each player.

85 Probie

When the Blackhawks signed free-agent forward Bob Probert in 1994, to say it raised eyebrows is putting it lightly. He was coming off a 1993–94 season in which he tallied just 17 points and racked up 275 penalty minutes in only 66 games, and the laundry list of off-ice issues he was dealing with was a mile long. In fact, the first year he was a "member" of the Blackhawks, Chicago paid $5,000 per week for him to be in rehab; hockey wasn't part of his life.

Bob Probert (left) pulls the jersey over St. Louis Blues' Tony Twist's head during a fight in the first period on February 8, 1996, in St. Louis. Probert's propensity for fighting may have led to his early death from chronic traumatic encephalopathy.

He had dealt with so many problems that most onlookers didn't see his great hands and smooth skating through the police reports and legendary penalty-minute totals. Most fans even today don't recall that, in 1991–92, Probert scored 20 goals in only 63 games with the Red Wings; the focus was instead on his 276 penalty minutes that year.

During his time in Detroit, Probert had been expelled from the NHL on two occasions, been caught trying to bring cocaine back into the U.S., had twice left rehab without authorization, and had even been deported from the United States.

But Chicago needed an enforcer to protect their scorers—especially Savard—and Probert was available. His approach was simple: do what it takes to help the team. In his article "The Enforcers," from *Blackhawks* magazine, Boron describes enforcing as being "about protecting your teammates, but it's also about changing the momentum of the game. A big fight, win or lose, can really spark your team. When you're down by a goal or two and you want to do something to turn the game around, a good fight or even just sticking up for your team can definitely change a game."

Probie brought that approach every night. In his first season in Chicago after his year in rehab, Probert showed the full array of talents that he brought to the roster. He played in 78 games, scored 19 goals, and added 21 assists as the Blackhawks made a run deep into the playoffs.

The following season, for the only time in his career, Probert played in all 82 games. His offensive production dipped to 23 points and his penalty minutes skyrocketed to 326—89 more than the year before.

Despite playing in only 14 games during the 1997–98 season because of a rotator cuff injury, the Hawks gave Probert, then 33, a three-year extension. During those three seasons, the Hawks received a return on their investment of only 18 goals and 37 assists. During the 1999–2000 season, Probert passed two significant milestones: 3,000 career penalty minutes and six years sober. The other notable footnote on Probert's Chicago career was that, on February 13, 1999, he scored the final goal in the history of the legendary Maple Leaf Gardens in Toronto.

Throughout his career, Probert was the protector of some of the great scorers of their eras. From Steve Yzerman in Detroit to Savard and Tony Amonte in Chicago, he had no problem letting people know that he was on the ice to protect his team's top offensive threat.

To this day, some of his fights are still the most viewed online. The site HockeyFights.com hosts a number of memorable fights,

Hawks All-Time PIM Leaders

In the long history of the Chicago Blackhawks, there have been some great fighters to wear the Indian-head sweater. Over the years, 10 players have reached a dubious benchmark while playing for the Hawks: 1,000 penalty minutes.

Here are the top 10 penalty-minute recipients in Blackhawks history:

- Chris Chelios—664 games played, 1,495 penalty minutes
- Keith Magnuson—589 games played, 1,442 penalty minutes
- Al Secord—466 games played, 1,426 penalty minutes
- Dave Manson—431 games played, 1,322 penalty minutes
- Phil Russell—504 games played, 1,288 penalty minutes
- Stan Mikita—1,394 games played, 1,270 penalty minutes
- Bob Probert—461 games played, 1,210 penalty minutes
- Pierre Pilote—821 games played, 1,205 penalty minutes
- Eric Nesterenko—1,013 games played, 1,012 penalty minutes
- Denis Savard—881 games played, 1,005 penalty minutes

including one that lasted almost two minutes against Marty McSorley from 1994. His fights against another great enforcer, Tie Domi, are the thing of legend, and rarely did he lace up his skates against Stu Grimson without dropping the gloves. At the end of his career, Probert was credited with being involved in 246 fights.

Probert was honored with a Heritage Night on February 22, 2009, and he dropped the ceremonial puck before Game 3 of the 2009 Western Conference Finals between the Hawks and Red Wings.

Unfortunately, those fights added up. On July 5, 2010, Probert collapsed and died suddenly from heart failure while on a boat with his family. A few months later, researchers at Boston University found the same degenerative disease, chronic traumatic encephalopathy, which has also been found in more than 20 deceased professional football players.

86 Johnny's West

Every fan of a team wants to feel like they really "know" their favorite players. Seeing a player in public or at an event always makes for a great story or photograph.

Seeing behind the curtain of the professional game—seeing how the players train—is something truly unique. Thousands of fans attend spring-training baseball games in Florida and Arizona to see how teams prepare for their seasons, and fans flock to open practices for NFL teams during their preseasons as well. But not many professional sports teams allow fans to see their team practice during the season.

To rhetorically answer the infamous rant made by basketball star Allen Iverson: yes, we're talking about practice!

A wonderful way for Blackhawks fans to see their favorite players in action without paying for game tickets is to attend an open practice at Johnny's IceHouse West.

Johnny's IceHouse opened in 1997 and has hosted many youth and adult leagues. It started a partnership with the Chicago Blackhawks that resulted in the opening of a second facility, Johnny's West, on February 1, 2010, at 2550 West Madison Street.

Johnny's West is the official practice facility of the Blackhawks and is also the location for the Blackhawks Prospect Camp and preseason training camp.

The open space at Johnny's West creates some incredible opportunities to see players in ways fans could never experience the Blackhawks at the United Center. If you want to stand and watch players going through drills at ice level, that's possible. The seating, though limited, is the equivalent of lower-100-level seating at the United Center, just elevated about 10 feet above the ice surface.

A sense of intimacy is created by watching the players when the lights and cameras are off. Getting a chance to see how hard the players work in a game is expected, but seeing the preparation that goes into that performance creates a relationship with players that not only makes a fan feel closer to the action but also leads to a greater appreciation for the amount of work it takes to be a professional hockey player.

Another aspect of practices that cannot be experienced through a television or from seats in an arena is observing the relationships between the players. In practice, the pressure is off, and players can have the ability to interact with each other on a personal level. Seeing the players joking around with each other, showing off, and encouraging each other is a reminder that hockey is still a game.

And while the team doesn't make any promises, some fans have been fortunate enough to get their favorite player's autograph after a practice session at Johnny's West.

On the Blackhawks' official website (Blackhawks.NHL.com), there is a schedule of open practices that fans can attend for free at Johnny's West.

87 Watch the Kids

It isn't quite the same as Christmas in July, but every year the Blackhawks open the doors of their organization in the middle of the summer so their hockey-hungry fans can catch a glimpse of what the future of the organization might be.

Some of the young men arrive on their summer break from college. Others fly in to Chicago from as far away as Russia, Sweden, Germany, and other European countries.

Some players have a nice professional contract signed and are trying to justify their salary to the team, while others don't have a contract and are desperately fighting for a chance to play the game they love for a living.

Some of the players were just drafted by the organization a few weeks prior, while others have been under control of the team for two or three years.

It is the annual Blackhawks Prospect Camp.

The function of the camp is for the team's management to see the talent in the system skate against each other. Some of the players are as young as 18, and others can be as old as 25 or 26; all of the players, though, just want to play hockey.

Blackhawks beat reporters from Chicago's media outlets attend the camp for the same reason as both the team's management and the fans. Who will be the next great scorer or shutdown defenseman to wear the Indian-head sweater?

For fans, the week is a fabulous look behind the curtain of professional hockey. There is no charge for fans to sit on the same bleachers as the team's head coach and general manager at Johnny's West, and the opportunity to see great hockey skill on display in the middle of the summer many times is the perfect remedy for the off-season blues.

Black Hawks Become Blackhawks

For nearly 60 years, the name of the team was the Chicago Black Hawks. Everything from the Stanley Cup engraving to hockey cards had the team's name split in half.

However, during the 1985–86 season, some digging through historical documents uncovered the original contract between Major McLaughlin and the National Hockey League.

It identified the Chicago franchise as the Chicago Blackhawks— one word. From that point forward, the team has been known as they are today: as the Blackhawks.

The players take part in a number of skill drills run by scouts and coaches of the Blackhawks. They are then placed onto rosters and scrimmage each other in a round-robin style tournament. There are fast line changes, smooth goals, penalties, and even fights during the games. All played at full speed because, after all, this is a tryout to play professional hockey.

The opportunity is given to the players to show management that they belong, and some players have made a strong enough statement that their lives have changed. In 2010 defenseman Nick Leddy anticipated a return to the University of Minnesota for his sophomore year. After impressing fans and brass alike, he received a contract and was brought into camp.

Leddy was on the United Center ice on Opening Night in October 2010, less than 17 months after he graduated from high school.

The hard part is the end of the camp when buses arrive to take players to locations other than Chicago. Some of the players are headed back to college without a contract. Others might be headed to juniors or the AHL in Rockford. Unfortunately, some are just sent home; many players arrive as free agents and leave with the same designation.

For fans interested in seeing some of the names and faces that will be skating for the Blackhawks at some point in the future, the Blackhawks Prospect Camp is an opportunity to do just that.

88 Rent-a—Hall of Famer

Many Chicago Blackhawks greats have unfortunately left Chicago at the ends of their careers. Glenn Hall, Steve Larmer, Pierre Pilote,

Denis Savard, Jeremy Roenick, Doug Wilson, and Chris Chelios were a few of the team's great—and, in Roenick's, Chelios', and (hopefully) Larmer's and Wilson's cases, future—Hall of Famers who played the best years of their careers in Chicago, only to leave in their careers' twilight.

However, the Hawks didn't only *donate* Hall of Famers. There have been a number of great players who played games in Chicago at the end of their great careers.

Probably the biggest name to come through Chicago as a rented superstar was Bobby Orr, who played only 26 games in two seasons—with a season out of the league because of injury—but still averaged more than one point per game. After all those incredible years in Boston, Orr just didn't have much left to give when he came to Chicago.

Perhaps the most infamous career to end in Chicago was Michel Goulet. After 11 great seasons with the Quebec Nordiques, he was acquired in a blockbuster, six-player trade at the deadline in 1990. What made the Chicago portion of Goulet's career noteworthy wasn't that he had nothing left in the tank but how his career ended.

Goulet gave Chicago two seasons of 65 and 63 points in 1990–91 and 1991–92, respectively, before his production fell off to 44 points in 1992–93. Late in the 1993–94 season, in a game against the Canadiens in the Montreal Forum, Goulet crashed into the boards headfirst in a horrific accident. He was knocked out on the play and suffered a severe concussion, which eventually forced him out of the game for good.

Like Orr, Sid Abel was one of the best of his time. He played parts of 12 seasons in Detroit before winding up in Chicago in 1952. He only managed to play in 42 games over the next two seasons, scoring only five goals, before hanging up his skates.

Of course Glenn Hall wasn't the only player the Blackhawks acquired from Detroit in 1957. Ted Lindsay was a great forward in Detroit who was run out of town because of the off-ice politics between the Detroit organization and Lindsay, who had the nerve to help launch the Players' Association. He was more productive than Orr or Abel was in Chicago, posting 123 points in 206 games. He walked away before the Hawks' Stanley Cup run in the 1960–61 season.

Some other Hall of Famers who had a cup of tea in the Windy City include Paul Coffey (10 games in the 1998–99 season), Jack Stewart (1950–52), Phil Housley (2001–03), and Allan Stanley (1954–56).

Arguably the greatest hand-me-down individual to impact the evolution of the Blackhawks organization was an owner. James D. Norris, whose father owned the Detroit Red Wings, was part of a group—including Arthur Wirtz—that purchased the Blackhawks in 1946 when Major McLaughlin passed away.

Despite the laundry list of great players to leave Chicago at the ends of their careers, Chicago accepted almost as many donations. Certainly Orr didn't have the impact on Chicago that Chelios did in Detroit, and Goulet didn't have the impact on Chicago that Roenick did in his various other stops before retiring. But the Blackhawks has been the short- and long-term home of some of the greatest names in the game's great history.

89 Hawks–North Stars Rivalry

During the 1980s there might not have been a better rivalry in the National Hockey League than the one that existed between the Chicago Blackhawks and the Minnesota North Stars. The rivalry between the cities was deeper than hockey; the Minnesota Vikings and Chicago Bears play in the same division as well. But the rivalry on the ice was the primary focus of the fans for a decade.

In the old Norris Division, the battle between the North Stars and Blackhawks was always heated. Between 1982 and 1986, the teams combined to win the division title in four of the five seasons, with each team claiming the top spot twice.

With Minnesota's Dino Ciccarelli, Bobby Smith, Mark Napier, and Brian Bellows doing battle against Denis Savard, Al Secord, and Steve Larmer, the teams had plenty of big names on the ice.

From the 1981–82 season until 1992–93, the Norris Division's playoff champion would face the Smythe Division's playoff champion in the Campbell Conference Finals. Of the 11 times the Campbell Conference Finals were decided in this format, the Blackhawks represented the Norris on six occasions, while the North Stars appeared twice.

But it wasn't only in the standings that the two teams battled each other. The Blackhawks and North Stars faced off in four consecutive postseasons. In 1982 the teams met in the division semifinals, and each team scored 14 goals in the four games. However, the Blackhawks won the best-of-five series three games to one. In 1983 the teams met in the division finals for the first time. The Blackhawks emerged victorious, winning the series four games to one, but only outscored the North Stars by six goals in the five games. In 1984 it was once again in the division semifinals. This best-of-five series required the maximum number of games, and the North Stars won the series. In the five games, the North Stars outscored the Blackhawks by only four goals. Finally, in 1985 they met in the division finals again. The Blackhawks advanced in six games but only outscored the North Stars by four goals in the series.

In the four postseasons, each of these series was one of the most physical in the entire NHL playoffs. The scoring margins bear witness to how close the contests were between the two teams, but the action on the ice was much more explosive than any box score could demonstrate.

There was a break in the two teams facing off in the postseason until 1990, but fans weren't disappointed when the two teams again faced off in consecutive seasons. The playoff format had changed since their battles in the early 1980s, and the division semifinals was a best-of-seven affair when the two teams squared off in the spring of 1990. The Blackhawks again won a close series, defeating the North Stars in the maximum seven games and only outscoring Minnesota by three goals in the series.

Perhaps the most heated and legendary series between the two teams came in the division semifinals in 1991.

90 The '91 Debacle

In October 1990 the Chicago Blackhawks began what would be one of the most striking seasons in the history of the franchise.

Head coach Mike Keenan was entering his third season behind the bench, and the first two had not come without turmoil. Because of a rift between the head coach and some of the more successful players on the roster, Keenan (also the team's general manager) traded fan favorite Denis Savard to Montreal for Chicago native Chris Chelios during the summer.

Dirk Graham, who Keenan named captain the year before replacing Savard, returned as the team's captain with perennial All-Star Steve Larmer, Doug Wilson, and Chelios serving as his alternates. As some of the team's stars, like Larmer, aged, some younger players started to emerge on the roster to add more explosive firepower to the team.

One of the rookies on the 1990–91 roster actually burst onto the scene in the 1990 postseason. Ed Belfour was a revelation in net, winning the Calder Memorial Trophy as the league's top rookie, the Vezina Trophy as the league's best goalie, and the William M. Jennings Trophy for allowing the fewest goals. In fact, he barely missed out on a sweep at the NHL Awards that year, finishing the runner-up to St. Louis' Brett Hull for the Hart Memorial Trophy as league MVP.

Another exciting young player whose presence played a large role in making Savard expendable was Jeremy Roenick. In his first full season in 1989–90, Roenick scored 26 goals and then put on a show in the playoffs, scoring 11 goals in 20 postseason games. For

Minnesota Helps Chicago

Was it irony or karma?

On April 10, 2011, Minnesota had a wonderful chance at redemption against the franchise they once loved. The Dallas Stars—yes, the former Minnesota North Stars—came into town for the final game of the NHL regular season, and the Minnesota Wild became a footnote in NHL history.

With a win and two points, the Stars would reach 97 points and qualify for the playoffs. With a loss, whether it came with one point in overtime or not, the Stars would be cleaning out their lockers on Monday.

Dallas had dominated the regular-season series and were playing well. The Wild were...bad. On paper, this game was a no-contest.

Earlier that Sunday, the Blackhawks had lost to the Detroit Red Wings in regulation, opening the door for the Stars to catch them in points and, with the tie-breakers in their favor, steal the playoff berth away from the defending champions.

But it wasn't to be. Minnesota stunned their former team, ending their season.

Was it payback for the Stars leaving the fans who adored them? Or was it a tip of the cap to Chicago for ending the Hawks' 1991 season prematurely? Either way, Chicago fans appreciated the effort from the Wild.

as good as he had looked before, Roenick's real coming-out party was the 1990–91 season; he jumped to 41 goals and 94 points and was one of the three Blackhawks representatives in the All-Star Game.

The Blackhawks hosted the 1991 All-Star Game at the Chicago Stadium. It was a memorable game, despite many fans in (and out) of Chicago feeling that Belfour had been robbed of a spot on the roster.

One of the Hawks to appear in the All-Star Game that year was Larmer, the steady veteran. This was the first season in Larmer's career that Savard wouldn't be on the ice with him, but he proved to be worthy of his All-Star nomination. Prior to 1990, only six times in the history of the franchise had someone eclipsed 100 points in a season; Larmer became the seventh, posting 101 points (44 goals, 57 assists) in his best season as a professional.

With all the incredible individual performances that took place during the season and the emotional spark provided to the fan base in Chicago by the All-Star Game, the momentum and talent was undeniable. Graham won the Selke Trophy as the best defensive forward in the league, and the Hawks barely snuck past the rival St. Louis Blues for the first (and only) Presidents' Trophy in the history of the franchise.

The table appeared to be set for the Blackhawks to make a serious run at their first Stanley Cup in 30 years. When the playoff brackets were released, the Blackhawks were the top seed in the Campbell Conference and the Norris Division champions. They would face the fourth-place team in the division, the Minnesota North Stars, in the first round in a great, heated series between rivals.

No series between Minnesota and Chicago was ever easy, and this was no different. In Chicago for Game 1, the two teams skated to a thrilling overtime conclusion. Unfortunately for Hawks fans, it was Minnesota that came away with the 4–3 victory. The

Blackhawks handled their business in Game 2, easily winning 5–2, and emerged with a close 6–5 win in Minnesota in Game 3.

After Game 3, though, the North Stars blew the best team in the regular season away. In the final three games in the series, the North Stars outscored the Hawks 12–2, including a shocking 6–0 shutout in Chicago in Game 5.

The North Stars rode the momentum of their upset all the way to the Stanley Cup Finals, but Mario Lemieux and the Pittsburgh Penguins won their first Stanley Cup championship.

Momentum wasn't only in Minnesota, though. The Pulford-Keenan regime continued to isolate the team's superstars, and the roster felt more turnover in the summer of 1991. The following season, the evolving Chicago Blackhawks didn't exit the playoffs as quickly—or quietly—as they had the year before.

91 The 1991 All-Star Game

One of the more emotional nights in the history of the Chicago Stadium took place on January 19, 1991.

The hockey game that took place was an exciting, high-scoring affair. In total, 16 goals were scored, 11 of which were from the home team. But on this day, it wasn't the Blackhawks hosting a rival; the National Hockey League's All-Star Game was played in Chicago, and the theater provided by the event was second-to-none.

It was the first time since 1974 that Chicago had hosted an All-Star Game, and it was arguably the most memorable midseason event in the league's history. As NHL president John Ziegler said before the game, "There's no other building, none of the fans like being in the Chicago Stadium. The roof's going to go off." And it nearly did.

When the All-Stars were introduced, there were a few notable ovations. Obviously the three representatives of the Blackhawks in the game—forwards Steve Larmer and Jeremy Roenick and defenseman Chris Chelios—received a strong show of support from their faithful fans. It was the first All-Star appearance for Roenick, who was one of the young stars in the league in 1991, while Chelios was voted a starter and named an alternate captain in his hometown.

But perhaps the strongest and most emotional response from the crowd during introductions came when a member of the visiting Wales Conference team was named. Denis Savard, who was a member of the Montreal Canadiens, was introduced and received a hero's welcome from the fans he had thrilled for a decade. It was obviously an emotional moment for Savard as well as the sold-out crowd at the Chicago Stadium, and it was only the beginning of a powerful performance from the stands that, in history's recollection of the event, overshadowed the game.

Once the players were lined up, the great Wayne Messmer assumed his regular position on the ice to provide the Canadian and American National Anthems. As had been the tradition in Chicago, the fans respectfully received "O Canada." But when the great organ at the old barn hit the first note of "The Star-Spangled Banner," the roar was unbelievable.

This All-Star Game happened to be taking place during the first war with Iraq: Operation Desert Storm. All of the players had decals on their helmets as a gesture of support for the troops from both countries who were fighting in the Middle East. Some players, including Wayne Gretzky, briefly asked that the game be skipped because of the unfolding events overseas, but the league pressed forward with the game only two days after the conflict began.

Thanks in large part to the advent of cable television, and now with YouTube preserving great moments in television history, the National Anthem at the Stadium that day might be the most remembered moment in the history of the building. Messmer did a wonderful job performing the song, but no one in the building would have known it; the applause from the crowd overwhelmed the performance.

There were flags hanging over the edge of the 300 level, and some fans even smuggled sparklers into the stadium. With all due respect to the incredible moments provided by Michael Jordan and the Bulls, this was the finest moment from Chicago fans in the Madhouse on Madison.

When the game ended, Leafs forward Vincent Damphousse won the Most Valuable Player award by scoring four goals; only Gretzky and Mario Lemieux matched that number at that time. Blues center Adam Oates had five points in the game but had to watch Damphousse take the MVP honors.

Hundreds of thousands of people have watched the National Anthem performance from the 1991 All-Star Game on YouTube, and it's something everyone should take a moment to watch again.

92 '92 Sweep

Following their Presidents' Trophy–winning 1990–91 season and subsequent implosion as the hands of the North Stars in the post-season, the 1991–92 season figured to be a fascinating season for the Blackhawks. It was also the 75th anniversary of the National Hockey League, and each of the Original Six teams celebrated by wearing throwback sweaters for certain games.

The regular season that year lived up to its intriguing preface. Eddie Belfour had company between the pipes in Chicago, as Dominik Hasek was suddenly competing for—and earning—valuable minutes. From an individual perspective, two Blackhawks had noteworthy seasons on the stat sheet.

Jeremy Roenick followed Steve Larmer's lead from the season before and passed the 100-point mark, scoring 53 goals and adding 50 assists; it was the first of three straight 100-point seasons for Roenick in Chicago.

On the other end of the spectrum, Mike Peluso broke Dave Manson's record for penalty minutes in a single season, piling up 408 minutes in the box in only 63 games.

As a team, the Blackhawks had a fairly disappointing regular season. They finished second in the Norris Division behind Detroit, totaling only 87 points, but still qualified for the playoffs. Once they were in the postseason, the game changed completely for the Hawks.

In a first-round matchup against their rivals from St. Louis, the Blackhawks lost a double-overtime thriller on the road to suddenly trail in the series two games to one. From that point forward, though, the Blackhawks made history.

The third game against St. Louis was the last time the Blackhawks lost for almost a month. The team ran off 11 straight wins, marching in dominating fashion all the way to the Stanley Cup Finals for the first time since 1973.

After a four-game sweep of Detroit, followed by a four-game sweep of Edmonton, the Blackhawks found themselves staring at the defending champions from Pittsburgh. Mario Lemieux, Kevin Stevens, and company also swept their way into the Finals, beating Boston in the Eastern Conference Finals.

Neither Finals series was even close, either. The Blackhawks outscored the Oilers 21–8, including an 8–2 opening-game

Sports' Longest Droughts

Twice the Blackhawks have had long championship droughts. They spent 23 years (1938–61) between their second and third Stanley Cup championships and broke the longest active drought between Stanley Cup championships in 2010, when they won the Cup again after 49 years. With their win in 2010, the Hawks passed the "honor" for longest Stanley Cup drought to the Toronto Maple Leafs.

However, neither drought was the longest in professional sports. Here are the longest active championship droughts in the big four professional sports in North America (as of Summer 2011):

- Major League Baseball: Chicago Cubs—1908
- National Football League: Arizona Cardinals—1947* (pre-Super Bowl)
- National Basketball Association: Sacramento Kings—1951
- National Hockey League: Toronto Maple Leafs—1967

There are also a number of teams in each league that have never won a championship: NHL (11), NBA (13), MLB (8), and NFL (14 haven't won a Super Bowl; seven haven't won an NFL Championship Game or Super Bowl).

blowout. Meanwhile, the Penguins outscored the Bruins 19–7 in their series, scoring five goals in each of the last three games.

When the puck dropped for the Finals, there was no question that the offense would be the story. Lemieux and Stevens ranked first and second in the NHL in scoring, and Roenick ranked in the top 10 as well. But, at least on paper, the advantage appeared to be in the Hawks' locker room. Belfour finished the year with the second-best goals-against average in the league, behind only Patrick Roy.

Unfortunately, the defending champs were just too much for the Hawks. Lemieux became the second player in league history to win consecutive Conn Smythe Trophies, leading the way to a second-straight sweep. The fourth and final game was an epic, heavyweight bout that, unfortunately for Blackhawks fans, ended in a 6–5 Penguins victory at the Chicago Stadium.

After the season, the dismantling of the team under Mike Keenan's regime continued, but Keenan's job as head coach did not. The Blackhawks removed one of Keenan's titles after the Finals, making him only the general manager and handing the bench to his hand-picked successor, Darryl Sutter.

Belfour's insecurity also played a factor in the roster that summer, as the Hawks dealt Hasek to keep their top netminder happy.

This was the last Finals series at the Chicago Stadium and the last time—until 2010—that the Blackhawks played for the Stanley Cup.

93 Pregame Plans

Despite sharing the first half of their season with the Bears, the Blackhawks don't have the same tailgating access before games. However, many fans like to make heading to a game a bigger event than just attending the game itself. Thankfully, there are a number of options available to fans to make a Blackhawks game a great experience.

Something every Blackhawks fan must do is enjoy pregame festivities at one of the great watering holes in the neighborhood surrounding the United Center.

Probably the most famous place for a pregame meal is the Billy Goat Inn (1535 W. Madison). In 1934, William Sianis bought the Lincoln Tavern for $205 with a check that bounced. Legend recalls that a billy goat allegedly fell off a truck and wandered into the bar. Sianis changed the name of the bar to the Billy Goat, grew a goatee, and acquired the nickname "Billy Goat."

The Billy Goat has a number of downtown locations now, but the original home of the "cheezborger" is something every Chicago sports fan needs to experience. Of course the Tavern became infamous because of its relationship with the Chicago Cubs—and their alleged curse—but the half-mile distance between the original establishment and the United Center makes it an easy, affordable pregame stop.

Another fantastic place to stop before a Hawks home game is Palace Grill (1408 W. Madison). This stop is known as much for its breakfast options as it is as a great place for anything from a burger to a steak sandwich. This is a smaller diner-style location with limited counter-only seating. Fans will find themselves having a great meal surrounded by Blackhawks memorabilia, and the Palace is just a quick cab ride from the U.C.

A third establishment to make sure to check out is West End Bar and Grill (1326 W. Madison). They have a great beer selection and lots of televisions that are always tuned in to great games. The food is a little bit more expensive than the Billy Goat or the Palace Grill, but the selection is trendy as well. West End is also a great place for fans who don't have tickets to simply watch the game.

In addition to these options, the Blackhawks have hosted regular roadwatch parties in recent seasons. These events are fairly well publicized, both through the team's website and Twitter, and there are always great giveaways and the Ice Crew shows up on occasion. These are always set up for a Hawks road game, and the atmosphere is fantastic, as Hawks fans take over the entire bar or restaurant.

94 Daze

How the Blackhawks received the 90th selection in the 1993 Draft may be as dubious as the career of the player who was selected with it.

As a fourth-round draft choice in 1993, the pressure wasn't too much for 6'6" Eric Daze to handle. He had put up a decent season in juniors but wasn't the fastest skater or a big hitter, despite his 222-pound frame.

After being selected, things blew up, though. With an NHL organization showing interest enough to select him, 66 games in juniors produced 107 points. The following season started in juniors again, but after putting up 99 points in only 57 games, his days in juniors were numbered.

For his efforts during the 1994–95 season, he won the CHL's Most Sportsmanlike Player Award as well as the Viscount Alexander Award, awarded to the Junior Male Athlete of the Year in Quebec. He was also a key contributor on the gold medal–winning World Junior Championship team in 1995. Eric Daze showed he belonged.

Jumping into the Blackhawks lineup in his rookie year of 1994–95, Daze scored 30 goals and 53 points in 80 games, adding eight points in 10 playoff games. He earned a spot on the NHL's All-Rookie Team and appeared to be destined for a long, productive career in Chicago.

The following three seasons saw his point total drop but remain consistent at 41, 42, and 42, respectively.

But the while the goal totals consistently stayed in the 20s, the games played started to become an issue. Daze missed a handful of games in the 1998–99 season, but it was in 1999–2000 that he

Eric Daze celebrates his third goal with teammate Phil Housley in this December 11, 2002, game against the New York Rangers in New York. The Blackhawks won 4–3.

missed a big part of the season (23 games). He still scored 23 goals but struggled physically the entire season.

Between 2000–01 and 2001–02 Daze emerged as one of the top goal scorers in the league. He scored as many goals in 2000–01 (33) as superstars Mike Modano and Teemu Selanne, and his 38 the following year tied Keith Tkachuk for seventh in the NHL.

He finished the 2001–02 season with his best numbers with the Blackhawks, registering 70 points and leading the Hawks into the playoffs for the first time in five seasons.

In 2002–03 Daze scored over 20 goals for the eighth and final time in the NHL, posting 44 points in only 54 games. During that season, Daze finally earned a trip to the NHL All-Star Game, and he performed well enough—two goals and an assist—to be named the game's Most Valuable Player; he was the first Hawks player to be named the All-Star Game MVP since Bobby Hull in 1971.

Unfortunately, the descent for Daze was faster than his rise to stardom. The next year he skated in only 19 games, scoring just four goals. His back had become a problem and was not allowing him to stay on the ice for very long.

In a span of five years, Daze had three surgeries to repair herniated disks in his back. None of the procedures proved to be much more than a Band-Aid, and his back ultimately took him away from the game for good after one final game in the 2005–06 campaign.

Daze was a polarizing figure to many Chicago fans because he didn't play the stereotypically gritty power-forward game expected from someone his size. Even though his wrist shot was lethal and he was one of the best in the league at depositing a one-timer, he rarely hit.

In only 601 games with the Blackhawks in parts of 11 seasons, Daze ended his career with 398 points, which ranks 23rd in franchise history. His 226 goals rank 11th in Hawks history, and his 34 game-winning markers are tied with Pit Martin and Tony Amonte for sixth in the team's long history.

Oh, and the pick that was used to select Daze back in 1993? It was the pick acquired with Stephane Beauregard when the Hawks decided against keeping their backup goalie: Dominik Hasek.

95 Toss Your Hat

There are a number of legends regarding the origins of the term "hat trick," and you'll witness a heated debate if you ask for the term's history if you're in some sections in Canada.

According to the Hockey Hall of Fame, the Blackhawks were involved in the birth of the term. In that account, Blackhawks forward Alex Kaleta was hat shopping in Toronto on January 26, 1946. He found a lid he wanted to purchase in a store owned by

Sammy Taft but didn't have enough currency in his pocket to cover the transaction. Taft agreed to waive the cost of the cap if Kaleta scored three goals against the Maple Leafs that night. Kaleta scored four, and the rest is history.

Another legend recalls that a hat store, Henri Henri in Montreal, originated the term at some point during the Original Six era. The store rewarded any player who scored three goals at the Montreal Forum with a free hat. On the list of great scorers to receive a free hat from Henri Henri are Blackhawks Bobby Hull and Stan Mikita.

Either way, the legend has evolved from a player being rewarded with a single hat to the ice being graced by hundreds.

In the 1970s fans began throwing hats on the ice to celebrate any player scoring three goals in a game. The NHL had to amend the rule book so that the home team would not be called for a minor penalty when hats hit the ice; Rule 63.4 now reads, "articles thrown onto the ice following a special occasion (i.e. hat trick) will not result in a bench minor penalty being assessed."

There have been a few notable hat tricks in Blackhawks history.

Michel Goulet reached the 1,000-point mark as a Blackhawk in Minnesota on his third goal of the game on February 23, 1991.

On February 22, 1996, Tony Amonte recorded the first hat trick in the United Center against the St. Louis Blues. It was the 53rd Blackhawks home game played at the United Center.

Here is a very simple breakdown of your obligation as a fan at the United Center if a Blackhawks player scores three goals: if you're wearing a hat, and your seat is within a conservative throw of the playing surface (read: 100 level), it is considered a good idea to toss your hat onto the ice.

If you're sitting in the 200- or 300-level seats, it's OK to keep your hat on your head. While many fans will still make the attempt to get their hat to the ice from further away, the odds of reaching

Brian Campbell skates through a sea of hats that were tossed on the ice after Patrick Kane scored a hat trick against the Vancouver Canucks in Game 6 of the NHL Western Conference semifinal in Chicago on May 11, 2009. Chicago won 7–5.

the ice in one throw are slim. The hat may eventually find its way to the ice with a little help, however.

There are a couple variations on the hat trick.

First, there is the "natural hat trick." This refers to a player scoring three straight goals. This event happens even more rarely, and when it happens, it is truly a special event. Jonathan Toews accomplished this feat on November 17, 2010, in Edmonton.

When this form of the hat trick takes place, your hat should end up on the ice.

The most famous hat trick in the league's history came off the stick of a Chicago player. Blackhawks great Bill Mosienko holds the NHL record for the shortest time to accomplish a natural hat trick; he scored three goals in 21 seconds on March 23, 1952.

In the event of a "Gordie Howe Hat Trick," however, your hat can stay on your head. This refers to a player being credited with a goal and an assist and getting into a fight in the same game. The irony is that this trick's namesake only accomplished all three in the same game on two occasions in 1,767 NHL games.

There have been 209 hat tricks in the history of the Blackhawks. Bobby Hull recorded the most three-goal games, with 24 in his Chicago career.

96 That's You in the Corner

Before the 2009–10 season, the Chicago Blackhawks and Bulls together made a substantial investment in the fan experience at the United Center by making some dramatic changes to the 300 level.

Instead of small signage and minimal viewing ability, the teams added large video screens above the concession areas. To anyone who had attended a hockey game before the large screens were put in, waiting to get back you your seat while a puck was in play became excruciating without the ability to see the action well.

But the bigger change that was made was actually addition by subtraction. Prior to 2009–10 the two teams agreed to remove seats in two opposite corners of the 300 level, starting at the third row, and carve into the concourse a premium bar area with televisions and high-end beer and alcohol options. The following summer, with a bump in income from a Bulls playoff appearance and a Stanley Cup championship in the respective owners' back pockets, the teams added two more matching areas in the other two corners.

For many fans, the ability to see a Hawks home game is hard because of one simple factor: the cost. Hockey isn't the cheapest sport to see, especially in Chicago. Thanks in large part to a secondary market that exploded with the team's success, it's hard to afford tickets to a regular-season or postseason game at the United Center if you aren't able to land tickets for face value.

With the addition of these four bar areas, standing room has become a more viable option for fans.

When there weren't options like the four bars to stand in, anyone with a standing-room ticket was ushered to a walkway behind/above the 300-level seats; basically, standing-room tickets afforded you the opportunity to see the ceiling of the United Center.

Now, however, there is a chance that, with a little luck and a quick run from the doors to the bar, you could have a unique viewing experience from what feels like the fifth row of the 300-level seating—seats that are usually significantly more expensive than a standing-room ticket.

Being at the United Center for a Blackhawks game is a special experience, and any night can provide memories for a lifetime. Chicago fans are arguably the best in professional sports, and the Blackhawks and Bulls organizations realized that there was more they could do to improve the experience for their great fans.

What makes hockey games unique is the willingness of fans to engage each other, both for a friendly high-five, a conversation about the game or, sometimes, to taunt someone wearing the wrong team's sweater. There aren't many venues in all professional sports that offer such a unique viewing experience to their fans.

In addition to the ability to interact with other fans, the sight lines from the bars are exceptional. In contrast to the standing-room area at the top of the building, where watching a game can feel like trying to get excited about an ant farm, these four areas provide a great look at the ice—and easily accessible libations.

Every fan should find a way to spend a game at one of the corner bars.

97 Blackhawks-Canucks Rivalry

In 1982 the rivalry didn't exist. In the semifinals, the Blackhawks met the Vancouver Canucks and were ousted in five games.

It was 13 more years until Vancouver and Chicago met in the postseason again, but that time the series was significantly more heated. The Blackhawks swept the Canucks in the Western Conference Semifinals but needed late, game-winning goals from Chris Chelios in Game 3 and Game 4 to advance.

The break between postseason battles extended another 14 years but returned with some of the most heated series in recent years. Between 2009 and 2011, the Blackhawks-Canucks rivalry became very similar to the series between the Hawks and North Stars in the early 1980s.

On March 29, 2009, the matchup between the Canucks and Blackhawks received what every rivalry needs: an injection of hatred. At the 5:50 mark in the third period, Hawks forward Dustin Byfuglien jabbed Canucks goalie Roberto Luongo in the head, and the two teams erupted into an all-time brawl.

Chicago's Ben Eager and Vancouver's Kevin Bieksa opted for a mixed martial arts approach, with each body-slamming the other to the ice during the fracas. On the other end of the ice, Vancouver's Alexandre Burrows opted for a less respectable approach, deciding to pull Duncan Keith's hair instead of throwing punches. When the dust settled, the one fight warranted 80 total penalty minutes, including six 10-minute misconduct calls.

The two teams met again one month later in the Western Conference Semifinals, and the baby Blackhawks were supposed to go quietly into the night. With a team of young players who, in most cases, were in their first postseason, a second-round appearance was supposed to be good enough against a veteran Canucks team. Byfuglien continued harassing Luongo, and the Hawks pulled off the improbable upset in six games.

When the 2009–10 postseason began, Chicago was suddenly a Stanley Cup contender with Vancouver. Not only were the two teams at the top of the league, but there was history between the two teams. Andrew Ladd won a couple ugly fights with Ryan Kesler, and Byfuglien continued making Luongo's life miserable.

After escaping a first-round scare from the Nashville Predators, the Blackhawks met the Canucks in the conference semifinals again. The Canucks came out and stole the first game in Chicago, chasing Blackhawks rookie goalie Antti Niemi after two periods. But the Hawks got hat tricks from Byfuglien in Game 3 and Jonathan Toews in Game 4—in which the Blackhawks scored six goals on Luongo again—to take control of the series. For the second consecutive season, the Hawks ended the Canucks' season in six games in the second round of the Stanley Cup playoffs.

When the 2010 season ended and the championship parade had been cleaned off Chicago's downtown streets, the dismantling of the Hawks roster began. One of the casualties was Byfuglien, who was traded to Atlanta with Eager.

On the final day of the 2010–11 regular season, the Hawks lost a home game to Detroit but still backed into the playoffs when the Wild beat the Stars; their first-round opponent would be the Presidents' Trophy–winning Canucks.

While the previous two seasons' series were good, this edition of the rivalry captured everything that is great about playoff hockey. An epic battle between two familiar opponents provided enough theater for a feature film.

Chicago was without Dave Bolland for the first three games of the series and lost all three. After being shut out in the first game, the Hawks battled back and were close in the second and third games but couldn't finish the job.

In Game 3 Canucks forward Raffi Torres—who was just returning from a four-game suspension for a head shot—leveled Brent Seabrook behind the Blackhawks' net. Seabrook struggled to get up and left the bench for some time but returned to the game. Torres hit him again later in the game, and clearly Seabrook was hurting.

After the game it was determined that Seabrook would miss Game 4 because of a concussion. However, Bolland returned to the lineup, and the series' momentum completely shifted.

The Blackhawks knocked Luongo out of Game 4 and Game 5, winning by respective scores of 7–2 and 5–0, and forced a Game 6 on Easter Sunday. Surprisingly, Luongo didn't start Game 6 but replaced an injured Cory Schneider in the third period. Rookie Ben Smith, who had played in only 11 NHL games prior to that night, scored the game-winning goal in overtime.

The Blackhawks were just the seventh team in NHL history to force a Game 7 after losing the first three games of a series.

Game 7 served as Corey Crawford's arrival on the leaguewide stage. He played the game of his life between the pipes for the Hawks, keeping his team in a 1–0 game despite Vancouver outplaying Chicago for most of the game. With less than two minutes left in regulation—and the Blackhawks season—Jonathan Toews borrowed a page out of Patrick Kane's history book from the first round of 2010. The Blackhawks captain scored a short-handed, game-tying goal from his knees to force overtime.

Unfortunately for Hawks fans, Chicago wasn't able to convert on a power play early in overtime, and an ugly turnover in the defensive zone led to a series-clinching goal for Burrows, who scored both of Vancouver's goals in the game but was also called for the overtime penalty. Crawford made 36 saves in Game 7, and finished his first postseason with an impressive .927 save percentage.

Where this rivalry goes in the world of a salary cap and free agency is anyone's guess, but it has developed into one of the most exciting—and physical—in the NHL.

98 Blackhawks' (Lack of) Media Exposure

For years, Blackhawks fans struggled though an inability to see their home team on television.

In 1982 Bulls and White Sox owners Jerry Reinsdorf and Eddie Einhorn founded Sportsvision as a new cable outlet to broadcast local Chicago games. For an additional charge, and with a converter box, fans could see some Bulls, Blackhawks, and White Sox games.

Over the coming years, the channel's ownership and name changed a number of times, and it eventually became a basic cable channel. But for a long time, the Blackhawks organization continued to resist the potentially exponential growth that television could afford the team.

Despite reluctance to show their product on television on a regular basis, the voice of Pat Foley became associated with Hawks games through the various incarnations of Sportsvision. In 2006, though, that relationship ended and, in many ways, fans left with him.

It wasn't until 2008 that fans were finally able to see their beloved Hawks on television on a regular basis. Starting with the 2008–09 season, things changed. The revolution that took place when John McDonough and Jay Blunk were brought on board was enhanced by the product on the ice, but consider the words of the team's general manager, Mike Smith, in 2004: "Revenue comes mainly from ticket sales. There are TV and radio contracts, advertising, and programs, but that's about it.... Memorabilia sales are not substantial revenue generators."

In complete contrast to his father's business model, Rocky Wirtz decided that engaging media would become a critical piece of the financial model of the team moving forward.

Blackhawks partnered with WGN television and Comcast SportsNet to bring home games to the viewing public. With Foley back in the mix and Eddie Olczyk providing color, the broadcasts have been an enormous success.

Of course, winning the Stanley Cup helps television ratings, too.

In February 2011 the Blackhawks and WGN-TV announced a five-year broadcast extension, guaranteeing Chicago that their Hawks will continue to be televised.

WGN Radio also took over as the flagship station for the Hawks beginning with the 2008–09 season, and signed a three-year broadcast extension with WGN in April 2010. Former Blackhawks forward Troy Murray currently provides the color commentary for radio broadcasts, and John Wiedeman brings the play-by-play.

The partnership between WGN and the Chicago Blackhawks was the first, and most obvious, sign that change was coming to the organization under the leadership of Rocky Wirtz. Even the online presence of the team is now one of the most dynamic in the National Hockey League, with the team itself producing video content for online consumption and television specials. BHTV has become an entertaining inside-look opportunity for fans to get to know their heroes off the ice.

But in 2007 even the thought of something like BHTV existing would have been considered as rational as Latin becoming a prominent language again.

Fans should be thankful for, and never take for granted, local broadcasts of Blackhawks games.

99 Bob Pulford

Perhaps the best summary of Bob Pulford's time in Chicago came in the Associated Press release on October 11, 2007, when he was reassigned by new owner Rocky Wirtz: "With Pulford in charge, the Blackhawks once won eight division titles and made the NHL playoffs 20 straight seasons. Last year, Chicago missed the playoffs for the eighth time in nine seasons."

As a player, Pulford was one of the top penalty killers of his generation on four Stanley Cup championship teams in Toronto. Late in his career, the Leafs traded him to Los Angeles, where he played his final two years and, after retiring, moved behind the bench as the Kings' head coach. In 1975 Pulford won the Jack Adams Award as the league's best coach when the Kings set a franchise record with 105 points in the regular season.

Early in his tenure, Pulford pulled all the right strings. His first run as general manager lasted from 1977 to 1990, during which time the Hawks were one of the most competitive teams in the NHL. In the first three years he was the team's general manager, he was responsible for drafting Doug Wilson and Jack O'Callahan (1977) and Keith Brown (albeit ahead of Ray Bourque in 1979). In 1980 Pulford put together arguably the greatest draft class in the organization's history, selecting Denis Savard in the first round,

Troy Murray in the third, and Steve Larmer in the sixth (120th overall).

In his early days in Chicago, Pulford also made a number of shrewd trades that improved his club as well, including the deal that brought Al Secord to Chicago during the 1980–81 season.

Between 1980 and 1990, the Blackhawks qualified for the postseason after every season. Unfortunately, Pulford's legacy—like many of the great players on the Blackhawks teams he put together during that decade—will forever lack a championship in Chicago. Indeed, not many great players won a title in that decade because only four organizations—the New York Islanders (four in a row), Edmonton Oilers (four in five years), Montreal Canadiens, and Calgary Flames—won a championship during the 1980s.

While the Hawks were making the playoffs each year between 1980 through 1990, Pulford's draft classes weren't nearly as successful. Probably the greatest diamond-in-the-rough he selected was Dominik Hasek, who lasted until the 10th round in 1983. But none of his first-round picks between 1981 and 1987—including Eddie Olczyk—made a long-term impact on the ice for the Blackhawks.

In fact, the only player he drafted to make a significant impact on the ice for the Hawks between 1981 and 1990 was Jeremy Roenick, the team's first-round pick in 1988. Because the minor league system in Chicago suffered a talent deficiency, Pulford had to keep the Blackhawks competitive through trades.

This led to some of the most painful divorces—for the team, but more for the fans—in the history of the organization. During Pulford's watch, Savard, Larmer, Olczyk, Hasek, Ed Belfour, Roenick, and Chris Chelios were just a few of the names that left Chicago in trades. Making matters worse, the only player of substance coming back in any of those trades was Chelios (for Savard).

Another harsh reality of the Pulford regime in Chicago was the turnstile behind the bench. While he was with Chicago, Pulford named himself the head coach on three occasions, replacing an existing coach personally. He spent parts of seven seasons as the Blackhawks' head coach, totaling 182 wins. Nine other men were, at some point, the head coach of the Hawks, but each of them had to look over his shoulder to see how long his time there would be.

The most powerful testimony to Pulford's lack of effectiveness in Chicago is that the only two seasons between 1977 and 1998 that he didn't serve as general manager or head coach were perhaps the best seasons from the team during that span; in 1990–91 the team won the President's Trophy, and after 1991–92 the team advanced to the Stanley Cup Finals for the only time while Pulford was associated with the organization.

At the end of the day, Pulford was the head coach of the Blackhawks for 426 games, winning 182. He ranks second in the history of the Blackhawks in both categories (through the 2010–11 season), and he was inducted into the Hockey Hall of Fame in 1991. Three men who played in Chicago during Pulford's tenure—Doug Wilson, Bob Murray, and Dale Tallon—are general managers of NHL teams, and Pulford's son-in-law, Dean Lombardi, is the general manager in Los Angeles.

A lot of wonderful, historic hockey was played in Chicago while Bob Pulford served the organization. But a lot of heartbreak and disappointment happened as well.

100 Fun Facts!

The colorful, sometimes unbelievable history of the Chicago Blackhawks is loaded with some odd, sometimes laughable, often-times random anomalies.

Everyone knows the gaudy numbers put up by Hull, Mikita, and Savard, but there were 61 players in the team's history who scored only one goal while with the Blackhawks. Some of the players to embody the team's marketing slogan of the 2009–10 season include great defenseman Jack Stewart, who was a four-time All-Star in the 1940s, and center Bruce Boudreau, who is now the head coach of the Washington Capitals.

Grant Mulvey is the youngest player in Blackhawks history to play in 300 games (22 years, 32 days). He also has the worst plus-minus rating in the team's history, settling in at -64 in 574 games with the Hawks. (The NHL started officially tracking players' plus-minus rating in 1968.)

In 1982–83 Al Secord scored 54 goals but racked up 180 penalty minutes. This was one of only nine times in NHL history that a player scored 50 goals and was whistled for more than 150 penalty minutes in a single season.

In 1991–92 Jeremy Roenick was credited with 13 game-winning goals. Only three players have ever been credited with more than 13 in a single season: Phil Esposito (16—twice), Michel Goulet (16), and Pavel Bure (14).

The same season that Roenick won 13 games, Mike Peluso piled up 408 penalty minutes. Only two players have ever been whistled for more in a single season: David Schultz (472 in 1974–75) and Paul Baxter (409 in 1981–82).

In 1988–89 Dirk Graham scored 10 short-handed goals. Only two players have scored more goals in a single season while trying to kill a penalty: Mario Lemieux (13 in the same season as Graham) and Wayne Gretzky (12 in 1983–84 and 11 in 1984–85).

Only four goalies in the history of the team have lost just one game as a Blackhawk netminder: Matt Underhill, Red Almas, Michel Dumas, and Marc Lamothe. Four goalies were able to stay undefeated in net while members of the Hawks while winning at least one game: Gilles Meloche, Sebastien Caron, Raymond LeBlanc, and Bill Dickie.

Stan Mikita is the all-time leader in games played for the Blackhawks, lacing up the skates 1,394 times. Only four forwards in NHL history have played more games with one franchise, and three were with Detroit. Gordie Howe (1,687), Alex Delvecchio (1,549), and Steve Yzerman (1,514) were longtime Red Wings, and John Bucyk (1,436) spent two decades with the Boston Bruins.

Mikita is also the all-time leader with 1,467 points as a Hawks player. Only four forwards in NHL history have scored more points for a single franchise: Howe (1,809—Detroit), Yzerman (1,755—Detroit), Lemieux (1,723—Pittsburgh), and Wayne Gretzky (1,669—Edmonton).

Tony Esposito won 418 games in Chicago, which is the second-highest total for any goaltender with a single franchise in NHL history. Only New Jersey's Martin Brodeur has won more games wearing a single sweater; he's at 625 and counting.

Ever since Major McLaughlin founded the Blackhawks and favored players born in the United States, Chicago has always featured some of the best U.S.-born players in the league. A handful of individuals who have been a part of the Blackhawks organization have been inducted into the United States Hockey Hall of Fame Museum: William W. Wirtz (administrator); William J. Stewart (coach); and Clarence Abel, Tony Amonte, Frank Brimsek, Cully Dahlstrom, Victor Desjardins, Victor Heyliger, Phil Housley, Virgil Johnson, Michael Karakas, Sam LoPresti, John Mariucci, Fido Purpur, Jeremy Roenick, and Doc Romnes (all players).

Finally, each time the Blackhawks have won the Stanley Cup, a Democrat has been in the White House. In 1934 and 1938 Franklin D. Roosevelt was in office. In 1961 John F. Kennedy was serving as president. And in 2010 Chicago's own Barack Obama was president. Not surprisingly, a Democrat was also mayor of Chicago each time the Hawks brought Lord Stanley's Cup home.

Sources

Associated Press. "1961 Stanley Cup Champions Chicago
Blackhawks in Video Clips and News Clips."
http://www.habseyesontheprize.com/2010/5/28/1491884/1961-
stanley-cup-champions-chicago (accessed April 1, 2011).

———. "Blackhawks Exec Bob Pulford Reassigned."
http://www.chicagobusiness.com/article/20071011/
NEWS07/200026708 (accessed April 13, 2011).

"Bobby Hull Streaks Past 50." http://www.nytimes.com/packages/
html/sports/year_in_sports/03.12.html (accessed April 7, 2011).

Boron, Brad. "Keith Magnuson." http://blackhawks.nhl.com/club/
news.htm?id=477074 (accessed April 13, 2011).

———. "National Anthem a Chicago Specialty." http://www.nhl.
com/ice/news.htm?id=388510 (accessed April 5, 2011).

———. "The Enforcers." *Blackhawks Magazine*, Winter 2009,
p. 94.

Botta, Chris. "Golden Years in Chicago Return for Bobby Hull."
http://www.aolnews.com/2010/03/05/golden-years-in-chicago-
return-for-bobby-hull/ (accessed April 5, 2011).

Burnside, Scott. "Do Original Six Teams Still Matter in the NHL?"
http://sports.espn.go.com/nhl/columns/story?id=2773591
(accessed March 14, 2011).

———. "The Original Six: Chicago Blackhawks." http://sports.espn.
go.com/nhl/news/story?id=2772473 (accessed April 15, 2011).

Cazeneuve, Brian. "Talking Chicago and Stanley Cups with Bobby
Hull and Stan Mikita." http://sportsillustrated.cnn.com/2010/
writers/brian_cazeneuve/06/08/hull.mikita.interview/index.html
(accessed April 5, 2011).

Chicago Blackhawks. "Blackhawks Extend Contract of Pat Foley
and Eddie Olczyk." http://blackhawks.nhl.com/club/news.
htm?id=547880 (accessed April 5, 2011).

Chicago Blackhawks Press Release. "Blackhawks Announce Return of Broadcaster Pat Foley." http://blackhawks.nhl.com/club/news.htm?id=476373 (accessed April 5, 2011).

Dreger, Darren. "Dreger: Quenneville Finds Spot with Blackhawks." http://www.tsn.ca/blogs/darren_dreger/?id=250762 (accessed April 11, 2011).

ESPN.com. "Wirtz Dies at 77; Helped Negotiate NHL-WHA Merger." http://sports.espn.go.com/nhl/news/story?id=3036711 (accessed April 15, 2011).

Hall, Glenn. Foreword to *The Blackhawks*, by Brian McFarlane. Toronto: Stoddart Publishing Co. Limited, 2000.

"Hockey: Hawk on the Wing." *Time*, March 1, 1968.

"Hockey: The Golden Goal." http://www.time.com/time/magazine/article/0,9171,842548,00.html (accessed April 7, 2011).

Inside the Minds: The Business of Sports—Executives from Major Sports Franchises on How a Team Operates Behind the Scenes. Boston: Aspatore, 2004.

Kane, Martin. "Hockey's Biggest Moment No. 51." http://sportsillustrated.cnn.com/vault/article/magazine/MAG1078310/index.htm (accessed April 7, 2011).

Kram, Mark. "A Hard Toe Right to the Jaw." http://sportsillustrated.cnn.com/vault/article/magazine/MAG1077196/index.htm (accessed April 7, 2011).

McErlain, Eric. "Hawks Fire Denis Savard." http://www.aolnews.com/2008/10/16/hawks-fire-denis-savard-after-only-four-games/ (accessed April 13, 2011).

McFarlane, Brian. *The Blackhawks*. Toronto: Stoddart Publishing Co. Limited, 2000.

McGourty, John. "Bobby Hull Thrilled by Brett Hull's Induction." http://www.nhl.com/ice/news.htm?id=505218 (accessed April 5, 2011).

———. "Pierre Pilote: Too Good to Be Forgotten." http://blackhawks.nhl.com/club/news.htm?id=477078 (accessed April 5, 2011).

Morreale, Mike. "Anthem in Chicago a Tradition Like No Other." http://blackhawks.nhl.com/club/news.htm?id=530513 (accessed April 10, 2011).

———. "Keenan's Tough Love Helped Shape Roenick's Career." http://www.nhl.com/ice/news.htm?id=534875 (accessed March 31, 2011).

Mulvoy, Mark. "An Old Custom at Customs." http://sportsillustrated.cnn.com/vault/article/magazine/MAG1084936/1/index.htm (accessed April 15, 2011).

———. "Little Big Man of the Black Hawks." http://sportsillustrated.cnn.com/vault/article/magazine/MAG1087327/index.htm (accessed March 29, 2011).

New York Daily News. "Sports' All-Time Coolest Uniforms." http://www.nydailynews.com/sports/galleries/sports_alltime_greatest_uniforms/sports_alltime_greatest_uniforms.html (accessed March 29, 2011).

NHL. "Official Rules—Rule 63: Delaying the Game." http://www.nhl.com/ice/page.htm?id=26355 (accessed April 7, 2011).

NHL Press Release. "Kane, Toews Among Top 10 in NHL.com Jersey Sales." http://blackhawks.nhl.com/club/news.htm?id=517491 (accessed April 14, 2011).

Pelletier, Joe. "Pierre Pilote." http://blackhawkslegends.blogspot.com/2007/03/pierre-pilote.html (accessed March 17, 2011).

"Remembering Bob Probert." *Blackhawks Magazine*, Fall 2010, p. 88–90.

Rosenbloom, Steve. "Hip, Hip, Huet for Rocky Wirtz." http://blogs.chicagosports.chicagotribune.com/rosenblog/2010/09/hip-hip-huet-for-rocky-wirtz.html (accessed March 21, 2011).

Sandomir, Rich. "Blackhawks Owner Reverses Team's Old-School Legacy of Failure." http://www.nytimes.com/2010/06/02/sports/hockey/02wirtz.html (accessed April 11, 2011).

Sassone, Tim. "How About a Dirk Graham Night?" http://blogs.dailyherald.com/node/1208 (accessed April 5, 2011).

Schardt, A.W. "The Black Hawks Are Now the Bright Hopes." *Sports Illustrated*, January 14, 1963.

Schwartz, Larry. "Hull Helped WHA into Hockey Family." http://espn.go.com/sportscentury/features/00014266.html (accessed April 7, 2011).

Schwarz, Alan. "Hockey Brawler Paid Price, with Brain Trauma." http://www.nytimes.com/2011/03/03/sports/hockey/03fighter.html?pagewanted=1&_r=1 (accessed April 8, 2011).

Seminara, Dave. "1938 Hawks: Champs—but no Cup." http://articles.chicagotribune.com/2010-06-01/sports/ct-spt-0602-38-blackhawks--20100601_1_hawks-nhl-history-davey-kerr (accessed April 5, 2011).

Shea, Kevin. "One on One with Bill Mosienko." http://www.legendsofhockey.net/html/spot_oneononep196507.htm (accessed April 17, 2011).

———. "Stanley Cup Journal." http://www.hhof.com/html/exSCJ10_02.shtml (accessed April 9, 2011).

Smith, Mike. "Building Success Through Sports Management." Chapter in *Inside the Minds: The Business of Sports—Executives from Major Sports Franchises on How a Team Operates Behind the Scenes*. Boston: Aspatore, 2004.

"Sport: Maggie the Policeman." http://www.time.com/time/magazine/article/0,9171,876858-2,00.html (accessed April 1, 2011).

"Sport: Stanley Cup: Apr. 16, 1934." http://www.time.com/time/magazine/article/0,9171,769858-1,00.html (accessed April 11, 2011).

Strom, Rich. "The Roenick Trade." http://articles.chicagotribune.com/1996-08-17/sports/9608170118_1_jeremy-roenick-roenick-trade-alexei-zhamnov (accessed April 17, 2011).

Suppelsa, Mark. "Mark Suppelsa's Closer Look—Bill Wirtz." http://marksuppelsa.typepad.com/closerlook/2005/11/bill_wirtz.html (accessed April 15, 2011).

Swift, E.M. "Odd Man Out." http://sportsillustrated.cnn.com/vault/article/magazine/MAG1011117/index.htm (accessed April 13, 2011).

Time magazine. "Scoreboard: Who Won May 7, 1965 http://www.time.com/time/magazine/article/0,9171,898764,00.html (accessed April 7, 2011).

Verdi, Bob. "The Verdict: Bill White Was a Defensive Stalwart, prankster." http://blackhawks.nhl.com/club/news.htm?id=546331 (accessed April 6, 2011).

———. "The Verdict: Chelios' Tale One of Longevity and Excellence." http://blackhawks.nhl.com/club/news.htm?id=545978&navid=DL|CHI|home (accessed April 4, 2011).

———. "The Verdict: Murray Broke Selke Mold." http://blackhawks.nhl.com/club/news.htm?id=513216 (accessed April 5, 2011).

Wittenberg, Harvey. *Tales from the Chicago Blackhawks*. Champaign, IL: Sports Publishing LLC, 2003.

Wolf, Bruce. "Strange Misadventures of the Stanley Cup." http://abcnews.go.com/Entertainment/WolfFiles/story?id=90991&page=1 (accessed April 14, 2011).